HELLENIKA

For Chris and Betty
In friendship!
Peter L.

HELLENIKA

HERITAGE AND HISTORY

by
T. Peter Limber

Second Edition, Revised

COSMOS PUBLISHING CO. INC.
River Vale, New Jersey
1997

For my children. And their children.
That they may know the story of their forebears.

Cover painting by **Hippolytes Ides**

Drawings by **Steve Edles**

Original map designs by the author

Library of Congress Card Catalog Number 97-77149
ISBN: 0-9660449-0-8 (paper, second edition)

Published in the United States by Cosmos Publishing Co., Inc.
P.O.Box 2255
River Vale, NJ 07675
Phone: 201-664-3494
Fax: 201-664-3402
e-mail: greekbooks@worldnet.att.net

Printed in Greece

Graecia capta ferum victorem cepit et artes intulit agresti Latio.

Greece, taken captive, captured her savage conqueror, and
brought the arts to rustic Latium.

Horace (65 BC-AD 8)

Καὶ τώρα τί θὰ γίνουμε χωρὶς βαρβάρους;
Οἱ ἄνθρωποι αὐτοὶ ἦσαν κάποια λύσις!

And now what shall become of us without barbarians?
These people were a certain solution!

Konstantinos Kavafes (1863-1933)

CONTENTS

LIST OF MAPS

PROLOGOS

Most people have pride in their ethnic origin, especially if it is from a single and recent source, and particularly if there is good reason to have pride in it — without diminishing in the slightest the merits of the country they themselves were born in or in which they live. If they can know something about it, an extra dimension is attained that can add spice to their life. In modern times, especially, when travel to the birthplace of one's ancestors is available to anyone, it is enjoyable to go there to see traces of its history and how it is today, learn something about it and feel a sense of kinship with it.

People of Greek heritage, of which I am one, have a very strong attachment to things Greek and to Greece itself. Why not? From childhood at home in America and in our schooling, we were exposed to the dramatic stories of Greek mythology, later to the ancient playwrights and philosophers, and to the excellence of ancient Greek architecture and art in general. We could see that everyone appreciated the culture of ancient Greece, not just those of us that were of Greek forebears. Nor was our exposure to things Greek limited to those of the Classical Age. My parents and their friends would discuss the role of the monarchy in Greece, and whether the country would be better off with or without it; they discussed the tragic events for Greece and the Greek people of 1922 (the catastrophe in Smyrna); and many other subjects about the country of their birth and its problems. How could they not pay attention to what was happening in Greece where so many of their relatives and childhood friends still lived? We kids paid less attention, having been born and growing up in America, and though we absorbed something about these matters, usually we learned only isolated pieces of that history and those political events, without continuity and with little understanding. As time went on we learned more, but by now we began to concentrate on what would be our future profession or business. The immigrant background of many parents coupled with the broad opportunities America provided made studies for the sake of intellectual satisfaction a less urgent (or nonexistent) pursuit in most families. Even though their children were born in America, many strove to succeed economically as a primary and all-pervasive goal, and education was bent to that singular purpose.

However fascinating a subject, coming to grips with Greek history and its heritage is a more formidable task than many are prepared to tackle. When I first visited Greece as a young adult in 1951, the country was still coming out of the devastating civil war that had followed World War II. One could not sit at an outdoor café in Athens without being subjected to pathetic pleas of countless beggars, many of them bearing the physical scars of that terrible conflict. But one could also sense an excitement in the air of a dynamic people finally liberated from the horrors of war. Being deprived of everything during that long period, did not stop the fertile Greek mind from working. I distinctly remember animated conversations with Greek friends until the wee hours in the summer night sitting at those sidewalk cafés in central Athens, sipping endless coffees in the cooling air, discussing ideas and philosophy, and, of course, politics; materialism and commercialism had not yet had time to return to daily life.

Starting at that time, I had to learn more about the history of my ethnic background. But it is no easy task. The list of books is endless, and not just those written by Greeks. Authors and historians from England, France, Germany, and many other countries have published numerous volumes on every aspect of the subject. While I was living in Athens, each time I picked up and read another book on Greek history I put a new facet on my knowledge of this intriguing subject. Nearly five thousand years of recorded Greek history is a very long time in which events take place, and especially to a vigorous people located geographically at an important world crossroad. Ancient and modern periods alike, provided stimulating reading.

I began to keep notes for my personal reference. Not finding a single volume that told the highlights of this endless topic, and in the realization that historians rarely write this kind of a treatise for the general reader, I soon began to think of producing a book for the many people that I talked with who expressed a desire to read such a volume if it were available. One other aspect also became obvious to me, searching through the landscape of this fascinating topic that stretched from Gibraltar to India. Historians in their books would mention place names, apparently in the certain knowledge that their readers were familiar with them. Sometimes they provided a few crowded and often not very well designed black-and-white maps. I thought to myself, the general reader would want as many maps as possible to gain a better understanding of where the events described took place, preferably in color, which makes them easier to understand by far. So I began to convert my thoughts and notes into narrative form that would summarize the highlights of Greek history and tell how the Greek people went from one stage to another during the long known period of their existence. And of course there would be many maps. Some of these I had to design myself from reading the histories, because many were not available elsewhere that I could find. Of course, in the process, I soon learned why historians do not pay more attention to this obvious element: maps are expensive to design, and even more expensive to produce in color. This volume shows that I persisted in my convictions.

It is much simpler to read Greek history as a student, or to be taught the subject, the knowledge of it is gained over that period of time that is normally devoted to learning. But life gets busy in adulthood and there are fewer moments that we can devote to such pursuits as the reading of history. The opportunity for broader understanding of complex events is usually lost. This book is designed to help retrieve that time, and bring to a general level of understanding that heritage that belongs to all people of Greek ethnic origin, wherever they were born or currently reside. Nor are other people neglected that simply love the reading of history in general, whatever their ethnic background, and particularly about a history as rich and stimulating as ours is.

This book may be read from beginning to end, or individual chapters may be referred to for information about specific periods. As the maps are designed to supplement these specific periods and events, reading the brief texts first and following the descriptions and places on the accompanying maps will provide the best understanding of the period.

The events described are based on historical facts and are presented in chronological order. Others are included because of their important bearing on Greek cultural development, such as *The Development of Greek Religion*, in Chapter Nine, or simply because they are interesting, as *The Olympic Games*, *The Parthenon*, and *Cleopatra*. Two sections are based on legendary or invented events: *The Trojan War*, which was made famous by Homer in the *Iliad* and the *Odyssey*; and the adventure story about the Argonauts and their quest for the Golden Fleece. Another reference to legend is a brief description of the Olympian family of gods in Chapter Nine. In the ancient world, mythology was the basis of polytheistic religion, and, during the Classical Period, these familiar legends were woven into the comedies and tragedies of the famous playwrights. So imaginative and intellectually satisfying were these religious beliefs that the Romans adopted them in their turn, starting in the second century BC. Though Christianity became widespread throughout the central and eastern Mediterranean and Balkan areas later, it took several centuries to entirely replace the old cultism.

If the reader gains enough knowledge of Greek history and Greek lore to suit his interests through this volume, this is adequate justification to have prepared it. If the reader is inspired enough to continue his reading of other books to learn additional details among the many woven into the rich tapestry of Greek history and the broad world it affected, an even greater service will have been rendered.

ACKNOWLEDGEMENTS

This volume has taken a long time to be prepared. To put the complexities of Greek history into a single volume there was much to be read, weighed, written, revised, researched, and rewritten. During the course of its preparation many people were helpful, and I would not like to leave out a mention of their valuable efforts. But, for the sake of brevity: My early draft was written while I lived in Athens, and that distinguished journalist, historian, and editor, John Lampsas, was helpful in many ways. Katherine Vanderpool, then editor of the *Athenian* magazine, was encouraging and gave much advice and aided with early organization of material, and book planning and production, particularly for the maps. My designs for the maps were redrawn and put into form for four-color printing by cartographer Nikos Zitis in Athens, who worked long and hard on the subject. I wore out secretaries and bored them to death typing drafts and retyping them. It was not until I returned to the United States and availed myself of the marvels of computers and word-processing software, that the entire project began to be placed under control. I also acknowledge that my title *Hellenika*, was borrowed by me from the book of the same name by Xenophon.

Also, while I resided in Athens, my research on this broad subject was greatly facilitated by the very large collection of volumes on Greek history in several languages available at that superb institution, the Gennadeion Library.

I was able to take advantage of the visit to Athens and consult and be guided in the preparation of the modern Greek history portion by Dr. Victor Papacosma, Professor of History at Kent State University in Ohio, an accomplished author and lecturer. Upon returning to resume living in the United States, I had the opportunity to have my manuscript critically read by the Rev. Dr. Demetrios J. Constantelos, Distinguished Professor of Greek History at Stockton State College, New Jersey, and a noted author of many books and numerous articles on Greek history. He was also encouraging and most helpful with his comments and generous with his limited time. My familiarity with specific aspects and details of Greek history were sharpened by many conversations on the subject with a number of other knowledgable individuals in Greece and in America. I am especially grateful to Albert McGrigor, my copy editor and an admirer of things Greek, who was able to breath some measure of coherence and bring under control that many-headed Hydra that was my manuscript. If errors remain, or if the material could have been better prepared, is no fault of the patient and able people I have named and others who remain nameless.

Steve Edles' work in preparing the painstaking sketches that grace this book also deserves special mention. The intention originally was to make simple little drawings to decorate the chapter headings, and Steve went well beyond that in his unbridled enthusiasm with the subject matter coupled with his unique talent.

I cannot close this acknowledgement without mentioning what borders on the saintly patience of my wife, Demetra, who was a "sometime widow" to my endless research and writing.

INTRODUCTION

W hen we refer to Greece, it is natural that we should think about the Greek peninsula and islands. Our modern minds are used to specific frontiers. But this volume describes the history of the Greek people, where they went and what they accomplished.

To better understand this narrative, there is a second dimension that should be kept in mind, and that is time. Three hundred years of American history, for example, seems a long time to us. It is difficult to come to grips with the many events that can take place and how they slowly evolve over a span of 5,000 years — the known period of history of the Greek people. One more element completes the setting, and that is the sparsity of population in ancient times. When Greek colonists searched for new places in which to settle they had a wide choice of unoccupied areas from which to select. Over a period of several centuries, travelling by boat along a coastline, they searched for a protected harbor or cove with fertile land nearby. There were many such places, and they established hundreds of communities from Gibraltar to the far reaches of the Black Sea. Later, resulting from the conquests of Alexander the Great, some settlements were established as far east as India.

These colonists carried with them more than their few worldly possessions; they brought the remarkable culture that had been already developed on the Greek peninsula and islands. Their mother country is an area of uncommon beauty, but relatively infertile and of limited resources. Yet in this atmosphere a number of distinct self-contained civilizations grew and developed and lasted for many centuries: the Minoan on the island of Crete, 2500-1400 BC; the Mycenaean on the Greek mainland, 1600-1100 BC. Both of these added to the high level of culture that was to be achieved in the many independent city-states in Greece and wherever the Greek people settled.

Usually the expression "Greek culture" brings to mind that of the Classical Period. This stems from the degree of attention given to the unique achievements of those times, disseminated repeatedly to many of us by numerous authors and lecturers, addressing themselves to the works of ancient Greek philosophers, poets and writers, and to the fine art works and architecture. Formerly, when a classical education was more important than the pursuit of business or technology, early Greek culture was even more pervasive. There are signs of its excellence everywhere: the Olympic Games, a modern revival of an ancient Greek athletic ritual in honor of religion and peace that began formally in 776 BC; architecture based on the design of Greek temples to give dignity and beauty to banks, court houses, opera houses and government buildings; semicircular Greek theatres carved into hillsides at universities, parks and elsewhere; major museums around the world that have large sections of admirable Greek arts dating from those ancient times.

More important than the physical arts are the thoughts of the ancient philosophers and authors, expressed in their writings and plays. These are still a basic source of material to provoke the thinking of students in schools and colleges. Modern playwrights have conceived the plots of some of their plays on variations on the themes of the comedies and tragedies of the ancient Greek authors. Stories of the Greek myths are widely familiar and are still being read. The philosophies of Aristotle, Sophokles, Plato, Sokrates, and others, have not been forgotten. And, in a recent example, speaking of Sokrates, the attraction of those times recently led a veteran senior journalist, I.F. Stone, to go to the trouble at the age of eighty, to learn to read ancient Greek. His purpose was to search primary sources in the original language and compile a description of the events leading to the death of that great philosopher.*

Nor were the Minoan, Mycenaean and Greek mainland civilizations the only examples of the accomplishments of these lively and creative people. We will learn in this volume about the Hellenistic Age, covering a geographical area of Greece, Asia Minor and Egypt, and lasting three hundred years. There were great achievements during this period as well, which people sometimes confuse with the Classical Age. This was to be followed by the eventual conversion of the eastern Roman empire into a Greek-speaking, Greek cultured kingdom that absorbed their Latin masters and lasted 1100 years.

What was the quality of this land and these people, wherever they settled, that led to these ageless and rich accomplishments? The reasons are complex and many factors must have contributed to the legacy. Certainly the prime mover must have been the atmosphere and physical qualities of Greece, an area of dramatic, even inspirational, natural beauty, with its rough mountains and fertile valleys and plains; large enough, surely, but also human-sized, surrounded by "wine-dark" seas (as Homer wrote); its many islands serving as stepping stones to areas and adventures beyond its own confines, and with a generally agreeable and invigorating climate.

In addition to the physical quality, there was the intellectual environment. A free person in Greece in ancient times could arrive at a state of mind where he could observe and reason; he could reflect, question, and speak freely, he could learn. The talented thinkers and the doers were

---

*I.F. Stone, *The Trial of Socrates* ; Little, Brown and Company, Boston, 1988.

supported and encouraged. A highly imaginative religion was developed. Human dignity and intellectual achievements were appreciated. Everyone could turn out during festivals to see and hear the poets and the plays. There was time to analyze and discuss them.

The small independent city-state, or *polis*, was the catalyst. Some ancient thinkers believed that a maximum of five thousand free citizens was the ideal size. This was where all the benefits that a person could provide for himself and his fellows, could come together. Slavery existed in Greece as in the rest of the ancient world, and it helped to give the people who could afford slaves the leisure to accomplish what they did. All these and other elements contributed to the unique achievements of the Greeks at that time, of so much value to future generations of mankind.

Not all of it was good, of course. There were many wars, for example, with their attendant cruelties. Battles had frightful casualty rates especially considering the hand-to-hand nature of the fighting. Sieges of cities refusing to surrender were often followed by the slaughter of men and boys, slavery for the women and children, and the looting and razing of the defeated polis. Captured soldiers were often put to work in mines or pulling oars or at other forms of hard physical labor.

But it took the Greek peninsula thousands of years before it emerged as a nation. At first, there were the independent city-states. These were sometimes grouped into regional leagues with a common goal, of which the principal leaders of their respective leagues were Athens and Sparta. These two cities became intense rivals, and this eventually led to the Peloponnesian War (434-404 BC). As a result, both these cities were greatly weakened and this prevented their being able to put their capabilities and assets into more admirable use. Sixty years later, Philip II of Macedonia, Alexander's father, was to emerge as the strong leader who managed by conquest or by treaty to temporarily unify a large part of the Greek peninsula for the first time, except for Sparta and her neighboring city-states, which continued to remain independent.

Over the next two centuries, the lack of lasting political unity among the Greek peoples continued without change, until the arrival in the Greek world of the Romans. In 146 BC, the Greek peninsula was conquered and unified by the armies of Imperial Rome. The Greeks remained under foreign domination from various masters for the next two thousand years, until 1832. It took until 1947 for Greece to emerge as the nation we know today.

Finally, it is worth repeating that the history of present-day physical Greece is only one part of the history of the Greek people. As this volume will describe and as the maps will reveal, the true history of the Greeks covers a broad geographical area. But more than geography, the history of these people is the triumph of energy, creativity, and an ageless culture. And from the same roots also grew tragedy.

Before ending this introduction, it may be of interest to comment on the origin of the words "Hellas" and "Hellene" and "Greece" and "Greeks." Both had their origins in the names of ancient tribes occupying the Greek mainland in antiquity. The Hellenes were an early tribe in southern Thessaly, the Graia in Boiotia. (*Graeci* is the Latin derivative of Graia.) Neither of these names was used extensively in early times to denote all of the people of the area. Those who lived in Athens were known as Athenians and those in Sparta, Spartans, and so on. The names Hellenes and Graia were woven into mythology by Hesiod in his *Theogony*, in which he describes the origins of the gods: Hellen was the son of Deukalion and Pyrrha; Graikos was the son of Thessalos. Each is variously described as being the father of the Hellenes, or Greeks.

It is practically impossible to trace the process of how the names were finally adopted to describe all these people. The Greeks have always called their country Hellas and themselves Hellenes. Western use of the words Greece and Greeks have come down to us from the Latin.

NOTES ON SPELLING

By tradition, many historians have adopted the Latinized forms of Greek personal names, similar to the Latin spellings of Greek words. For example, *Odysseus* in Greek became *Ulysses* in Latin; *Hercules* in Latin was *Heracles* in Greek, or more properly *Herakles*. But a number of them favor a closer transliteration from the Greek originals. This may lead to confusion for the general reader, especially when the names are sometimes used in their altered Latin form. This book favors Greek spellings. Yet, even this has its practical limits; it does not seem useful to be so dogmatic on the subject if respecting the Greek spelling can lead to confusion. Thus, for example, the Latin name of the large Greek island of *Crete* is used rather than the Greek name for it, which is *Krete* (pronounced *"Kriti"*), since the Latin is the more familiar term. Likewise *Mycenae* is preserved for the same reason, although the Greek spelling *Mykene* or *Mykenai* is at least recognizable.

A note on some of the differences between Greek and Latin spellings will help in clarifying the spelling of familiar Greek names and may be of some linguistic interest.

Greek has three letters all having the same *e* sound (as in *me*), these being the *υ* (*upsilon* in English, or, more correctly, *ypsilon*), the *ι* (iota), and the *η* (eta). These were adapted into the Latin script as *y*, *i*, and *e*, respectively. Also, because in Greek the *y* and *e* sounds at the beginning of a word are slightly aspirated, they have been transliterated into English with an *h* preceding them, as in *Hydra* (the island) or *Hera* (wife of Zeus). These conventions are followed in this book.

The Greek *κ* became a *c* in Latin and was so adopted in English. This resulted in the place-name *Kyrenaika* in Greek being written as *Cyrenaica*, and *Kirke* becoming *Circe*. In this book, *Kyrenaika* is used, but *Circe* is used in its Latin form because the Greek spelling alters the familiar name too much. In another example, *Corfu*, the Greek island, is called *Kerkyra* by the Greeks, and Herodotos referred to *Corcyra* (as it was then called), or more properly, *Korkyra*. *Corfu* and *Korkyra* are both used in this book, as appropriate.

Another change involves diphthongs. These are the two-vowel combinations pronounced in modern Greek as one sound, and in ancient Greek as two, (as for example, *οι*, pronounced *o-ee* then, and *ee* now), that usually appear in their Latin forms as:

    αι   (pronounced in modern Greek *e* as in *met*) was written in Latin *ae*;

    οι   (pronounced *e* as in *me*) became *oe* ;

    ου   (pronounced *oo* as in *boot*) became *u*;

    ευ   (pronounced *eff* in Greek) became *eu* but often pronounced as *you* in English (as in *Euboea*), or *ee-uh* (as in *Odysseus*);

    αυ   (pronounced *aff* in Greek) became *au* which is pronounced in English as *awe* (as in the name *Pausanias*).

The Greek *o* at the end of a name became a *u* in Latin, as in *Herodotus* or *Miletus*. These and other similar names are used in this book in their Greek forms, i.e., *Herodotos* and *Miletos*. In other cases, where the Latin *u* is in fact the Greek *ov*, as in *Peleus*, remain unchanged. But *Byzantium*, is usually shown in its Latin spelling because of its broad familiarity, (rather than the Greek *Byzantion*).

The Latin *ch* sound such as in *Aeschylus* (in Greek, *Aischylos*), is the closest the Latins could come to the Greek χ, which is not an *x* at all but an *h* sound. This spelling has been kept throughout the book. Similarly, the Latin *ph* for the Greek φ (pronounced f) was written as two letters because the Greek letter was originally aspirated. This spelling is used in the book.

I trust linguists and historians will be tolerant of my choices, dwelled on here in order to familiarize the reader with how they came into the language rather than how they were altered in Latin. In any case, the index in this book lists both spellings and offers a cross-reference.

A NOTE ON NAMES

As indicated in the preceding, Greek spellings for Greek names of people or places are favored in this volume, rather than the Latinized versions. The reasons are certainly justifiable, in the opinion of this and a number of other authors, as will be described. Another area of possible confusion for the general reader who might have occasion to refer to one history book or another, is that the names of persons (especially) have also been subjected to translations, and by no means uniformly. For example, the Roman leader Marcus Antonius has been called by many historians Mark Antony, and sometimes Mark Anthony. The line of the Macedonian Greek kings of Egypt have been called by historians by the name of the founder, Ptolemy; the name in Greek is *Ptolemaios*. Likewise, the eastern successor king called Seleucid in English is *Seleukos* in Greek.

Why some names have been left relatively unchanged by historians, and others translated or written in Latinized forms, is not clear. The name of that famous Roman emperor commonly written in English as Constantine is in Latin, *Constantinus* (and *Konstantinos* in Greek). Why historians did not translate (that is, Anglicize) other Roman Emperors' names is a mystery.

There is no formally adopted general rule on the subject. But it seems useful in the opinion of this author that the casual reader of the milennia-long history of the Greeks and the impact they made on world culture should be aware of the Greek spellings of Greek names, and not just their Latin adaptations. Therefore, this volume respects the Greek spelling where appropriate, but not when it would distort the familiar usage too much.

References to the names of Roman emperors poses another question. Should the use of Latin names always be preferred? There were western emperors at Rome and eastern emperors at Constantinople. Certainly when they were Latins, the Latin spelling should be respected, even in the mention of the name of the emperor Theodosius who had a purely Greek name, *Theodosios.* But the western empire was lost to invasions of Germanic tribes, and the east was Hellenized and the common language (*lingua franca* in Latin) was Greek. The language of the original Christian church founded in Hellenized Judea was always Greek, and in many other ways the Greek language was dominant. This became so prevalent that during the reign of Heraclius (in Latin, or *Heraklios* in Greek)(AD 610-641), the emperor decreed that the official language would be Greek since it had been so for a very long time unofficially, anyway. Should historians use the Greek spelling of the eastern emperors' names only from that time on, or at some time earlier? And many were Greek names anyway, like *Theophilos* (AD 829-842), why should it be written in the Latinized form, Theophilus?

Would the place of birth of the emperors be a clue to as to what might be a correct usage? From one point of view, even if they were not born in Italy but elsewhere in the vast empire, they were no less Roman. The eastern empire was known as the Eastern Roman Empire, and the capital was called New Rome, even if it was later called Constantinople. But it is most likely that when the emperors were referred to in writing at the time when people began using the Greek language, their names were spelled as written in Greek. Hence, this is the usage employed in this volume. Both the Latin and the Greek spellings are cross-indexed.

One

Prehistoric
Greece

BOOK ON THE HISTORY OF GREECE PUBLISHED before 1875 would have contained little material about the Greeks prior to the first millenium BC. The author would have mentioned that a number of peoples inhabited the Greek peninsula during Neolithic times prior to the third millenium BC, such as the Pelasgians — whom historians consider to be "pre-Greek." The first "Greeks" were Indo-Europeans who gradually migrated west from the Anatolian plains into Europe, some continuing south into the area we now call Greece. They easily replaced or absorbed the few Stone Age inhabitants of the Greek landscape. The author would have identified these invaders as Dorians, Aeolians, Ionians, and other related tribes. Some of these settlers traded with Egypt and the East and began to develop into a civilization. Little else of historical importance about this early period would have appeared in such a book. However, it would no doubt have included descriptions about Greek mythology, another important part of what was then known about early Greek history. But it would probably have been difficult for the reader of that history book to understand clearly how much of what he was reading was factual and how much was embellished storytelling of the ancient poets and bards.

Foremost among the ancient heroic epics that have come down to us are the two best-preserved books from those times, Homer's *Iliad* and his *Odyssey*. The *Iliad* is about the war between the Peloponnesian and mainland Greeks who united against the leaders of Troy in Asia Minor and their allies; this conflict was supposed to have taken place about the middle of the thirteenth century BC. The *Odyssey* describes the adventures of one of the Greek leaders in trying to return home from Troy to his island kingdom of Ithaki (Ithaca). The books contain much about the people of prehistoric Greece: their lives and attitudes, their religion and beliefs, and their relationships with each other. (Homer's writings are covered in more detail starting p.13). These and other, later sources, originally handed down from generation to generation in the form of narrated stories, added to our early knowledge, there being no written language in the Greek peninsula and islands in those prehistoric times.

Then came the archeologists. Only about a hundred years ago they were to discover the remains of two highly developed and distinct civilizations that had existed in ancient times on the Greek peninsula, Crete and eastern Asia Minor. The descriptions that follow relate how they were discovered and what they were.

HEINRICH SCHLIEMANN
(b.1822-d.1890)

O ne of the prominent figures to make their mark in nineteenth century archeology was Heinrich Schliemann, a wealthy German merchant steeped in Homer since childhood. In 1868, at age 46, he retired from commercial activities and arrived in Greece to devote himself full-time to his archeological studies. Schliemann was convinced that Homer's stories were based on true events — that Homer was narrating actual historical facts. Schliemann believed, for example, that the ancient city of Troy had existed and the Trojan War took place. His plans for Greece began with his marriage to a 17-year-old Greek girl of a good but modest family in Athens. The bride had been found for him in traditional Greek style as he had requested, and the marriage arranged through her uncle who had known Mr. Schliemann. Sophia was to be of great help to him, and she participated in all his work to come, although Schliemann himself was a linguist and had already learned Greek.

The area we now call Greece, it must be remembered, had been under Ottoman Turkish occupation for nearly four centuries. The liberation of the Peloponnese and part of the mainland came only in 1832. Other areas still continued under Turkish rule. While the Ottomans had permitted some archeological investigations to take place in these territories, probably entirely by foreigners, it was not easy to obtain a *firman* (royal decree) to conduct this work. Also, in those times the Turks bargained for a good-sized share of any treasure that might be found, apparently with very little regard for its historic value. These are some of the circumstances that Schliemann faced upon his arrival in Athens.

But Schliemann was determined to find the city of Troy, and he managed to obtain the permission of the Ottomans to dig in the area he had identified from his studies; this area he located in Ottoman Asia Minor at a place near present-day Hissarlik. Schliemann financed, planned, and organized the dig entirely on his own, being guided by his conviction by what Homer had described. He hired workmen to excavate under his direction. Luck was on his side, and his workmen eventually came upon the remains of an ancient city. They continued digging and finally uncovered successive layers of this ancient city built and rebuilt over the same area at least nine times during a period of what would turn out to be 2000 years. In 1873, Schliemann's laborers finally uncovered a burial ground containing a large treasure of impressive gold artifacts. Schliemann promptly announced to the world his finding of King Priam's palace in Homer's Troy.

By 1876, inspired by his findings at Troy, Schliemann moved his investigations to an area he identified on the Peloponnese in a part of Greece that had by now been liberated from the Ottomans. He believed this area to have been the location of ancient Mycenae, the city of King Agamemnon, leader of the expedition against Troy, all as described by Homer. He was again fortunate, late in the year, to unearth royal tombs filled with one of the largest deposits of gold treasure and other precious objects of antiquity that had ever been discovered.

Schliemann continued his investigations in other areas as well, but with less spectacular results than the first two, until his death in 1890. Although scholars do not agree with his methods and conclusions in many important details, Dr. Schliemann and his assistants and collaborators opened the way to greatly expanding the world's knowledge of ancient Greek history. The process continued with the efforts of other archeologists, in no small measure inspired by Schliemann's lectures and writings that had electrified world attention at the import of his discoveries.

Did the findings of Schliemann uncover the Troy of the *Iliad* and the tomb of King Agamemnon at Mycenae, converting into reality Homer's tales of mythology, as he dramatically announced? Apparently not, according to later studies. None of the impressive findings provide evidence confirming that the stories of the Homeric epics actually took place as described. There is no indication that any of the cities built at the site called Troy was ever destroyed by an army of Greeks as described in the *Iliad*, even though evidence was found of destruction of the cities by various means, earthquakes, fire, and the hostilities of nameless invaders. The names Troy and Agamemnon exist only in Homer, so far as anyone has been able to prove. But there surely were rich royal tombs unearthed at Troy and Mycenae, and evidence of a well-developed civilization.

SIR ARTHUR EVANS
(b.1850-d.1940)

The likelihood of the presence of the remnants of an ancient civilization at Knossos, on the Ottoman-governed island of Crete, was evident for some time, and small artifacts of a fairly sophisticated craftsmanship had been found at that site by local people. But the Ottomans refused to allow anyone dig at Knossos, and the requests of a number of persons had been refused, including Schliemann's. It was only in 1890, after Crete became autonomous but still under Ottoman suzerainty, that Arthur Evans, a British archeologist, was finally able to purchase the Knossos site at his own personal expense and begin to dig. Before long, it became evident that an even older, distinct and even more sophisticated civilization than the Mycenaean had existed in the area.

Evans devoted the rest of his life and most of his fortune to digging at this site, working from 1900 to 1914, and, after the interruption of World War I, from 1920 until 1932. In 1928, Evans made a gift of his Knossos site to the British School of Archeology, located in Athens, but he continued to devote his time lecturing and writing about the Minoan civilization until 1940 when he died, aged 90. For his efforts he was knighted in 1911, and won many other honors.

One of the curious facts about Knossos is that a large quantity of clay tablets were uncovered at that site on which were two distinct kinds of "writing." Evans called the two Linear "A" and "B." Linear A is an older hieroglyphic writing, that has never been deciphered. Many clay tablets with Linear B script were also found at Mycenae and other sites, thus it was concluded to be a Creto-Mycenaean writing. When Sir Arthur lectured on this subject in England in 1936, one of his listeners was a 14-year-old English schoolboy, Michael Ventris, who resolved then and there that he would be the one to decipher the unknown script. Ventris was a determined dreamer. Beginning his work after World War II, and aided principally by John Chadwick, a linguist from Cambridge University, and using army code deciphering techniques, by 1956 they were able to substantially interpret the script. Though the contents of the tablets were found to be mostly records of trading and the storage of goods, this and other information found on them has contributed to our knowledge of those ancient times. Most importantly, this is the first written source to be found of an ancient Greek language.

These and other archeologists and historians have contributed to our knowledge of these two distinct ancient Greek civilizations, the Minoan (c. 2600- c. 1400 BC) and the Mycenaean (c. 1600-c. 1100 BC). Very recently and within a short time, these scholars extended our knowledge of Greek history back two thousand years. The Minoan civilization on Crete and the Mycenaean on the Greek mainland were not long separated from each other. Evidence shows that they traded peacefully with one another until about 1450 BC, when, for some reason, the aggressive Mycenaeans invaded Crete and subjugated the Minoans for a period of time, gradually replacing them.

What were these civilizations?

THE MINOAN AGE
(c.2600-c.1400 BC)

The Minoan Age coincided with the period historians call the Bronze Age of Greece. It was Sir Arthur Evans who coined the term "Minoan" after King Minos of Crete, a mythological ruler of the island kingdom who is first mentioned in Homer's *Iliad*. But whether Minos actually existed is unknown; rather, the name (or word "Minos") meant "ruler" in the language spoken by the Minoans.

It is not clear from where the first Cretan settlers came, but it is generally believed these earlier Neolithic people (Stone Age people who preceded the Bronze Age) were gradually overtaken by a people who migrated there shortly before 2600 BC from the area of present-day Libya and from the Nile River delta. Some evidence also shows they mixed with others who came from eastern Asia Minor starting a little later. In this place and peaceful atmosphere, the culture developed quickly and brilliantly.

The Minoan civilization was restricted to the island of Crete, and while Knossos was the principal palace-city, there were a number of other towns with lesser but still splendid palaces. The Minoans traded extensively with Egypt as well as with other Eastern civilizations. Minoan outposts were established on other islands nearby, such as in Kythera and Thera, and there is evidence of trade with communities on other Greek islands and the mainland. Indeed, commerce and trade were the root of Minoan economic success. Minoan Crete became a thalassocracy; that is, a maritime power (in Greek, thalassa, ocean; kratos, nation).

The high degree of development of Minoan Crete is expressed by the extensive rich and attractive palace complexes* built principally at Knossos, Phaistos, and Mallia beginning around 2000 BC, as well as by the graceful painted vases and urns, the gold jewelry and carved gems, fine weapons, the extensive, well-executed wall paintings, and other artifacts showing skill, imagination, and beauty. The early Minoan palaces were severely damaged by earthquakes around 1700 BC, but they were rebuilt on an even grander scale. These are the buildings made known to us by the archeologists, especially the main palace at Knossos in its partial modern reconstruction designed by Evans.

Around 1450 BC, all the palaces were destroyed by severe earthquakes centered at the island of Thera to the north (See *The Cataclysms at Thera* p.8). Phaistos and Mallia were abandoned, but Knossos was again rebuilt and reoccupied, only to be destroyed by sacking just after 1400 BC, apparently this time by Mycenaean invaders. The Minoan civilization seems to cease about the same time.

THE MYCENAEAN AGE
(c.1600-c.1100 BC)

The Indo-Europeans who settled in southern Greece and gradually developed into the Mycenaean civilization are regarded by archeologists and historians as the first true Greeks.** Their language, identified by Evans in its written form as Linear B, was an early form of Greek. As we have seen, Linear A, a Minoan language, has never been deciphered. The

---

*"Complexes" is the right word. Found to have extensive and intricate passages, provides a clue about how the well-known ancient myth came into being describing the adventures of Theseus, the labyrinth, and the Minotaur.

**"Indo-Europeans" is a general name given to tribes that lived in central Asia, some of whom gradually migrated westwards and settled in Europe. Though evidence has been found of the presence of Neanderthal man in Greece dating many tens of thousands of years BC, modern man dates several thousand years BC, migrating from the area of southern Russia. The evidence of their origin comes from primitive stone tools and other artifacts, as well as language.

Mycenaeans had agricultural skills; but it was not until they became a seafaring people that they flourished. Trade with the Near East, the Minoans, and the Egyptians exposed them to the cultures of these more advanced civilizations, which they absorbed and blended with their own. The Mycenaeans' accumulation of wealth and the growth of their cities were explosive. Homer called Mycenae "rich in gold," and Schliemann proved this when he excavated the royal shaft graves and beehive tombs. Nor was this the only site of rich Mycenaean finds.

Although Mycenae was the principal city (hence the adoption of its name by modern historians to identify the civilization), it was not the capital city; indeed, there was none. Separate city-states or regions had their own kings and palaces. Impressive Mycenaean sites have also been found at Tiryns and Pylos in the Peloponnese; at Athens and Thebes in central Greece; and at Orchomenos and Iolkos in Thessaly; among many others. During its zenith, in the thirteenth and twelfth centuries BC, about 400 Mycenaean settlements had been established. Some of these rivaled the Minoan in their degree of culture and refinement.

Among the Minoans, the king's palace complex was placed on a prominent site, near but separate from the community. But among the Mycenaeans, the palace stood in the center of the city, closely surrounded by the community, and, often, by heavy stone fortifications. The Minoans had been peaceful people. The Mycenaeans, being aggressive, lived in a less secure atmosphere and fearful of possible attack by their neighbors, on whom they also preyed at times. Eventually, it was through hostilities that the greatly developed Mycenaean civilization finally came to an end. A number of events contributed: a reduction of overseas trade due to a downturn in the economy in the east; unrest and war between rival Mycenaean communities; invasions from northern barbarian tribes, and from "sea-peoples" from the east (so-called by historians because they arrived by boat). Mycenaean communities greatly declined as people left insecure areas to seek safety elsewhere, or they died out altogether. The later invasions of the Dorians, another strong tribe from the north, finalized the decline by the end of the eleventh century BC. The southern Greek peninsula was plunged into a "dark age" for the next three centuries, although evidence shows that the Mycenaean civilization continued in a subdued fashion in many areas during this period (c.1100-c.800 BC).

THE CATACLYSMS AT THERA
(c.1500-c.1450 BC)

The island of Thera (present-day Santorini) is situated in the Aegean Sea, about 75 miles (120 kilometers) due north of the coast of Crete. Inhabited since the third millenium BC, it maintained close contacts with the Minoans as well as with the Greek mainland, and was highly developed. The island was originally circular in shape, with a volcanic cone in the middle several hundred feet high.

Around 1500 BC, and over a period of years, a series of what had to be enormous volcanic eruptions and explosions took place centered on Thera itself, ending with the final violent collapse into the sea of about one-half of the island's total ground surface. In its place a huge undersea crater was left (called in modern times a *caldera*), 1300 feet (400 meters) deep and 35 square miles (90 square kilometers) in area. This spectacular event has been thoroughly studied by modern vulcanologists, geologists, archeologists, and other specialists, who have examined the site and the surrounding area and have evolved a likely description of the phenomenon.

The eruptions would have been accompanied by violent earthquakes and ear-shattering explosions. Great volumes of sulphurous fumes, poisonous gases, and superheated steam would have been released in dense clouds. Enormous quantities of lava, rocks, and pumice would have been heaved up and blown around over a large area. Especially during the last violent explosion, so much volcanic ash would have been blown into the air and atmosphere above, that an area of at least 250 miles (400 kms) across would have been plunged into utter darkness. This would have lasted at least a day even after the eruptions stopped, and it would have taken several days to clear completely. Because of the then prevailing wind direction the darkness would have lasted even longer at the northern coast of Crete, 75 miles (120 kms) distant. Measurements taken in modern times by drilling in the sea bottom and on land show that volcanic ash was deposited in varying thicknesses up to several feet over an area of 100,000 square miles (260,000 sq. kms.) bearing toward the south-east carried by the prevailing winds. It has been estimated that the sound of the final explosion would have been so great, it would have been heard as far west as the eastern coasts of the United States and Brazil; as far south as South Africa; and as far east as China.

The gases and fumes would have combined with the moisture in the air and resulted in acid rains over Thera and the surrounding area. Torrential rainfall from condensing steam and other atmospheric disturbances would have drenched a wide area. The sea rushing in to fill the caldera formed by the violent implosion, would have produced huge seismic waves (*tsunamis*, a Japanese word), the height of which have been estimated by some experts at 650 feet (200 meters) at the source. Such force would have sent them long distances in all directions. They have been estimated to have still been 25 feet (7 m) high at the present-day Israeli coast, 550 miles (900 kms) distant.

All life still remaining on Thera would have been destroyed, incuding all vegetation. Archeologists, historians, and other experts have also carefully studied the effect of the Thera eruptions on the surrounding areas. The nearest site was that of the Minoan civilization on Crete, which had been flourishing for more than a thousand years by this time. Although the experts do not agree on all the details, there is much evidence to show that the Minoan civilization was very much affected by the events at Thera. The huge seismic waves would have drowned a large number of people as well as collapsing buildings already damaged and weakened by the earthquakes. Much agriculture would have been destroyed by the volcanic ash fallout, and at least some of the area would have

MAP 1.0 THERA CATACLYSMS (c. 1500-c. 1450 BC)

Preceded by many strong earthquakes, a high volcanic cone rising from the center of this round island exploded around 1500 to 1450 BC. About half the land surface collapsed into the sea. More earthquakes, large seismic waves, acid rains, ash deposits, and other devastation affected large areas of the Mediterranean, including the highly developed Minoan culture on Crete, to the south.

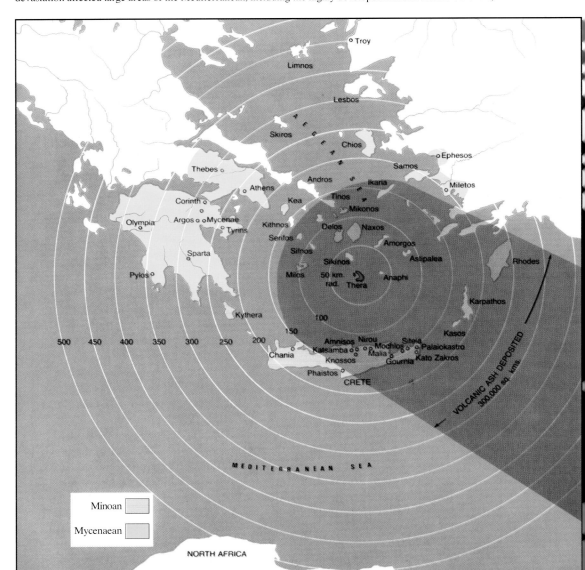

Troy

Limnos

Lesbos

Skiros

Chios

Ephesos

AEGEAN

Thebes

Samos

Andros

Ikaria

Miletos

Athens

Tinos

Corinth

Kea

Mikonos

Olympia

Argos Mycenae

Kithnos

Delos

Naxos

Tyrins

Serifos

Amorgos

Sparta

Sifnos

Sikinos

Astipalea

Rhodes

Pylos

Milos

50 km.
rad.

Anaphi

Thera

Kythera

Karpathos

100

150

Kasos

200

Amnisos Nirou

Siteia

VOLCANIC ASH DEPOSITED

250

Katsamba

Mochlos

Palaiokastro

300,000 sq. kms

500   450   400   350   300

Chania

Malia

Kato Zakros

Knossos

Gournia

Phaistos

CRETE

MEDITERRANEAN SEA

Minoan

Mycenaean

NORTH AFRICA

MAP 1.1
ISLAND OF THERA

All life on Thera was destroyed during the eruptions and explosions of the volcano. The resulting undersea basin, or *caldera*, is 1300 feet (400 meters) deep. Many years later two small burnt rock islands rose up in the center, which remain to this day. Seismic activity of far lesser intensity continues, but the island is inhabited and is a prime touristic attraction.

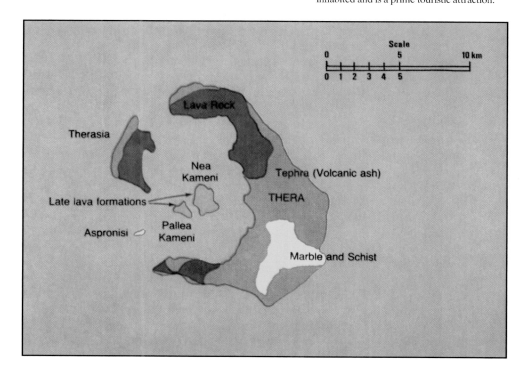

remained infertile for years. Not to be underestimated was the fearful psychological effect on the frightened survivors, shaken by the frequent earthquakes, explosions, and other phenomena that would have continued over a period of years. Many of these people would have left Crete to settle elsewhere. Though enough population remained to somewhat rebuild what was destroyed, whole areas were abandoned, and new areas were built more simply. The Minoan civilization gradually declined, and the survivors eventually mixed with the Mycenaean Greeks who began to settle in Crete. By the end of the the fifteenth century BC, Minoan civilization died out altogether and was supplanted by the Mycenaean.

Many references to flooding during this period have come down to us through legend and mythology in the few ancient texts extant describing devastation in such areas as Attica, Boiotia, Argos, the Aegean islands from Samothrace to Rhodes, and along the Asia Minor coast. Egyptian records show a sudden interruption of foreign trade with the area of the eastern Mediterranean.

References are also found from the same ancient sources about "floating islands," which probably refer to thick masses of floating pumice on the sea, which material had been spewed up by the volcano. These islands must have remained on the Aegean for years, moved about by winds and currents. Homer's *Odyssey*, as well as the story of the Argonauts by Apollonios, describe related events: giants throwing huge boulders are a more satisfactory and dramatic explanation for volcanoes spewing rocks, which the ancients would not have understood and which stories became more melodramatic with the telling — whether Thera or Vesuvius, near both of which Odysseus had some of his adventures. "Days turned into nights" by the gods are better thus explained for the sky heavily filled with fine black volcanic ash. The Argonauts throwing a clod of earth into the sea, given to them by Triton the god of the sea, by which act Thera was supposed to have been originally created, explained the appearence of new islands in the sea suddenly forced up from the sea bottom by volcanic action. Considering the times, more scientific explanations were lacking, and these vivid descriptions more dramatically satisfied the imagination and fitted the prevailing traditions.

The force of the final Thera cataclysm has been studied carefully by many specialists. A comparison has been made with Krakatoa, an island in the Sunda Straits between Java and Sumatra in the Far East. This volcanic island, of remarkably similar characteristics as Thera, exploded in 1883 under conditions that allowed ample scientific observations. Krakatoa created seismic waves that achieved heights of up to 130 feet (40 meters) at their origin, and even 50 feet (15 m.) high 50 miles (80 kms.) away. These spread in all directions causing destruction of 300 coastal towns and villages, with over 36,000 people drowned or otherwise killed. Yet Krakatoa lost only 9 square miles (23 sq. kms.) of its original surface compared to the 35 square miles (90 sq. kms.) lost by Thera. Its caldera is about 900 feet (280 m.) deep compared to the 1300 feet (400 m.) at Thera. This is not to conclude that the Thera cataclysm was as great as four times that of Krakatoa. However, there is no doubt that the Thera cataclysm and related effects are one of the greatest, if not the greatest, such volcanic phenomena to have taken place anywhere in the world in recorded time.

Thera has remained volcanically active since antiquity. Since then, a number of spectacular but less devastating tectonic events have occured causing considerable damage to the island and to the surrounding area. This geology has caused some burnt islets to have been pushed up in the center of the caldera, and they remain to this day. The last volcanic action on Thera occured in 1956, causing a major earthquake.

The Lost Atlantis

The eruptions at Thera have led scientists to speculate on whether the legendary *Atlantis* — said to have been the center of yet another great ancient culture that was supposedly swallowed by the sea — was in fact at Thera. Reference to Atlantis was originally made by Plato (428-347 BC) in his *Dialogues*, his *Timaios and Critias* referring to the "lost kingdom of Atlantis." Some eminent scholars make a case for Thera as its location, basing their theories on a combination of the existence of the advanced Minoan culture also prevalent on the island and the destruction caused by the earthquakes and eruptions. Of course, other locations have also been proposed as the site of Atlantis. But Atlantis, if it ever existed, remains undiscovered. Aristotle, who examined the subject some years after the death of Plato (who had been his teacher), concluded: "The man who dreamed it up made it vanish."

THE HOMERIC EPICS
The Trojan War

No other pieces of literature from ancient times were better known or influenced the Greeks more than the *Iliad* and the *Odyssey*. Scholars and historians have been trying to match fact and legend ever since their discovery. They are among the earliest examples of Greek written literature in poetic form; ordinarily, such epics were passed by word of mouth from generation to generation. Indeed, the style approximates oral rather than written speech. It was sung or recited by singers and poets to their attentive audiences.

The *Iliad* and the *Odyssey* represent the beginning of a revived Greek heroic tradition in which imaginative and dramatic events are presented majestically. These descriptions are richly and emotionally drawn — they are not mere adventure storiers. These books having been written and copied over and over from ancient times, they were passed to an ever wider audience uniformly. They describe deeds that took place in the prehistory of Greece, and they paint a fascinating picture of what life must have been then. Not the least

MAP 1.2 TROJAN WAR

According to Homer, Paris, a Trojan prince, abducted Achaian Queen Helen from her home in Sparta and carried her off to Troy. To bring her back, the Achaians gathered thousands of men, sailing from Aulis in 1186 ships. The Trojans assembled their allies from Asia Minor, Macedonia, and Thrace. The war lasted ten years.

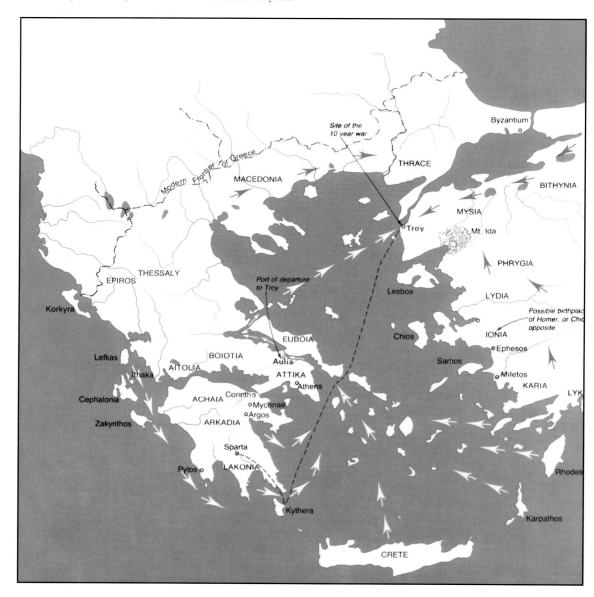

is their importance as a repository of Greek mythology; these books describe the hierarchy and character of the Olympian family of gods, thus becoming the "Bible" of the eighth century BC. They provided a synthesis of the diverse religions and beliefs of ancient Greece.

These two famous epic poems are attributed to Homer, and the events they describe are presumed to have taken place around the thirteenth century BC. It is generally agreed that Homer probably lived around the eighth century BC, and it is assumed he came from a Greek-occupied area known as Ionia, as central western Asia Minor was called in those times, or possibly from the Greek island of Chios opposite. Appearing at the end of the three centuries (eleventh to eighth BC) which some historians have called the "Dark Ages," Homer's works helped to rekindle and inspire the Greek spirit.

The *Iliad*

The *Iliad* tells the dramatic story of the war of the Achaians (a people living in the Peloponnese) against the city of Troy on the Asia Minor coast. This was provoked by the abduction of Helen (*Eleni*), wife of King Menelaos of Sparta, by Paris, son of King Priam of Troy. Paris had gone to Sparta from Troy to attempt to arrange the return of King Priam's sister, who, the legend says, had been carried off to Greece many years before. He arrived in Sparta to find that King Menelaos was away, and he was received by his wife, Queen Helen. Paris was immediately taken by the beauty of Helen, who was also smitten by the handsome Paris.

This was the fulfillment of an event that had occured some years before when Paris was pasturing his cattle on Mount Ida near Troy. He was approached by three goddesses to settle an argument they were having among themselves, namely, which one of them was the most beautiful. Hera, the wife of Zeus, told him if he selected her she would help him rule the richest realm on earth. Pallas Athene, goddess of wisdom, offered to make him the wisest and bravest among men. And Aphrodite, goddess of love, offered to give him the most beautiful woman on earth to be his wife. Paris chose Aphrodite over the other two. Helen was the woman to whom Aphrodite guided Paris. Thus the stage was set for the dramatic events that were to follow.

Forgetting the purpose of his mission to Sparta, Paris stormed the palace of King Menelaos with his men and forced Helen (not entirely unwillingly) to leave with him for Troy. When Menelaos returned and learned of the events, he called on his many friends to join him in the rescue mission. This was to be led by his elder brother, Agamemnon, King of Mycenae. Thousands of men gathered, and 1186 ships sailed for Troy and a war that was to last ten years. Of course, the Trojans also gathered together their allies against the invading Achaian forces. According to Homer, even the gods took sides. The Greeks had the support of Hera and Pallas Athene, losers of the beauty contest; and they were also supported by Poseidon, Hephaistos, and Hermes. The Trojans had Ares, Apollo, Artemis, Leto, Xanthos, and the contest winner, Aphrodite.* (See also the table on Olympian gods in Chapter Nine.)

The *Iliad* actually describes only four days of the war, but in the narration, Homer manages to convey the story of the ten-year long event. The war raged with brave exploits on both sides, and the heroes slaying each other in individual duels. It finally ended in victory for the Achaians and the destruction of Troy through the ruse of the wooden horse, conceived by the shrewd Odysseus, king of the island kingdom of Ithaka. Explaining this event briefly: the war was a stalemate even after the ten years it lasted, with the Achaians unable to penetrate the walled defenses of Troy. Odysseus finally proposed a plan whereby the Achaians would be seen by the Trojans to elaborately prepare for departure on their ships, as if they were giving up the war. They would also build a huge wooden horse and roll it on wheels to the main gate of the city, as a gift in tribute to the Trojan defenses. But inside the horse which was hollow a troop of picked warriors would be hidden. The Greek allies adopted the plan and proceeded with it. When dawn broke the Trojans saw that the enemy ships had ostensibly departed, and found only the enormous wooden horse left in front of their gates, which they finally opened and rolled it inside. That night the concealed Achaians descended from the horse and opened the gates to their companions who had crept back during the night and were hiding under the walls. They rushed in and stormed Troy, destroying it at last.

Schliemann's Troy and Mycenae

As already mentioned (p.4), Heinrich Schliemann was a determined enthusiast of the story and was convinced that Troy had existed and that the war had actually taken place as described by Homer. He amazed the world when he actually discovered the ruins of an ancient city in the spot he determined by his careful analysis of the Homeric texts. Digging down, he found a large cache of finely crafted gold artifacts. He announced them to the world as being from King Priam's palace. In the same manner, when he later found the even more impressive gold objects in the tombs at Mycenae, including a gold funeral mask, he dramatically cabled the Kings of Greece and Prussia, "I have looked upon the face of Agamemnon." Subsequent studies have refuted the emotional statements of Dr. Schliemann but not the importance of his discoveries as related to Greek history. Nor is there any need to confirm as factual the epics of Homer in fine detail. The narratives

* **Hera:**	queen of the gods, wife of Zeus	**Apollo:**	god of the sun
Pallas Athene:	goddess of wisdom	**Artemis:**	goddess of the moon
Poseidon:	god of the sea		and of the chase
Hephaistos:	god of fire	**Leto:**	mother of Artemis and Apollo
Hermes:	herald of the gods.	**Xanthos:**	god of rivers
Ares:	god of war	**Aphrodite:**	goddess of love

depicted those times and attitudes, and Homer undoubtedly used even older source material in creating his works. The Schliemann discoveries in many ways have confirmed the legends.

The *Odyssey*

Of all the Greek heroes who survived the ten-year-long Trojan War, only Odysseus was to take another ten years to finally arrive at his kingdom of Ithaka, an island off western Greece. The tale of his misfortunes — the adventures and wanderings he suffered and his troubles upon reaching home at last — is told by Homer in exquisite detail in the *Odyssey*.

Homer's hero Odysseus is a fascinating personality, and his character as described in both the *Iliad* and the *Odyssey* has been frequently analyzed and used by writers throughout the ages. Odysseus is depicted as a wise leader and resourceful, cunning, brave, a good fighter, a source of good advice, yet a liar when it suited him. His unpredictable nature and hero quality give special interest to Homer's tale of his attempts to return home. Was he selected by the gods to suffer these additional ten years because of his leadership role in the war and his having devised the means for the Greeks to win it? The *Odyssey* describes his adventures as he was forced to wander with his men-at-arms all over the Mediterranean.

The following paragraphs are numbered according to the events as they appear on Map 1.3:

1. Odysseus leaves Troy with his men in twelve ships. The wind carries them north to Ismaros, on the Thracian coast, the area of the Kikones people. The Greeks sack the town (for booty?) and kill the men, dividing the women and spoils among themselves. They are driven off by other Kikones, losing some of their comrades in the fighting — not a very auspicious beginning.

2. They sail south to the Peloponnese, and when they round Cape Malea to turn northwest to Ithaka, a fierce storm blows them southwest across the Mediterranean for nine days to the island of Djerba, off the Tunisian coast, the land of the Lotus-Eaters. The lotus fruit was said to induce a desire to remain there forever. The group manages to resist the temptation and flees taking with them by force two companions who had eaten the fruit.

3. They sail north, arriving finally at an island called Nisida (assumed by some to be present-day Capri) and anchor in a sheltered bay. In one of the boats, Odysseus takes twelve men to explore the opposite shore, where they are discovered by a Cyclops, one of the one-eyed giants who lived there. This Cyclops, named Polyphemos and said to be a son of Poseidon, traps them in his cave and eats six of them for his meals. Odysseus and his men finally manage to blind him while he sleeps and they are able to escape from the cave. The Greeks flee from the place while the raging and blinded giant throws huge rocks in their direction (Vesuvius erupting?), and their vessel is nearly smashed and sunk.

MAP 1.3 ODYSSEY

Odysseus, one of the Achaian leaders, was to take ten years following the end of the Trojan war to manage to arrive from Troy to his island kingdom of Ithaka. Homer describes the many adventures he and his men suffered enroute. Were the gods punishing Odysseus for having thought up the ruse of the wooden horse by which means the Achaians had won the war?

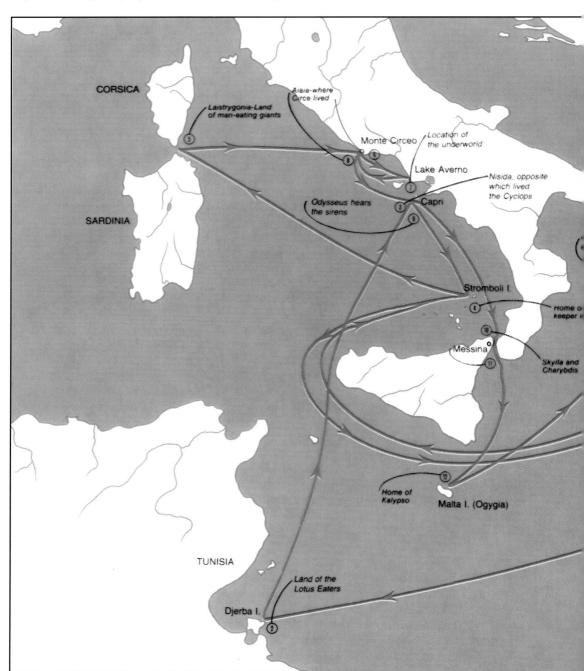

CORSICA

Laistrygonia-Land of man-eating giants

Aiaia-where Circe lived

Monte Circeo

Location of the underworld

Lake Averno

Nisida, opposite which lived the Cyclops

SARDINIA

Odysseus hears the sirens

Capri

Stromboli I.

Home o keeper

Messina

Skylla and Charybdis

Home of Kalypso

Malta I. (Ogygia)

TUNISIA

Land of the Lotus Eaters

Djerba I.

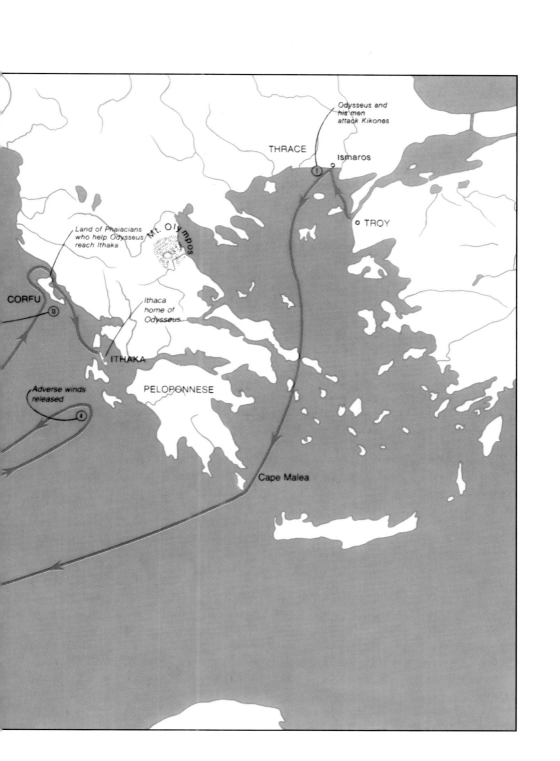

Odysseus and
his men
attack Kikones

THRACE   Ismaros

TROY

Land of Phaiacians
who help Odysseus
reach Ithaka

Mt. Olympos

CORFU

Ithaca
home of
Odysseus

ITHAKA

PELOPONNESE

Adverse winds
released

Cape Malea

4. Proceeding south toward their homeland, the vessels come upon a "floating" island (Stromboli?), ruled by Aelos, keeper of the winds. He takes pity on the Greeks and helps them on their way with a gentle breeze, making them a gift of a tightly bound large bag, which they are not to open. They sail for nine days and nights, nearing the Greek coast at last. While the others sleep, one man is overcome with curiosity and unties the bag, releasing the fierce winds that blow them all the way back to the island from where they had come. This time Aelos refuses to help them.

5. They row for seven days (in the wrong direction), arriving at last at Laistrygonia (between present-day Sardinia and Corsica), where they discover they are in a land of man-eating giants. They rush to escape, with more than a thousand giants chasing after them and throwing large boulders. The boulders strike and sink all their ships except that of Odysseus, which was anchored in a sheltered spot. Many men are lost, and the remainder escape by crowding onto the single vessel left to them.

6. They row to the island of Aiaia (perhaps Monte Circeo, a promontory northwest of Naples, not an island at all), which some of the men explore, meeting the beautiful goddess Circe (*Kirke*), who turns them into swine. While Odysseus is constantly imploring her to have them restored as humans again, he lives with Circe for a year, fathering her son, Telegonos. Odysseus finally succeeds in persuading her to set them free.

7. Circe advises Odysseus to visit the underworld to seek guidance for his safe journey home. He and his men set sail for Hades (possibly Lake Averno, a small lake on the mainland opposite Capri).* While the men wait outside, Odysseus enters alone and finds the ghost of his mother, who had died while he was away all these years; that of Agamemnon, who was killed by his wife Klytemnestra and her lover Aigisthos when he arrived in Mycenae from the war in Troy; and those of many of the other dead heroes of the war who had been his companions.

8. Odysseus is given advice by his dead companions in Hades about what he must do if his journey home is to be successful. Also, that he and his men must first return to Aiaia, to bury one of their comrades who had been killed in a fall before they left to visit Hades; this they do.

9. Before they had left Circe, she had warned Odysseus of another danger in his path toward home. Sailing south he would have to pass by the island of the Sirens (Capri or Galli?) whose song beguiles the listener to land, but where he would meet his death. He was warned to plug the ears of his companions with wax; he was also told that if he wished to hear the song of the Sirens he should have his men tie him to the mast, which they did. Though he implores them to

---

*Some interpretations of Homer have them sail to Hades at the Straits of Gibraltar before they return from where they had left, and all this in one day!

release him when he hears the song as they pass, they row on and escape.

10. Farther south they arrive at the next point of danger, the whirlpool of Charybdis and the crag of Skylla (at the Straits of Messina between Sicily and the toe of Italy). On Skylla lived a monster with twelve long rubbery arms and six long necks with hideous heads. Though the crew manage to escape the physical dangers of the crag and the whirlpool, the monster snatches and destroys six of the men.

11. Passing these dangers at last, the ship puts into a safe harbor near present-day Messina. The men had only rested there for one night when a storm comes up that lasts for a month. Though warned during Odysseus' visit to the underworld not to touch the beautiful cattle there, the men sacrifice one of the animals to appease the gods and to eat, for they are starved. This brings on more trouble when they depart a week later. In a storm, the infuriated Zeus destroys the ship with a thunderbolt, and all the remaining men are drowned except Odysseus, who had been away when the animal had been sacrificed. He floats on the stormy sea on a makeshift raft for nine days and ten nights until at last it lands him on the island of Ogygia (perhaps present-day Malta).

12. On Ogygia lives the nymph Kalypso, who is eager to comfort and tend Odysseus from these strenuous adventures. Though Homer has our hero crying every day that he was unable to depart for his island, he stays for seven years with Kalypso and fathers three children for her: Nausithous, Nausinous, and Latinos. At last the god Hermes persuades Kalypso to help Odysseus leave for home. This she finally does, first having provided him with a set of tools with which he built a boat.

13. Odysseus sails east for 18 days, arriving at last within sight of the mountains of the island of Scheria (Corfu). But the sea-god Poseidon sees him on his fragile craft, and still angry at Odysseus for having blinded his son Polyphemos the Cyclops, sends a storm that destroys Odysseus' boat and throws Odysseus into the sea. Three days later, and with great effort, he finally beaches himself on Scheria, the island inhabited by the Phaiacian people. Upon hearing of his many ordeals, the Phaiacians treat him kindly and give him many gifts and a ship and sailors to transport him to Ithaka, where he arrives at last.

But reaching home did not end the adventures of Odysseus for he now had to rid his palace of 112 suitors, who had been gathering there for years eating him out of house and home while wooing his faithful wife, Penelope, who refused to believe that Odysseus would not return. Finally, together with his brave son, Telemachos, whom he had left twenty years before as an infant, and some faithful swineherds, they slay the suitors, and Odysseus and his family are at last reunited.

A NOTE ON THE TROJAN WAR STORY

So impressed and inspired were ancient authors by details of Homer's stories of the Trojan War and the adventures of Odysseus striving to return home, that they continued and embellished Homer's legends and characterizations in their own writings. This is sometimes confusing as many modern authors describing the Greek myths link some of the events related to Troy as created by Homer, in a single narrative with elaborations by other ancient authors. This does not diminish the drama of those legends, but it is of interest to comment about two of the major details.

For example, Homer refers a number of times in his *Iliad* to the abduction of Helen by Paris that was the cause of the Trojan War. But these meager references to an all-important incident did not completely satisfy other authors. They developed the story at greater length of how he was led to do this by the incident of his having been caused to select the fairest among the three goddesses and the consequences of that choice. The legend was written about by a number of other authors, including a clear account by the Greek tragic playwright Euripides, writing 400 years after Homer. This became known as The Judgement of Paris and is contained in Euripides' play *The Trojan Women*.

In another prominent detail, the device of the huge wooden horse created as a ruse to penetrate at last the walled defenses of Troy, thought up by Odysseus, is only referred to by Homer in a few lines in the *Odyssey* and not at all in the *Iliad*. Other authors were fascinated by and elaborated on this detail over the centuries, but a very complete version of this incident is is contained in the epic poem Aeneid of the Latin poet Virgil, also inspired by the Homeric legend nearly 800 years later.

Other events directly based on these legends by Homer were also written about by (mostly) Greek authors centuries later, especially during the Classical Period. These included manner of the death of the Achaians' greatest hero Achilles, what happened to Prince Paris, the drama of the return of Helen to her husband Menelaos and to Sparta, what took place on the return of King Agamemnon to Mycenae, and many other details and stories. So stimulating were these legends of Homer, that people did not want them to end, and the ancient tragic playwrights and poets made their marks accommodating this desire. Not that the urge to follow Homer failed to inspire modern authors, as well, too numerous to mention. An outstanding example, patterned closely on the style of Homer, was the epic poem *The Odyssey - A Modern Sequel* by Nikos Kazantzakis, written in the 1950's.

Two

The Archaic Period
(c.800-c.600 BC)

MIGRATIONS AND SETTLEMENTS

WHETHER BECAUSE OF THE DORIAN INVASIONS or natural catastrophes or a combination of these, the brilliant Mycenaean world and the reduced settlements that remained decayed and eventually lost their identity. Mycenaean Greeks and other Hellenic ethnic groups and tribes then living on the Greek peninsula were displaced by the newcomers and were driven south, east, and overseas to the Aegean islands and the Asia Minor coast in search of new locations in which to settle themselves. This process took place over the period c.1100-c.800 BC.

As the migrations were largely forced by hostilities, whatever economic and other benefits and developments had been enjoyed by these people in their former settlements had to be left behind, and a new beginning had to be forged elsewhere. There followed the long, slow growth process of developing their communities in the new locations. What might have taken a few years to accomplish in more modern times was to take generations to realize in those ancient times.

Between the luminous heights reached by Mycenaean civilization in the twelfth century BC and the brilliant period of a much broader Greek world of the fifth century BC, there was a period of "dark ages. " Yet, during this unstable and low economic period, the foundations were laid for the explosive growth that was to follow. The eastern settlements that were founded and were to grow in this time-span have left their permanent mark on Greek history. These included, those on the large islands of Rhodes, Samos, Chios, and Lesbos; and in the coastal cities of Halikarnassos, Miletos, Priene, Ephesos, Smyrna, and Kolophon. Many elements contributed to their growth: after the initial refugee movements, more peaceful migrations took place, and the prevalence of that peace. The mixing of populations and much trade brought forth a vitalizing exchange among them. For example, these Greeks borrowed their alphabet from the Phoenicians, then added vowels of their own. They reestablished the art of writing That had been lost during the early period of migration. The spoken Greek language (albeit with many dialects) reached a degree of uniformity and became the common language of all these people. The Greeks also learned how to make iron, a process developed earlier by the Hittites that they had carefully guarded from others.

Their well-shaped pottery, characteristically ornamented with geometric designs, was traded (as uncovered by archeologists) over a broad area. All this led to a rise in the economies of these independent Greek communities, which also encouraged the development of the arts. These arts became a mixture of the styles then prevalent in the east and the west.

Critical was the fact that Athens was never conquered by the Dorians. While it did not flourish as it was to do beginning in the sixth century BC, it maintained its Greek culture and had continuous contact and trade with the newer eastern Greek cities, thus contributing to the preservation of the mother culture.

Finally, the Archaic Period (c. 800-c. 600 BC), brought forward a series of events that were to lead to the "Golden Age" of the Greeks. Greek presence and influence had greatly expanded following a movement of peaceful colonization extending farther east along the Propontis (Sea of Marmara) and the Euxine (Black) Sea, as well as increasingly westward along southern Italy, Sicily, and on to the coasts of present-day France and Spain. Many of these independent colonies were to become prominent in later times. It is at this time that we see the rise of monumental architecture used for public buildings that were also finely decorated, the plain but dignified Doric order appearing in the west and the Ionic (a mixture of Greek and eastern forms) appearing first on the island of Samos. Intellectual progress was made possible by the rise in literacy through the reintroduction of writing, Homer and Hesiod formalized the hierarchy of the gods in their written texts. The ritual of the Olympic games began formally in 776 BC and was enacted every four years, during which time all Greeks put aside their differences and participated, in respect of religion and peace. All these and many other significant experiences together with independence, self-reliance, free thinking, and the economic growth of the settlers, soon led to a broadening of political awareness, power, and the evolution of the city-state, the basis of Greek democracy, the springboard to yet new growth.

THE CITY-STATES AND THEIR FORMATION

It is not difficult to see how a tribe of early people under a leader chosen for his qualities eventually evolved into a city-state. Settling down in an area of good water and agricultural potential, populations grew, and this growth eventually led to the development of concentrations of people, as well. We can now imagine how an area, composed of several of these adjacent communities, evolved to where one became the center. When governing the community became a full-time job, and especially when specialized functionaries were required to look after the particular needs of the people, a seat of government became a necessity. The process continued until finally the independent settlement became known as a village, town, or a city; or, in Greek, a *polis*. Building the center on a hill or high place (for visibility and security), it was called an *akropolis* (that of Athens being a well-known example), with the rest of the community built around its base. Some poleis (*pl.*) remained small, but those near large tracts of arable land grew considerably larger. The *polis* of Athens together with its rural support area, for example, covered all of the large Attica peninsula. Likewise, Sparta. Thebes, Corinth, and Argos, among others, were poleis that covered large areas.

Only when the *polis* was large enough was it able to provide its citizens with services and administration, education, the arts, and many other benefits. Plato was of the opinion that a *polis* of about 5,000 free citizens was the ideal size*. This was only a theory, of course, and many cities by Classical times had grown considerably larger. The city-states of Athens, as well as Akragas and Syrakuse in Sicily, had over 100,000 people; Samos, Corinth, Korkyra, and Argos had between 60,000 and100,000; and more than 20 other Greek cities around the Mediterranean had between 25,000 and 60,000.

In those times a community was small enough so that the leading citizens all knew each other; as a result they were expected to participate in and perform their civic duties. This obligation was limited mostly to the land-owning free citizens who had the civic privileges as both a right and duty. Excluded from this group were the citizens of lower rank, as well as foreigners, women, and slaves. Concerning this last category, slavery was established at that time to create a labor force, as it provided household help as well as a means to wealth by providing manpower to work farms and mines and to labor at artisan crafts. This practice gave the privileged Greek males the economic strength and free time to participate in the affairs of the *polis*.

The tribal leader whose role evolved into becoming the monarch (from the Greek words for "sole ruler"), a title that usually became hereditary, was often replaced by the *oligarchy*, that is, "rule by the exclusive few." The development of writing enabled custom to be codified into laws, and government ceased to depend on the arbitrary judgements of the ruler or rulers, although the application and interpretation of these laws remained in the hands of the oligarchs. Nevertheless, the concentration of population in a roughly defined area (there were no formal borders then), with its support systems, laws, and government, led to its developing into an independent city-state. These city-states traded with each other, combined into leagues when it suited a larger purpose, and sometimes warred on each other — an event that took place all too frequently in those archaic times.

The amount of arable land being limited, and this being the source of wealth, it followed that the relatively few large landowners made up the ruling class. But the growth of the polis also led to a vast increase in trade, and the production of goods with which to trade, these leading to new sources of wealth which also became available to others. Therefore wealth became the source of power rather than just land-ownership. This wealth could be realized by anyone who had the intelligence and daring and was willing to work hard enough; it was not just inherited. The minting of coinage, which began around the middle of the sixth century BC, an eastern development soon adopted by most of the Greek city-states, also made the conveyance of wealth available to an ever larger number of the population.

---

*The expression "Free citizens" did not include women, children and slaves. Thus, a city of 5.000 free citizens could number 25-30.000 inhabitants.

These and other developments gradually brought about a pressure from a wider number of people, and especially people at a lower economic and social status, to broaden their rights as well as their participation in political activities. Sometimes the *demos* (people) retaliated against oppression by removing the oligarchs by force; then one of their own might assume the rule, a demogogue. Any person, from the demos or the opposing aristocracy, who rose to power in this manner was called a"tyrant" (*tyranos* in Greek), meaning at that time only that this person had absolute power, not pertaining to the good or bad quality of his rule, the word not having the negative connotation then that it has now.

Athens was slowly evolving under oligarchic rule in the eighth and seventh centuries BC, the principal ruling members of which were called "archons," originally three in number, becoming nine in the seventh century. Yet, Athens was still a long way from evolving the democratic process with which it was to become identified, although it was much farther along in this development than other city-states. For some time, a serious condition stemming from land-ownership and population growth had become apparent on the Attica peninsula. The smaller land-holders doing subsistence farming, unable to operate their properties economically, mortgaged them to the wealthy larger owners. This led to a condition where many small farmers were unable to pay their debts, often losing their land and being forced to work as bonded serfs. Many among these were sold into slavery abroad to satisfy their debts. So threatening became the social unrest, as a result, that it finally led to an agreement to mediate the differences between the aristocrats and the commoners rather than risk revolution. This resulted in a change of laws and was the first important reform leading to the rise of Athenian democracy.

THE REFORMS OF SOLON

Т he man unanimously selected in 594 BC by the archons and representatives of the demos to conduct the critical conciliation was Solon (c. 638-c. 558 BC), a leading and gifted Athenian stateman from a wealthy merchant family. He was elected archon and given extraordinary powers to difuse the situation and introduce new laws that would ensure long-lasting economic, political, and social changes. His first decision was to set aside most of the laws of an earlier archon, Drako. So severe had been those laws that in modern times the word "Draconian" has become synonymous with "unnecessarily harsh." Solon then established reforms to cancel the debts on lands and free the owners from the oppressive yoke of an unpayable mortgage. Further, no longer could anyone secure a debt on another's physical person. He freed those sold off as slaves for their debts, although the details of how this was accomplished if some had been sold abroad is not clear.

Most important were his constitutional reforms. These affected a compromise between the haves and have-nots, and for the first time power was taken away from the oligarchs constitutionally, while granting the lower classes the right to participate in the conduct of government. Solon divided the free citizens into a pyramid composed of four classes based on a formal survey of their wealth. Wealth now became the measure, not merely hereditary landownership. The four classes constituted a Popular Assembly who elected nine archons to serve annually, the candidates coming only from the highest class. A Popular Court was established for the first time by Solon to which anyone could bring suit, and judgement was by a jury and not by magistrates as before. Solon also created a Council of Four Hundred, consisiting of 100 elected from each of the four classes, the function of which was to prepare the agenda for the meetings of the Popular Assembly. Guardianship of the law and general supervision were entrusted to an upper chamber called the *Areiopagos,* consisting of all the archons upon retiring from their terms. They were to serve in this chamber for life.

Thus, the lower classes now had a voice in government and a means of redressing their abuses, and the highest class was broadened to include the wealthy as well as those with hereditary rights. These and many other reforms identified Solon as the Father of Democracy. Even so, the nobles were dissatisfied with the loss of some of their powers, and the lower classes felt that not enough power had been given to them.

GREEK SETTLEMENTS ABROAD
(eighth to sixth centuries BC)

So much of Greece is on or near the sea that exploring areas beyond their homeland became for the inhabitants a natural pursuit from the earliest times. Heavy seas and small boats notwithstanding, in those early times it was far easier to cover long distances on water than on land, and especially when guided by land masses in the form of the islands of the Aegean Sea or by sailing coastwise. Thus, there was plenty of room for the oppressed and the adventurous: the northern coast bordering on the Mediterranean stretches many hundreds of miles from Gibraltar to the Dardanelles, and the same body of water proceeds into the Sea of Marmara and the far reaches of the Black Sea; the south side of the Mediterranean likewise proceeds from Gibraltar along Africa to the coast of Palestine.

The Minoans began trading with the peoples of the Asia Minor coast and Egypt dating from the second millenium BC. The Mycenaeans who followed several centuries later established many colonies in the east. We have seen in the beginning of this Chapter how the Dorian invasions that began in the twelfth century BC forced the Greeks to seek new settlements abroad. The new communities established were almost totally independent of the places from which they came. They tended to be located along a coast where a natural harbor was available, together with enough fertile land nearby to provide subsistence. The settlers traded with other nearby peoples. When the Asia

THE PRINCIPAL GREEK COLONIES
EIGHTH TO THE SIXTH CENTURIES BC

YEAR (BC)	FOUNDED BY	LOCATION						
		Black Sea	Hellespont/ Propontis	Greece	Italy	Sicily	Libya/ Egypt	France
756	Miletos	Trapezos	Kyzikos					
c.750	Chalkis/Eretria				Pithekoussai (Ischia)			
c.750	Chalkis				Kyme			
c.734	Chalkis					Naxos		
c.733	Corinth					Syrakuse		
c.730	Eretria			Mende				
c.730	Eretria			Methone				
c.729	Naxos (Sicily)					Katane (Catania)		
c.729	Naxos (Sicily)					Leontini		
c.728	Megara					Megara Hyblaia		
c.725	Kyme/ Chalkis					Zankle (Messina)		
c.720	Zankle/ Messinia				Rhegion (Reggio)			
c.720	Achaia				Sybaris			
c.716	Zankle					Mylai		
c.708	Achaia				Kroton			
c.706	Sparta				Taras (Taranto)			
c.700	Sybaris				Posidonia			
c.688	Rhodes/Crete					Gela		
c.685	Megara		Chalkedon					
c.673	Lokris				Lokri			
c.670	Miletos		Abydos					
c.660	Megara		Byzantion					
c.654	Phokaia		Lampsakos					
c.654	Klazomenai			Abdera				
649	Zankle					Himera		
640	Corinth			Leukas				
c.630	Thera						Kyrene	
c.629	Miletos	Sinope						
c.628	Megara Hyblaia					Selinos		
625	Corinth			Ambrakia				
625	Corinth			Anaktorion				
c.610	—						Naukratis	
c.601	Samos		Perinthos					
c.600	Phokaia							Massalia (Marseille
c.600	Corinth			Potidaia				
c.600	Corinth	Apollonia						
c.600	Miletos	Pantikapaion						
c.598	Syrakuse					Kamarina		
c.580	Gela					Akragas (Agrigento)		
c.560	Phokaia				Alalia			
448	Athens				Thurii			

Minor coast had no more such new sites, new settlers moved north into the Sea of Marmara and farther east along the Black Sea coast.

About the same time, Greek immigrants spread to the west into central and southern Italy, and into eastern Sicily, the western tip of which had already been settled by Phoenicians from Carthage, the great Phoenician city nearby in Africa. The Greeks avoided the populated Etruscan coast of west-central Italy and pushed along the Italo-French coast and beyond into southern Spain. They also established themselves in Egypt and in the area of Kyrenaika, that bulge in the north African coast nearest Crete. If competition with the Phoenicians had not been a problem, the eastern Mediterranean basin would have had many more of these Greek settlements.

Many of these communities grew into city-states and remained in Greek hands for many centuries. In this manner the Greek language and culture spread throughout the Mediterranean, and began the process of "Hellenizing" the ancient world. When major troubles came to these overseas Greek cities, they came less from their immediate neighbors than from the established "barbarian"* cultures. From the east came the Persians, who desired access west to the Aegean; and from the west, the Carthaginians, with whom the Greeks competed for trade and colonies. Much later, of course, trouble also came from the Romans, who were consolidating their country to the south. Though these cities eventually ceased being entirely Greek as they lost their independence over the centuries, a Greek population continued to remain in these cities, often as strong minorities who managed to maintain their ethnic background.

Specific references to these Greek-populated cities and areas and how they evolved from ancient to modern times is contained in various sections of this volume. Because of their long histories, a brief summary will be of interest:

The Greek cities of the Asia Minor coast, mostly along the Aegean coast from Troy to Halikarnassos, were settled over a period of two or three centuries starting about the eleventh century BC. Despite occupation by the Persians in the sixth century BC, by Romans in the second century BC, and Ottomans in the fourteeenth century AD, the populations of these cities had a large Greek presence for more than twenty-five centuries, gradually declining in numbers under Ottoman rule, especially after 1922, as a result of the GrecoTurkish conflict of 1919 to1923.

The Black Sea. Starting even earlier than the eighth century BC, Greek traders continued settling eastwards along the Hellespont and the Propontis (Sea of Marmara) through the Bosporus and beyond. The Milesian Greeks came first establishing Kyzikos and Trapezos in 756 BC. The Megaran Greek settlers followed, building on the strategic site of the Bosporus the cities Chalkedon, in 685 BC, and Byzantion (Byzantium), in 660 BC. Over the next hundred years or so, the Black Sea was ringed with Greek settlements. Many of these lasted for centuries, though they suffered frequent attacks from various peoples;

---

*"Barbarian," in Greek *várvaros*; that is, someone speaking what sounded like "var-var-var," an unintelligable sound —not Greek. The connotation of "uncivilized" and "without culture," soon followed.

these incidents are described elsewhere in this volume. The last to lose its independence was the heavily fortified Greek Empire of Trebizond, finally conquered by the Ottomans in AD 1461. Even so, Greeks remained in the area, although in declining numbers.

Byzantium (in Greek *Byzantion*), was settled in 660 BC by Greeks from Megara, a city near Athens. The Romans built the city of New Rome (Constantinople) in AD 330 on the same site, as the capital of the Eastern Roman Empire. However, the largely Greek character of the city remained, since Greek was the *lingua franca*. Its prominence and wealth became ever greater during Byzantine times, especially after the Western Roman Empire collapsed. The city was captured by the Ottoman Turks in AD 1453, but Greek population and influence remained substantial, declining slowly until more recent times when the Greeks on the peninsula declared and fought for their independence from the Turks in 1821 to 1833. When Turkey was declared a republic finally in 1923, the name of the city was changed to Istanbul, from the Greek "εις την Πόλιν" "to (or at) the city," there being no doubt as to which city was being mentioned.

Cyprus (*Kypros* in Greek), started as a Greek settlement of Aegean colonists from the ninth century BC. Its relatively small size prevented its remaining independent and its strategic location encouraged conquerors: Assyrians, Egyptians, Persians, Romans, Arabs. English, Franks, Venetians, and Turks. The strategic location giving any occupier a close look at Turkish geopolitical ambitions, it was occupied and remained under the British in various forms since 1878. Cyprus was finally given its independence in 1960. Throughout all these centuries, the island remained mostly Greek in culture and language, desiring union with Greece from the time the mother country itself became independent. The Turks, of course, did not favor a traditional enemy (Greece) so close to its southern flank. In 1974, the renewed quest for *enosis* (union) with Greece triggered an invasion and occupation of the northern 40 percent of the island by Turkish forces on behalf of a Turkish minority of less than 20 percent of the total population, living then in communities dotted over the entire island. Cyprus remains divided as of this writing.

Italy and Sicily. Chalkis and Eretria, ancient cities on the island of Euboia, were founded by Greeks seeking trading routes to the west. These Greeks also established trading posts on the west coast of Italy, starting in the mid-eighth century BC, that gradually grew into colonies. Prominent among these were Pithekoussai (the island of Ischia), Kyme (in Latin *Cumae*, near Naples), and Neapolis (Naples). These in turn and other Greek cities established additional colonies on the southern coast of the Italian boot and its toe. These became so prominent during Classical times that they were called collectively *Magna Graecia* (Greater Greece) by the Latins.

Colonies on the strategic island of Sicily soon followed, Chalkis first establishing Naxos on the eastern coast and these colonies and other Greek cities from the mainland founding yet others. Nearly all the coastal area was ringed with Greek colonies, some of which became important Greek colonies such as Syrakousai (Syrakuse), Gela, and Akragas (modern Agrigento). Early in the sixth century Syrakuse became the most prominent city in Europe, even more important than Athens at that time, and remained so for the next two hundred years. There were many wars between these Greek cities and those of the Carthaginians (Phoenicians) who had even earlier settled on the western tip of Sicily. But most of the island was completely Hellenized for centuries, gradually declining as Greek cities after the Roman occupation during the third and second centuries BC. Ancient Greek temples were reconstructed and are still relatively well preserved in Sicily; and Greek artifacts, handsomely displayed, fill the many museums throughout the island, the Sicilians being proud of their ancient Greek heritage.

Egypt and Libya. There is much evidence of Greeks trading with Egypt starting in the middle of the second millenium BC. Trade increased very early in the eighth century BC, but without the Greeks establishing settlements. Greek traders finally settled Naukratis in 610 BC, on the westernmost branch of the Nile River near the Mediterranean. Greek farmers settled Kerene, in present-day Libya, in 630 BC, the area becoming known as Kyrenaika as more cities were established along this coast, including Euphesperides (Bengazi). These were gradually absorbed into the Roman Empire starting the first century BC. Greeks continued to remain in these cities in declining numbers over the centuries. It was a nationalistic shock to Greeks living in Egypt when Gamal Abdul Nasser in 1952 required that anyone resident in Egypt must take Egyptian citizenship or leave. Many left, and many others took Egyptian citizenship while retaining their Greek citizenship as well.

France and Spain. A number of Greek settlements were founded here around 600 BC, the most important being Massalia (Marseilles), and some smaller cities near the present Franco-Spanish border and farther south along the Gulf of Valencia to Cape Nao. In 350 BC, Massalia founded Nikaia (Nice). These declined as Greek cities after the Roman occupation, which began in the middle of the third century BC.

THE GREEKS AND THE PHOENICIANS

The history of the Phoenicians and their settlements in the Mediterranean is itself of great interest, but this volume deals only with the important contacts they had with the Greeks in early times and the impact they made on Greek history.

The Phoenicians were an ancient Semitic people known to historians as Canaanites ("from the land of Canaan," in the Near East), and their roots go back to several thousand years BC. The Greeks first called them *Phoinikes*, from the name of a fabulous bird found in the Middle East and Egypt, the "phoenix," which had a golden red color, for these people were somewhat

MAP 2.0 GREEK COLONIES (eighth to the sixth centuries BC)

The Greeks colonized an estimated 400 settlements throughout the Mediterranean and the Black Seas, especially during the period eighth to sixth centuries BC. The principal mother cities from which the colonists came are shown as well as the principal independent colonies they founded.

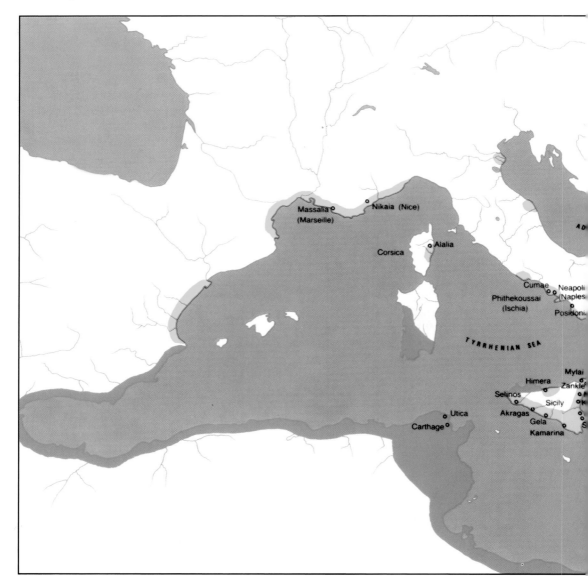

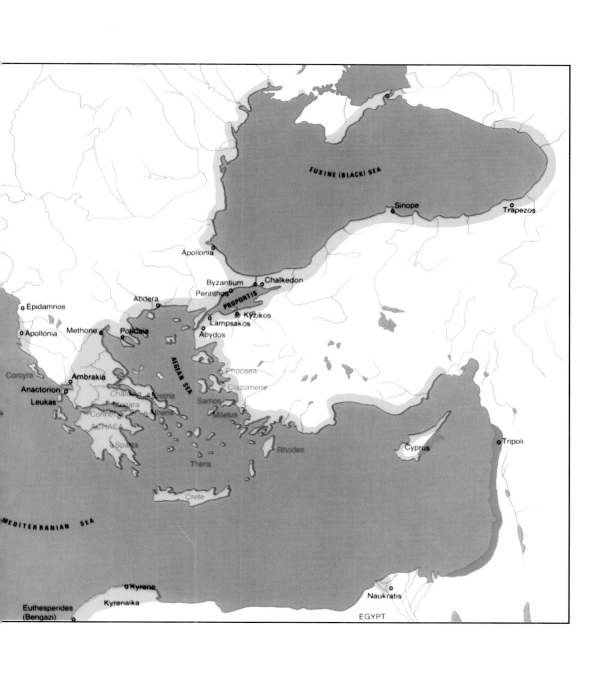

EUXINE (BLACK) SEA

Sinope

Trapezos

Apollonia

Byzantium Chalkedon
Perinthos
PROPONTIS

Abdera Kyzikos
Lampsakos
Abydos

Epidamnos

Apollonia Methone Potidaia

Corcyra AEGEAN SEA Phocaea

Ambrakia Clazomene

Anactorion Chalcis Eretria

Leukas Megara Samos

Corinth Athens Miletus

ACHAEA

Sparta

Rhodes

Cyprus Tripoli

Thera

Crete

MEDITERRANEAN SEA

Kyrene

Naukratis

Euthesperides Kyrenaika
(Bengazi)

EGYPT

tan-colored. The name stuck. The Romans Latinized the word and called them *Poeni*, hence the English word "Punic" referring to the Phoenicians in Carthage, their great city in North Africa across from Italy. The Phoenicians occupied the coastal strip in the eastern Mediterranean between the present-day cities of Iskanderun and Gaza. As their numbers increased, they began to migrate, and it was natural they should explore towards the west. Their explorations were made possible by the existence at that time of huge forests of firs and cedars on the mountains behind them nearby to the east from which material they built ships. This enabled them to trade early with Egypt, which was barren and treeless but highly developed.

The Greeks first came into contact with the Phoenicians through Mycenaean exploration and trading during the fourteenth century BC. Both the Mycenaeans and the Phoenicians had established colonies in Cyprus as well as in Rhodes. In Crete, which had become Mycenaean in the fourteenth century BC, traces of extensive Phoenician trading have been found and signs of colonies. Trading also took place with the Greek mainland. No doubt the extensive Mycenaean presence in the Aegean and the eastern Mediterranean kept the Phoenicians to exploring and settling along the North African coast, initially bypassing Greece, southern Italy, and Sicily.

Carthage (near modern-day Tunis) was founded in the beginning of the eighth century BC and soon grew into their principal Phoenician city. Other cities were developed by them nearby as well, and the Phoenicians also established colonies on the western tip of Sicily, the Greeks occupying the rest of this large island. They were uneasy neighbors. When the Persians occupied the Phoenician homeland in the Syro-Palestinian coast at the beginning of the fifth century BC, Carthage and the other Phoenician colonies had already become a dominant force in the central Mediterranean. Because of their intense commercial rivalry with the Greeks, when the land-based Persians decided to attack mainland Greece, the Phoenicians were ready to supply them with large naval contingents and men. They helped the Persian King Darius in his attack on the Greek cities of Ionia in 490 BC and supplied nearly a quarter of Xerxes' fleet at the battle of Salamis in 480 BC. (For the story of the Persian Wars, see p.38).

Carthage was strongly influenced by Greek culture. But the Phoenicians also helped contribute to the Greeks' rapid development. The Phoenicians had devised an alphabet as early as the fifteenth century BC. Contacts between them and the Greeks over a long period led the Greeks to adopting it by the eighth century BC. An important refinement of the Greeks, however, was the addition of vowels to the Phoenician alphabet, which had consisted only of consonants (as is the case with all Semitic languages).

The Persian occupation of the Phoenician homeland in the east was replaced by Alexander's own conquests of the area in 332 BC. Greek rule of the area continued under the "successor" kingdoms as described in Chapter Four. When Rome conquered Carthage and the other North African cities by 146 BC, having already conquered Sicily, Sardinia, and Corsica earlier, the Phoenicians passed into history.

RELATIONS WITH PERSIA

(Sixth Century BC)

T
he effect of relations between Greeks and Persians on the course of Greek history cannot be underestimated. Starting in the beginning of the sixth century BC, the mainland Greek cities began to feel the threat of the Persian Empire's westward expansion. Independent Greek cities that lay along the Asia Minor coast on the Aegean Sea had been occupied, and this was to be followed by the invasions of Greek island cities and towns and by attacks on the Greek peninsula itself.

These events for the first time made the Greeks realize that their traditional separate, independent existence could not stand against a vast, organized, and aggressive foe. Even so, this constant threat and these attacks still did not result in any long-lasting cohesiveness between the Greek city-states, especially Athens and Sparta.

The Persian conquests of all territories in their area west to the Aegean brought into close proximity to the mainland Greeks a presence that would influence the politics and relations between the Greek city-states for the next two centuries. However, Persia also became the new frontier for the Greeks from the mainland, islands, and eastern cities, Greek architects and builders, sculptors, physicians, teachers and scholars, poets and philosophers, and others, offered their services and skills to the Persian nobles and royal patrons. Greek mercenaries served in and trained Persian armies. Greek political exiles often took refuge in Persia, and similarly some key Persians escaped punishment for political disloyalty in their own country and bided their time with Greek rulers. The highly developed Greek culture found a fertile field in Persia, and likewise Persian culture influenced the Greek. Later, the subjugation of Persia in turn by Alexander and his successors brought Hellenization to this vast eastern area, and in some areas this influence lasted eighteen centuries, even through Roman rule.

How did the Persian expansion to the west take place? Neighboring the Greek Asia Minor coastal cities was the kingdom of Lydia, the ruler of which in 560 BC was Croesus (*Kroisos*, in Greek), who was said to be one of the wealthiest persons in antiquity (hence the saying, "as rich as Croesus"). Campaigns begun by Croesus' father and continued by him resulted in the incorporation of these Greek cities into the Lydian kingdom, by conquest or treaty. However, they remained nominally under their own rule while having to pay tribute. Croesus was very impressed with the Greeks and gave lavish gifts to Greek temples, and to oracles such as at Delphi. He also made a friendship pact with Sparta.

But the spreading imperialism of the Persians under the ambitious Cyrus I soon reached westwards. The Persians first conquered the kingdom of the Medes, in 549 BC, which lay on their western border. Continuing in the same direction, in 546 BC they took Sardis, the capital of the Lydian kingdom, and added that country to their empire. The Greek cities thought at first that this would give them an opportunity to gain their independence from the Lydians, but one master was replaced by an even stronger one, and their resistance soon revealed they were in no position to hold out against such a powerful conqueror. All Asia Minor came into Persian hands, but not the Greek islands nearby, as the Persians at first had no fleet nor experienced seamen. This was soon to be remedied. Persian aggression and Greek resistance was to result in a number of armed conflicts between them over a 67 year period to 479 BC, all of them in Greek territory.

We owe a large part of what we know about the wars between the Greeks and the Persians (546 to 479 BC) to Herodotos, born in the Asia Minor Greek coastal city of Halikarnassos in 484 BC. He travelled extensively throughout the Greek world, including Asia Minor and Egypt, compiling the first written history ever known, in nine volumes. (The total is equivalent to a single modern book in length. It was the practice of ancient authors to divide their narratives into "volumes," similar to our use of chapters.) While not comprehensive on the subject, several of the volumes cover the Greco-Persian Wars from Cyrus in 546 BC to Xerxes about 480 BC, and Herodotos gives us rich descriptions of the events. His *Histories* are considered well-written and interesting. As a Greek, it is understandable that Herodotos would generally favor the Greek view of the conflicts. Modern scholars believe that Herodotos reported reasonably accurately; however, he also assumed many legends to be facts and tended to exaggerate certain details, especially figures. But in his unique book for the times he provides many contemporary, eyewitness accounts. He died in 425 BC in Thurii, a Greek colony in southern Italy.

THE PERSIAN WARS
(546-479 BC)

As we have seen, the first phase of the conflicts between the Greeks and the Persians began with Cyrus invading the Greek cities of Asia Minor, which had been for some years under a fairly comfortable subjugation by Croesus of Lydia. Except for Miletos, which accepted the

MAP 2.1 GREEKS AND PERSIANS I (546-492 BC)

Cyrus the Great, monarch of the large Persian kingdom in the east, began to conquer the independent western kingdoms of the Medes and the Lydians, in 549 to 546 BC. The Greek city-states on the Asia Minor coast also began to be absorbed, and the Persians began to explore farther west.

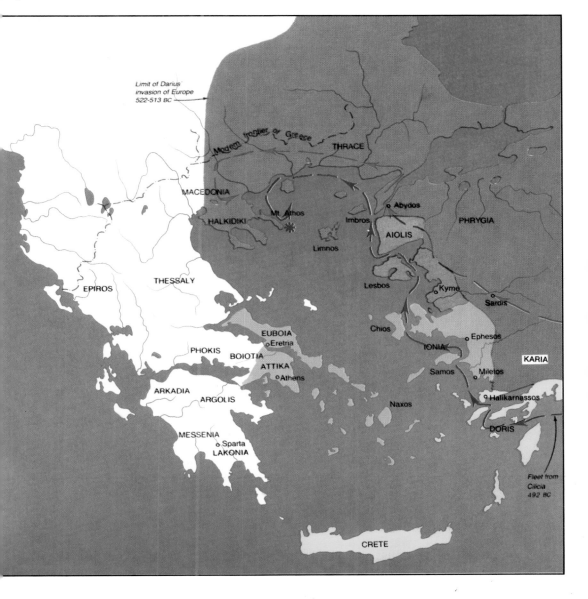

new invader without putting up a fight, the rest of the Greek cities resisted with various levels of intensity but always independently, which brought on their downfall, one by one. Cyrus then proceeded north and east to consolidate the rest of his kingdom, which success earned him the title of "the Great."

Polykrates, tyrant of the island of Samos in the Aegean Sea close to the Asia Minor coast, was a strong Greek ruler who had extended his influence on neighboring Greek islands and some parts of the Greek-occupied area known as Ionia on the Asia Minor coast opposite. He had come to power in 540 BC and achieved great works and prosperity for his island kingdom. Avoiding any conflict with the Persians while they were sweeping through the Greek cities, he concentrated more on organizing the Greek islands under his leadership. He built a strong fleet and controlled the neighboring seas. But his strong hold lasted only until the Persians were ready to proceed west. Polykrates was tricked by the Persian satrap (from the Persian word meaning "viceroy" or "provincial governor") into making a visit across to Persian-occupied Ionia in 522 BC, where he was treacherously killed. The Persians now took Samos, gaining its strong navy. The neighboring Greek islands of Chios and Lesbos soon submitted as well. Darius then decided to invade European Thrace, his armies crossing the Bosporus on a bridge of boats built under the direction of Mandrokles, a skilled Samian engineer. The Persian armies explored the area north to the Danube River, even crossing it at one point and penetrating into Scythian-occupied territory. After this excursion they retreated, with Darius returning to Persia, leaving the area under the charge of one of his generals, who carried the invasion on into Macedonia by 513 BC. On his way back to Persia, Darius also subdued the Greek islands of Limnos and Imbros, which, together with Thrace, facilitated Persian access to the European continent.

THE IONIAN REVOLT

By 499 BC, after 47 years under Persian domination, a revolt broke out in Ionia starting at its largest city, Miletos. Within a year, aided by fleets from Athens and Eretria, the revolt spread, and the Greeks successfully attacked the city of Sardis nearby, that had become the capital city of the Persians. The Greek cities on the mainland coast and the islands off Asia Minor now joined in, and the revolt spread from the Bosporus all the way south to the area across from Rhodes, as well as on the large island of Cyprus. Victories were gained by both sides over the next six years, but the Persians had a unified command where the Greeks had courage but were disorganized and had fewer resources. The Persians were slowly gaining back their conquests. Finally, between Miletos and the islet of Lade nearby, a vast naval force of Greeks met an even greater force of Persians aided by the Phoenicians. The resulting Persian victory virtually ended the revolt, though the Persians wisely left the rule of the reconquered area in Greek hands under democratic conditions. The economy of the Greek Asiatic cities nevertheless declined rapidly, but a useful consequence was the delay by the Persians to attempt further advances on Greece, and a realization on the part of mainland Greeks that a unified command and a strong fleet were going to be necessary for their survival, as the succeeding events were to prove.

PERSIAN EXPEDITIONS AGAINST THE GREEKS

The Persians now decided to invade the Aegean region and the Greek mainland. The first of these expeditions was led by Darius' son-in-law, Mardonius. He set off in 492 BC, with a large land force and a fleet, both proceeding from Cilicia in southern Asia Minor to meet in Thrace and proceed together to Macedonia. The fleet, in rounding the peninsula now known as Mount Athos, was caught in a violent storm, which (according to Herodotos) sank 300 Persian ships and 20,000 of their men were drowned. While these figures are regarded as exaggerated, in any event a large force must have been lost, as the remaining fleet and the army both turned back, not having much furthered Persian aims.

Marathon

By 490 BC, a new Persian expedition against the Greeks started again from Cilicia. Its purpose was to teach a lesson of Persian supremacy to the Cycladic Islands in the center of the Aegean and to punish Athens and Eretria, which had aided the Greeks during the Ionian revolt. Persian revenge was harsh. Some of the settlements were completely destroyed, and the rest were subjugated, as were the cities of Eretria and Karystos on Euboia. The Persians then continued west, arriving at Marathon, a plain along the coast, good cavalry country for the Persians and barely a day's march from Athens. The Athenian forces under Miltiades, aided by a contingent of Plataians, though greatly outnumbered, took the offensive and charged the Persians, who had their backs to the sea. Greek aggressiveness and tactics carried the day, and the Athenians won a stunning victory, with the remaining Persians fleeing in their ships. Though Herodotos' figures are also exaggerated as to how few Greeks (10,000, he writes) defeated a vastly superior Persian army (100,000), most modern historians estimate that the

- - -> Persian naval force 490 BC	- - - - Xerxes land armies
- - -> Xerxes naval force 480 BC	✱ Naval battles or disasters

MAP 2.2 GREEKS AND PERSIANS II (490-479 BC)

The Greek cities in western Asia Minor revolted against continued Persian occupation. These cities were being aided by the Greek island kingdoms in the Aegean Sea and Greek cities on the mainland. As a result, the Persians decided to invade the area. Though greatly outnumbered, the Greeks drove the Persians back to their homeland.

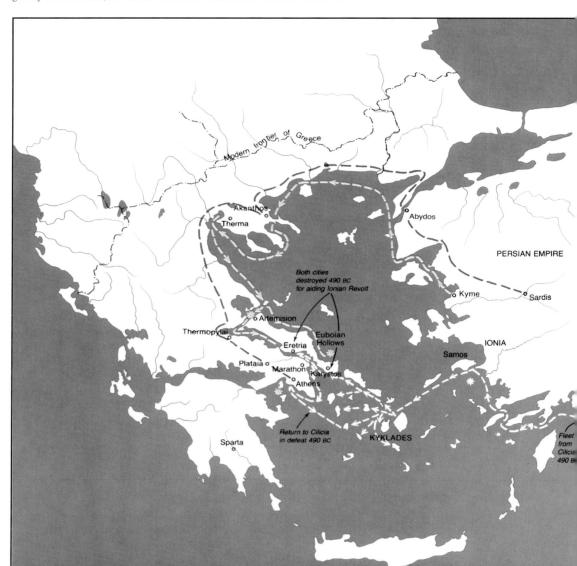

Modern frontier of Greece

Akanthos
Therma
Abydos

PERSIAN EMPIRE

Both cities
destroyed 490 BC
for aiding Ionian Revolt

Kyme
Sardis

Artemision

Thermopylai
Euboian
Hollows
Eretria

Plataia
Marathon
Karystos
Athens

IONIA

Samos

Return to Cilicia
in defeat 490 BC

KYKLADES

Sparta

Fleet
from
Cilicia
490 BC

Persians may have numbered perhaps 20,000. It was the news of this victory that a Greek runner carried to Athens about 25 miles away that has led to the gruelling foot-race celebrated as "the marathon."

While appearing to head east, the Persians instead rounded Cape Sounion to attack Athens while the Greek forces were still in Marathon celebrating their victory. The Greeks detected this ploy and quick-marched back, showing themselves in battle readiness on the beach at Phaleron, on the coast fronting Athens, at which sight the Persians turned east once more and departed for Asia. In some measure, a signal said to have been flashed from a nearby hilltop, which was interpreted as a sign that the Spartans were also on the march to aid the Athenians, may have helped persuade the Persians to retreat.

Xerxes' Campaign

The defeat at Marathon did not dampen Darius' determination to return and punish Athens as well as her ally Sparta, and this time he prepared accordingly. A revolt in Persian-held Egypt and the death of Darius himself in 486 BC delayed this campaign, which was subsequently carried forward by his son Xerxes. Even so, the preparations took a long time and included building twin bridges across the Hellespont at Abydos. More bridges were thrown across rivers and other bodies of water along the long overland route. A canal was said to have been dug across the lowest and narrowest point on the Mount Athos peninsula to avoid a repeat of the disaster suffered by Mardonius in 492 BC. (This is very much doubted by historians, as no signs of the possible existence of such a canal has ever been found in the area.) Roads were built and stores of food were placed at suitable locations under guard. Herodotos again reported far greater numbers of the enemy invading the Greek peninsula than any modern historian would accept; still, it must have been a large and formidable force.

In 484 to 483 BC, while all these preparations were taking place, a stroke of luck greatly aided the Greeks to successfully meet the Persian threat. In an old silver mine at Lavrion, on the Attic coast near Athens, new rich ore layers were discovered. It was this silver that enabled Athens to build a fleet of 200 triremes (long, narrow vessels propelled by three banks of oars) at the urging of the archon and military leader, Themistokles, which fleet was to be decisive in winning the battle of Salamis a few years later.

Thermopylai

The Persian aim was to conquer all of Greece. To achieve that purpose, the Persians assembled their armies at Sardis and their vast fleet at Kyme, which two forces proceeded together, one on land, the other on water. At the beginning of their march, they were largely unopposed, a number of Greek cities giving in to the numerous and feared enemy. Upon reaching the northern end of the island of Euboia, the Persian fleet split, half

MAP 2.3
GREEKS AND PERSIANS III

(480-479 BC)

Another invasion of the Greek peninsula by the Persians resulted in major land battles at Thermopylai and Plataia and critical naval battles at Salamis and between Samos and Cape Mykale. The Greeks were victorious once again, and the Persian invasions of the Greek world ceased.

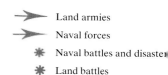

Land armies

Naval forces

Naval battles and disasters

Land battles

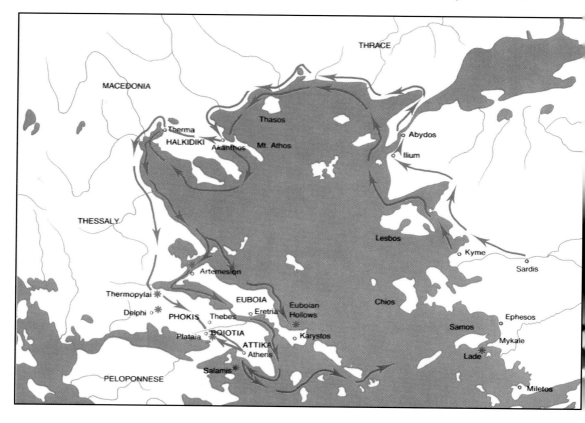

proceeding south along the exposed eastern coast of the large island, and the remainder turning westward to sail down the inland waters between the island and the Greek mainland. But the Greek fleet was waiting for them at Artemision at the northern end of the island, and they fought with great losses for both sides but with no decisive victory for either. Another part of the Persian fleet was lost in a storm off the Euboian Hollows.

The Persian armies continued their way south rounding the Malion Gulf, where they came to the narrow pass between Mount Kallidromos and the Gulf, known as Thermopylai, arriving there in August 480 BC. The Greek forces retreated south, leaving behind King Leonidas of Sparta with 300 of his elite Lakedemonian *hoplites* (from the Greek word *hopla*, i.e., "arms," therefore a heavily armed elite Greek foot-soldier), aided by several hundred other Greek volunteers, to hold the pass as long as they could.

Much has been written by Herodotos and others about the battle of Thermopylai, where Greek honor and determination stood for three days and nights against an overwhelming Persian invading force. The end was inevitable, the death of Leonidas being offset by the death of two of Darius' sons, brothers of Xerxes. The Greek sacrifice is well remembered by the epitaph written for the fallen heroes by Simonides, a famous court poet of the time, that translates: "O stranger, notify the Lakedemonians that we lie here obedient to their laws." A stark marble monument so inscribed still marks the spot.

Salamis

By September, 480 BC, the large Persian fleet that had moved down the inland waters between the Greek mainland and Euboia sailed around Cape Sounion toward Athens and Piraeus. Nearly the entire population of Athens was evacuated to nearby islands, and the Greek forces moved into a last-ditch position at the Isthmus of Corinth. The Persians entered Athens and quickly overwhelmed the small garrison that had been left to guard the Akropolis. Xerxes had his revenge on Athens at last.

The next Persian objective was to destroy the Greek fleet, which was holed up in the protected waters of the island of Salamis opposite Piraeus. The Persian fleet sailed over for the final battle. On a hilltop on the Attic shore, Xerxes and his court made themselves comfortable to watch the action. The Greek fleet, instead of being cornered, had prepared themselves in accordance with the strategy plotted by the Greek admiral Themistokles, to draw the larger Persian ships into confining waters. The tactic worked, and on September 23, 480 BC, the fierce naval battle took place. The Greeks were victorious, losing 40 ships against 200 by the Persians.

When the Persians lost their naval protection, they decided to withdraw from Athens and the Attica region. Xerxes led one army back north and east around the way he came, on the long road to Sardis. Another Persian army put down a revolt of the Greeks at Chalkidiki; and Mardonius camped in Thessaly for the winter. What was left of the Persian fleet sailed across the Aegean and moored in Samos and in Kyme.

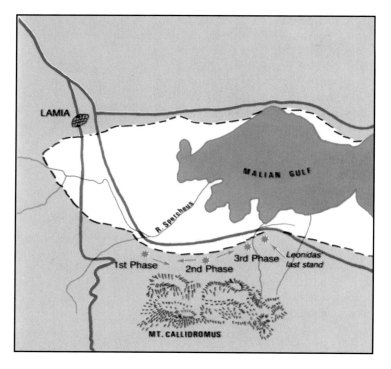

MAP 2.4
THERMOPYLAI

At a narrow defile at Thermolylai, a small Greek force led by the Spartan King Leonidas heroically withstood for three days the assault of a very large Persian army, until they were all killed.

‒ ‒ ‒ ‒	Former shoreline
———	Present Road
✳	Land battles

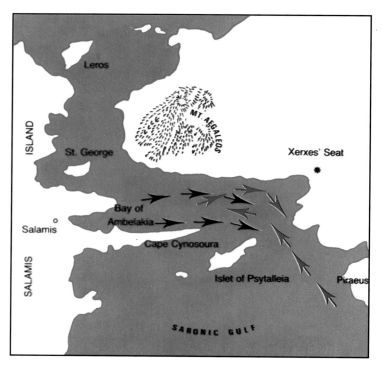

MAP 2.5 SALAMIS

The greatly outnumbered Greek fleet lured the large Persian naval force into the confining waters between the island of Salamis and the mainland near Athens, where the more maneuverable Greek ships were able to defeat them.

➤	Greek fleet
➤	Persian fleet

Plataia

Mardonius' army was on the march again in late Spring of 479 BC, re-entering Athens a second time in June, the population of which had again been evacuated. This time the Greeks mobilized an army under the Spartan general Pausanias, nephew of the dead Leonidas and regent to his young son. The opposing armies met on the large plain of Plataia, north of Athens. This complicated battle lasted three weeks and ranged over a wide area. It ended in victory for the Greeks and the slaughter of many of the Persians, Mardonius included. Although many Greeks took part, the heroes were Pausanias and his trained and disciplined Spartan professionals.

Mykale

Without losing their momentum, in the last days of September 479 BC, the Greeks sent a large fleet that had been assembled at the island of Delos, in the central Aegean, to Samos, to meet the remaining Persian navy still in Greek waters after these many months of conflict. The Persians sailed for the Asia Minor coast at Mykale opposite, where they beached their vessels and set up a land defense. Another bloody battle resulted in victory for the Greeks, at which signal the Ionian Greek cities again revolted and finally freed themselves from the Persian yoke.

While it would take some years for the Persians to quit the Aegean and Thrace altogether, the battle of Mykale marked the end of Persian armed aggression in the area. But this was not to be the end of Persian involvement with Greek affairs that would continue for three more decades.

The wars between Greeks and Persians produced many significant results. One was to finally bring together many of the independent Greek city-states into alliances (one of these was the Delian League under Athens, which was to have much impact on Greek history). It also sharpened the rivalry between Athens and Sparta that was to result in devastating wars between them later. Nor was this to be the last time the Greeks and the Persians would oppose each other. (See Chapters Three and Four.)

Three

The
Classical
Age
(c.600-323 BC)

FROM SOLON TO PERIKLES:
"THE GOLDEN AGE"

OME HISTORIANS REFER TO THIS PERIOD AS "THE Golden Age" of the Greeks, which brings to mind the glorious temples and fine sculptures, the great tragic and comic plays, the poets and other writers, the mind-stirring thinking of the philosophers, and the achievements of the early scientists and mathematicians, among much other evidence of genius. Indeed, as a time of art and learning, it was a golden period of development that comes down to us still vibrant and alive and fills even modern man with awe.

No less an achievement was the process of introducing democracy, around the sixth century BC, to a people who had been ruled arbitrarily for many centuries by kings and oligarchs — and making that democracy work. So advanced was this concept that it would take many centuries to be applied equally fully anywhere else. Yet it is the basis of nearly all governments today.

Still, the term "Golden Age" is somewhat misleading because it shuts the mind from remembering that in this period of 164 years — from the start of the reforms of Solon in 594 BC to the death of Perikles in 429 BC — many tragic events also took place. If the Greeks were able to survive these events, the "Golden Age" was formed in a crucible of fire. In addition to the numerous small wars between the city-states throughout this period, there were the Persian invasions of 490-479 BC, and the disastrous defeat of Athens' forces in Egypt in 460 BC, while trying to help that country free itself of Persian occupation. The Peloponnesian War of 430-404 BC tragically culminated the long rivalry of Athens and Sparta and greatly weakened both of these cities, especially Athens. The enlightened Athens also dealt ruthlessly with defecting members of the Delian League. It seems that war was the principal language of diplomacy at that time. Finally, the devastating plague that befell Athens in 430 BC and lasted two years, carried off one-third of its population and Perikles himself, the leader under whom the "Golden Age" reached its zenith. Fortunately, it is the rich creativity of the period that has remained as its legacy, and the development of democratic government, begun in Athens under Solon, continues to this day.

PEISISTRATOS AND KLEISTHENES

Continuing the history of the formation of democracy, Solon's laws were formally planned to remain unchanged for one hundred years. (See *The Reforms of Solon* p.28). To give the laws a chance to become established on their own merit and not by virtue of his leadership and interpretation of them, Solon also exiled himself from Athens for ten years, starting around 593 BC. He travelled to Cyprus, Egypt, and Asia Minor.

That Solon's democratic reforms could have lasted, considering how radical they were and what developments they set in motion, would have been beyond reasonable belief in that place and in those times. Yet it was 34 years before a change away from orderly democratic rule took place in Athens, through the seizure of power by Peisistratos in 561 BC. This happened more as a result of the personal relationships of strong men seeking power than from any failure of Solon's reforms.

Peisistratos was a benevolent tyrant who ruled Athens from 561 to 527 BC. Twice driven into exile by oligarchs who wanted to return to power themselves, Peisistratos managed to return each time. Of significance is that he did not change the reforms of Solon and even encouraged them. Nor did he tamper with Solon's constitution. He also continued and expanded on Solon's economic policy of limiting agricultural exports, that only benefited the large landowners, and he encouraged the establishment of trades and artisan skills, which created a sizeable new level of commerce involving a much broader crossection of the people. Peisistratos adopted the use of coins (from Lydia) at this time, no small contribution to the expansion of trade. He promoted the arts and introduced large festivals available to all, for which Athens was to become famous, as it was for its fine temples and public buildings, also begun at this time.

The years 510 to 507 BC saw a continuation of the struggle for power and how that power should be applied. Rule by oligarchy might have returned to Athens, but instead, in 507 BC, one of her archons, Kleisthenes, won against his principal rival, but only with the help of the *demos* (people). Kleisthenes showed great political skill in reorganizing the Athenian state and broadening even more the application of power, to where true representation of the people in government was established for the first time in history. The archons remained, but they were now to be elected by a much broader crossection of the people and, most important, were held accountable to them. As a further safeguard, Kleisthenes created a system of exile in order to insure against the rise of a tyrant, called ostracism (the word comes from *ostraka*, clay shards, on which a name was scratched voting to exile an individual, cast by a quorum of 6,000 Athenian citizens so authorized, meeting annually; the exile was for a ten-year period, but without loss of citizenship or property). The quality of Kleisthenes' reforms were such that it took twenty years for the first person to be exiled under the system. Solon and Kleisthenes were the two leading creators of Athenian democracy, without which the Golden Age of Athens could hardly have been realized.

THE RISE OF ATHENS

Athens and Sparta, the two leading city-states, were close rivals both before and during the Persian Wars. While for the most part they cooperated together against the common enemy, Sparta concentrated mostly on her relations with her neighbors in the Peloponnese. She had become leader of the defensive Peloponnesian League as early as 550 BC, which had included all of the area's city-states except the city of Argos, her strongest competitor.

Sparta's military tradition had been well applied for all the Greeks against the Persian invader. But she would not give the Greek cities of Asia Minor any gurantees of support against the Persians. Some of these therefore began to conclude treaties with Athens. Gradually, by 478-477 BC, The Confederacy of Delos, otherwise called the Delian League, was created in perpetuity with Athens as its leader, the members including many other Greek cities in addition to those of Asia Minor. It is important to be reminded that the Persian threat did not end with driving their defeat of Greek territory at the battles of Plataia and Mykale in 479 BC. Persian garrisons were still in Thrace many years later, as well as on a number of strategically placed Greek islands in the Aegean. The Greek coastal cities of Asia Minor continued to have troubles with the Persians. Athens pledged herself to protect the Delian League members from the enemy, for which purpose they paid to Athens a formal tribute, each according to their economy and size, or they provided a certain number of manned ships. The island of Delos in the center of theAegean became headquarters and provided the League's name; and the treasury was kept there. This system of making annual payments to Athens for defense purposes was unique in Greek history. By comparison, payments to the Peloponnesian League by its members were sporadic and were made to the League, not to Sparta.

Athens was victorious in a number of battles with the Persians after 470 BC, proving that she was indeed capable of protecting the members of the Delian League. The Persians were forced out of the Aegean for the first time in 80 years. The reduction of the Persian threat led to defections of some of the League members, such as the islands of Naxos (c. 470 BC) and Thasos (466 to 463 BC). These islands were invaded by Athenian forces and made to rejoin, being fined heavily as a warning to all members to remain loyal.

The southern half of Euboia was coerced by Athens into joining the League, because of its strategic location. The number of city-state members climbed rapidly from perhaps 200 at this time to nearly 400 by 430 BC or so. Membership being permanent, Athens was gradually turning the alliance into an empire.

THE AGE OF PERIKLES
(461-429 BC)

In the sections preceding, we saw how democracy began to flourish in Athens. We also saw how Athens was able to forge the unity of a large number of the independent Greek city-states by creating and dominating the Delian League. Perikles, starting in 461 BC, now provided the leadership qualities that developed and brought together the political, financial, and cultural attributes that made Athens the unparalleled and unforgettable classical civilization that it became. This period was to be the zenith of the Golden Age.

Perikles hailed from an aristocratic Athenian family. His father, Xanthippos, led the final naval victory of Athens against the Persians at Mykale; his mother came from a leading noble family. Born in 495 BC, Perikles became active in Athenian political life at an early age, being only 23 when he was appointed public prosecutor against the then leading archon Kimon, a prominent Athenian statesman and military leader whose opponents were trying to dislodge from a position where he dominated Athenian politics over a fifteen-year period. Participating in this action and to further other political reforms, Perikles worked closely with the senior archon Ephialtes. In 461 BC, the success of Ephialtes, assisted by Perikles, furthered importantly the democratic process in Athens, and caused Kimon, who opposed their views, to be ostracized. It also resulted in the assassination of Ephialtes in the same year, at the hands of the aristocracy whose remaining power he destroyed. Perikles became the inheritor of both these political mantles.

A number of events just before this time enabled Athens to gain even more influence. The success of the Athenian-led Greeks against the Persians was proved once again, resulting in the Greek cities of Asia Minor joining the Delian League. A large naval force led by Kimon met the Persians at the Eurymedon River off the south central Asia Minor coast, and wiped them out. But Athens was less fortunate when she responded in 460 BC to support a rebellion by the Egyptians to free themselves from Persian domination under which they had suffered beginning in 525 BC. The ill-fated expedition lasted six years, and ended with the destruction of the Athenian forces. However, this and other encounters over two decades finally led the two powers into signing the "Peace of Kallias," in 449 BC (named after an Athenian statesman), in which the Persians agreed to remain east of the Greek Asia Minor cities and to keep their navy out of the Aegean, and the Athenians agreeing they would not attack Persian territory.

A nagging problem at this time was the constant rivalry of Athens with Sparta. This reached a climax in 457 BC, over a dispute as to who would dominate Boiotia. Their armies met at Tanagra near Thebes, and Athens was defeated. But two months later Athens sent another army that recovered the territory. Two years later, an Athenian fleet blocked Spartan moves northward by taking the islands of Zakinthos and Kephallonia as well as some of the strategic area north of the Gulf of Corinth. The two rivals fought again at Delphi in 448 BC, and in other battles between 447 and 446 BC. Finally, Perikles managed a formal Thirty Year Peace treaty with Sparta around 446 to 445 BC, bringing peace to Athens.

In 454-453 BC, during the war with Persia over Egypt, the Athenian leaders moved the headquarters of the Delian League from Delos to Athens, along with the treasury — for safekeeping. The use of these accumulated funds, a substantial amount by this time, enabled Perikles to add to the prestige of Athens by means of a building program that transformed the capital into a beautiful and inspiring city for the enjoyment of all Greeks and visitors. To strong complaints of league members as to this use of their funds, Perikles answered that Athens had promised to protect them against the enemy, which she was doing, and Athens could decide how the funds could be used.

The Persians had destroyed most of the Athenian shrines when they invaded Athens in 480 BC, and most likely this is what prompted Athens to use the league funds for this purpose. Perikles' new building program, continued the works begun by Peisistratos and Kimon. Beginning in 449 BC, it was planned to make the Akropolis in the center of Athens, an attraction on a monumental scale. It was at this time that the present Parthenon was built (447 to 438 BC), under the direction of the sculptor Pheidias, who also made and directed the making by others of the beautiful friezes, and the colossal gold and ivory statue of the city's patron-goddess, Athena, standing inside. (See the section on *The Parthenon* which follows.) Many other of the impressive structures and sculptures on the Akropolis and around it were also installed at this time. Nor were these the only public structures ordered to be built by Perikles. The beautiful temple to Poseidon, on a promontory at Cape Sounion, was also constructed in 444 BC, giving visitors arriving by sea an introduction to the splendors they would find in Athens, or a last look to remember it by as they departed. The temple of Zeus was built at Olympia (470-455 BC), and Pheidias created the enormous gold-and-ivory seated statue of Zeus that adorned its interior (after 430 BC). This statue was considered to be one of the "Seven Wonders" of the ancient world. (See p.104)

In this atmosphere, the intellectual and artistic life of Athens blossomed. There were great festivals at which the tragic plays of Aischylos. Sophokles, and Euripedes were performed in the great semicircular theatres at the base of the Akropolis. The outstanding individuals who left their marks on the Periklean Age include: Anaxagoras, the philisopher-scientist, a close friend and advisor of Perikles; Hippodamos, the architect-planner who laid out Piraeus, as well as Thurii, the panhellenic city-colony in southern Italy promoted by Perikles on behalf of all the Greeks; Pindar the poet; Herodotos the historian; Protagoras the Sophist philosopher, well-received at that time; Hippocrates, the "founder of medicine." These and many more contributed to the splendor of the Periklean age. (See Table on p.61)

Not the least of Perikles' achievements, at least from Athens'point of view, was that of keeping the league members together under her leadership, even after Persia was no longer a threat and in spite of Spartan rivalry. Certain court proceedings were reserved to be heard in Athens, which contributed to Athens' hold on the other city-states. A coinage law passed in 450 BC attempted to unify the currency among League members. While Athens was always helpful to cooperating members, she was harsh to rebellious ones. The revolt of Samos was one example, in 441 BC, which for a time threatened to bring the Persians back into the Aegean on the island's side. But Athens prevailed after a long siege, and Samos was severely punished. The bitter consequences were not forgotten by the other members.

But two events brought tragedy and an end to the Golden Age of Athens: the Peloponnesian War, which began in 431 BC, and the devastating plague of 430. (The War between Athens and Sparta is described starting p.65). Both the War and the plague are described in eyewitness detail by General Thukydides (455-400 BC) in his well-regarded *History of the Peloponnesian War*. The plague raged in Athens for two years, and about one-third of the Athenians died of it. Perikles was removed from office in the late summer of 430 BC, everyone blaming him for the war and other accumulated grievances, and even for the plague. Although he was brought back again in the spring of 429, he had already contracted the plague himself and died of it three months later.

THE PARTHENON

The Parthenon, crowning the hill of Akropolis in the center of Athens, is the greatest symbol of classical Greece. Because of its prominence and attraction to all visitors to Athens, and the controversy regarding its debasement, some details regarding its history are offered to the reader.

No other architectural monument of this period has been so admired or so minutely studied, for it represents the ultimate sophistication reached by the architects and sculptors of that time, and, for that matter, of any time. Built between 447 and 438 BC, it remained substantially intact for more than 2,000 years, suffering its greatest damage only in the last 300 years or so.

In a way, the existing Parthenon owes its existence to the Persians, who, invading Athens in 480 BC, destroyed the buildings that had originally stood over the Akropolis. As mentioned before, Perikles decided to raise a new, magnificent temple to Athena, the city's patron-goddess, as a symbol of the revival of Athens. He appointed Pheidias, the most famous sculptor at the time, to be in charge of planning and overseeing the project, and named Iktinos and Kallikrates to be the architect-builders. The material used throughout was white marble, from the quarry of Mount Pentelikon, 11 miles (18 kilometers) to the northeast of the city.

Much of the remarkable beauty of the Parthenon begins with the extreme care taken with details of its architectural design. The rigidity of the simple Doric order of the temple was softened by a number of minute corrections made to please the eye: the marble platform on which the temple rests, measuring about 100 by 230 feet (31 x 69 meters), was raised slightly in the middle from the horizontal, to correct what would have been the optical illusion of dipping slightly in such long straight dimensions; the tapered, fluted columns were bulged slightly to prevent their looking squeezed in the middle if they had been cut exactly straight; the corner columns were made a little thicker than the others to correct another error of the eye. All the outer columns (8 at the ends and 17 at the sides) were made to lean in slightly, such that their centers extended would have met at a point several thousand feet above in space, in order to prevent their appearing to be leaning out. Other similar corrections were made by its skilled architects and builders to enhance the optical perfection of this structure. That these corrections were possible to be made with the primitive measuring instruments of the time can only add to our wonder.

More than eighty sculptors worked on the decorations that adorned the upper part of the temple (see drawings, next page). These consisted principally of groups of fully sculptured figures at the two triangular pediment ends; 92 heavily sculptured *metopes* (Greek for "forehead" or "brow"), rectangular slabs between the triglyphs decorating the faces of the horizontal sections resting on the columns; and a continuous frieze in low relief decorating the beams and walls along the top of the inner row of columns and walls. Inside was the 40 feet high (13 meters) standing figure of the goddess Athena leaning on an upright spear, sculptured by Pheidias himself. All exposed flesh parts were carved from ivory; and the rest (robes, helmet, shield) of sculptured heavy gold sheets estimated that together would have weighed more than a ton. In the style of the times and to relieve the starkness of the white marble, the figures on the metopes and friezes were painted in colors, and paint was used to decorate other parts of the temple, especially the ceiling and eaves. Some writers have said that the whole may have been somewhat garish, compared to the dignified and weathered beige ruin of today. But the Parthenon must have been magnificent then, perched on the highest point on the rock of Akropolis, its sparkling bulk visible without obstruction or distraction by anything else in the area in all directions as far as the eye could reach.

If it remained substantially intact for 2,000 years, how did it get to the sad state it is in today? Firstly, during the reign of Roman Emperor Justinian I (AD 527-565), the statue of Athena was carted off to Constantinople. It had been already destroyed there by 1203, before Constantinople was occupied by the Franks, but the exact details are unknown. The Parthenon itself was converted into a church during the Christian era (seventh century), then into a mosque following the Ottoman occupation (sixteenth century). The first major disaster to the temple occured on the evening of September 26, 1687, during the Turko-Venetian war. The Turks were using the Parthenon to store gunpowder, and a stray shell fired by a Venetian gunner struck the temple and blew it up, destroying practically all of the interior and several of the outer columns in the center of the structure on each side. In addition, Francesco Morosini, the victorious Venetian commander, tried to remove the sculptures from the west pediment; his careless workmen dropped them, and they were smashed. He did manage to take a number of other sculptured pieces fairly intact from various parts of the Parthenon, which he sent to Venice to commemorate his victory.

One section of the frieze was removed in 1787 and sent to France by French agents of the Compte de Choiseul-Gouffier, where it is now displayed

THE PARTHENON: DETAILS

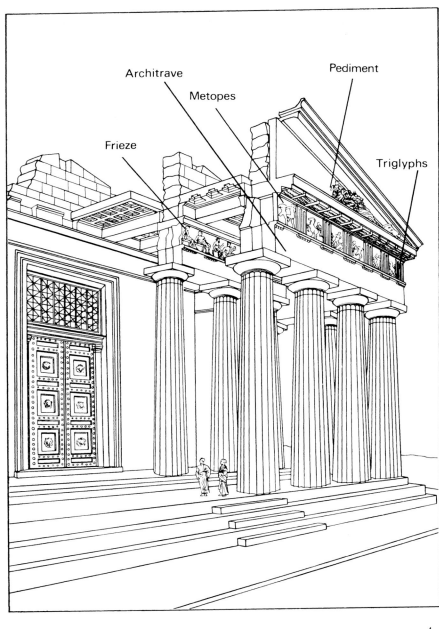

Architrave

Metopes

Pediment

Frieze

Triglyphs

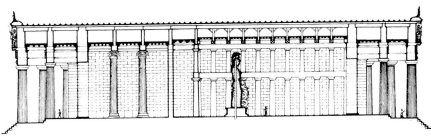

at the Louvre Museum. Other pieces were taken by various travellers to Athens, and many others were heavily damaged in the effort to remove them. But the greatest denuding of the Parthenon occured in 1801, when Lord Elgin, British envoy extraordinary to the Turkish government at Constantinople, obtained a permit (or *firman*, in Turkish) to study the sculptures, Greece being a part of the Ottoman Empire at the time. This firman was granted to Elgin by the Turkish government in gratitude for the British victory shortly before against their enemy Napoleon who had invaded Egypt, then another part of the Ottoman Empire. The permit allowed Lord Elgin to "study, measure and make molds, and to *take away pieces from the grounds*" (my emphasis). A self-serving interpretation of this clause led Elgin's helpers with his concurrence to remove the best pieces from the temple itself and prepare them for shipment to England, and not to just study them locally. The representatives of the Turkish government in Athens did not interfere. As a result, Elgin removed 17 metopes (33 others were ruined in the explosion; 41 remaining at the Akropolis are all in poor condition; one is in the Louvre). Also removed at this time was whatever sculptures remained from the east pediment and some fragments found from the ruined west pediment. The process of their removal caused further substantial damage to the Parthenon.

The frieze, considered to be the finest example of classical Greek sculpture, originally measured over 525 feet (160 meters) in length. The Akropolis Museum now houses 176 feet of it (54 meters), Lord Elgin having removed 247 feet (76 meters). Most of the rest was lost in the explosion of 1687. A number of fine sculptures from other parts of the Akropolis were also taken away by Lord Elgin, including one of the Karyatids (female figures) from the Erechtheion, another small temple near the Parthenon.

The Greeks say variously that Elgin "stole," "snatched," or "purloined" the sculptures and bear his memory a particular grudge. Elgin's motives originally appear to have been to study the great art, having been a scholar of classical sculpture and architecture. The opportunity afforded by the firman, his zealous companions, and his unique position brought about by the politics of the time, and the casualness of the Ottoman officials, were apparently overwhelming, and he undertook a mass removal. The expense to Lord Elgin was considerable, and despite his frequent appeals the British government refused to become involved. These costs were considerably increased when the crated marbles being sent to England — as arranged by Elgin on a British naval brig — sank in a storm while rounding Kythera, an island off the Peloponnese. The salvage operation took more than two years to accomplish. Elgin tried continuously to sell the collection to the British government, without success, as the expense was ruining him. Thirteen years later they reluctantly accepted — at about half the original cost he had incurred.

Elgin finally had to leave England and live in France to escape his debtors, and he lived there the rest of his life. The marbles were eventually taken to a specially prepared wing of the British Museum in London, where they may be seen today, admirably displayed. That these pieces may have been saved from further destruction or removal by other foreigners is no comfort to Greek pride.

SOME PROMINENT FIGURES OF THE GOLDEN AGE

The Table that follows shows some of the better known figures who lived during the two-and-a-half centuries or so of the the Classical Age of Greece, and especially during the Golden Age of Athens under Perikles.

So much has been written about Athens and its Golden Age that the perception of many readers has been clouded about how long and how broad the Golden Age of the Greek world really was. Personalities in certain cities such as those in Athens took the political lead and others as in Sparta were prominent in military prowess. The outstanding intellectual and artistic personalities of the period, however, hailed from cities throughout the Greek world stretching from Asia Minor across the Greek islands and peninsula to southern Italy and Sicily. Many of them travelled widely during their lifetimes to other Greek cities, as well as to Lydia and Persia, and disseminated their knowledge broadly, in turn gaining experiences that contributed to their creative work. They were not isolated or "ivory tower" thinkers or early scientists; many of them were also statesmen and military leaders. Many participated in affairs of state, in relations with other city-states or other countries, and fought in wars.

Great festivals were held throughout the Greek world to provide opportunities to the poets, lyricists, and playwrights to present their latest works. People eagerly gathered to see and hear them, and the artists' efforts were awarded highly-esteemed prizes and honors in formal competitions. We have only a glimpse of those times of brilliance and genius. Much of the result of their thinking and studies was not written down at all, or was lost entirely and only described in part by others, or only fragments were discovered. It is estimated that a very small percentage of their literary works was ever found. So good was what did come down to us that it is tantalizing to think about what has been lost.

Monumental public building programs sponsored by rulers gave architects and sculptors the opportunity to show their creations and beautify their cities. The excellence of these accomplishments provided the inspiration for the work of generations of Greeks to come. We still admire that genius, not only in terms of what they achieved in that very early time, but for its own timeless sake.

One interesting illustration of the broad appreciation of genius and intellect in the Classical Greek world (during the period around 650 to 570 BC) is that of a group known as the "Seven Sages." This group originally included: **Bias** of Priene (a city north of Miletos on the Asia Minor coast); **Chilon** of Sparta; **Kleoboulos** of Lindos in Rhodes; **Periander**, tyrant of Corinth; **Pittakos** of Mytilene on Lesbos; **Solon** of Athens; and **Thales** of Miletos. The Sages were known for their judgements, wise sayings or axioms, eloquence, poetry, philosophy, and nobility. Stories about their individual or collective wisdom were widely circulated from city to city, and they were extensively quoted. People flocked to hear them whenever any of them had occasion to visit their city. The practice of listing other groups of seven sages continued to later times.

Some Prominent Figures of the Golden Age (BC)

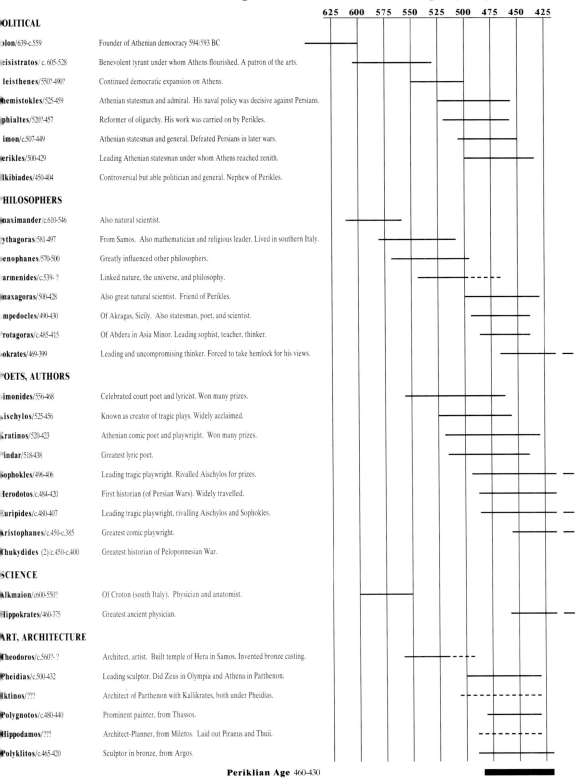

| | | 625 | 600 | 575 | 550 | 525 | 500 | 475 | 450 | 425 |

POLITICAL

Solon/639-c.559 — Founder of Athenian democracy 594/593 BC

Peisistratos/ c. 605-528 — Benevolent tyrant under whom Athens flourished. A patron of the arts.

Kleisthenes/550?-490? — Continued democratic expansion on Athens.

Themistokles/525-459 — Athenian statesman and admiral. His naval policy was decisive against Persians.

Ephialtes/520?-457 — Reformer of oligarchy. His work was carried on by Perikles.

Kimon/c.507-449 — Athenian statesman and general. Defeated Persians in later wars.

Perikles/500-429 — Leading Athenian statesman under whom Athens reached zenith.

Alkibiades/450-404 — Controversial but able politician and general. Nephew of Perikles.

PHILOSOPHERS

Anaximander/c.610-546 — Also natural scientist.

Pythagoras/581-497 — From Samos. Also mathematician and religious leader. Lived in southern Italy.

Xenophanes/570-500 — Greatly influenced other philosophers.

Parmenides/c.539- ? — Linked nature, the universe, and philosophy.

Anaxagoras/500-428 — Also great natural scientist. Friend of Perikles.

Empedocles/490-430 — Of Akragas, Sicily. Also statesman, poet, and scientist.

Protagoras/c.485-415 — Of Abdera in Asia Minor. Leading sophist, teacher, thinker.

Sokrates/469-399 — Leading and uncompromising thinker. Forced to take hemlock for his views.

POETS, AUTHORS

Simonides/556-468 — Celebrated court poet and lyricist. Won many prizes.

Aischylos/525-456 — Known as creator of tragic plays. Widely acclaimed.

Kratinos/520-423 — Athenian comic poet and playwright. Won many prizes.

Pindar/518-438 — Greatest lyric poet.

Sophokles/496-406 — Leading tragic playwright. Rivalled Aischylos for prizes.

Herodotos/c.484-420 — First historian (of Persian Wars). Widely travelled.

Euripides/c.480-407 — Leading tragic playwright, rivalling Aischylos and Sophokles.

Aristophanes/c.450-c.385 — Greatest comic playwright.

Thukydides (2)/c.450-c.400 — Greatest historian of Peloponnesian War.

SCIENCE

Alkmaion/c600-550? — Of Croton (south Italy). Physician and anatomist.

Hippokrates/460-375 — Greatest ancient physician.

ART, ARCHITECTURE

Theodoros/c.560?- ? — Architect, artist. Built temple of Hera in Samos. Invented bronze casting.

Pheidias/c.500-432 — Leading sculptor. Did Zeus in Olympia and Athena in Parthenon.

Iktinos/??? — Architect of Parthenon with Kallikrates, both under Pheidias.

Polygnotos/c.480-440 — Prominent painter, from Thassos.

Hippodamos/??? — Architect-Planner, from Miletos. Laid out Piraeus and Thuii.

Polyklitos/c.465-420 — Sculptor in bronze, from Argos.

Periklian Age 460-430

THE PELOPONNESIAN WAR
(431-404 BC)

The nearly seven decades of Persian threat had brought about a forced cooperation if not a political unity among the traditionally independent Greek city-states against a common enemy. The end of that threat in 479 BC released the growing rivalry and antagonism of the two leading city-states, Athens and Sparta.

There were many fundamental differences between these two city-states. Sparta was land-locked and looked mostly to its immediate surroundings unless forced to do otherwise. Athens was near the sea on the Attika peninsula and was traditionally taken up with interests on both sides of the Aegean as well as in northern Greece. Their modes of government were also different: Athens pursued the democratic form of government she had developed, while Sparta continued its oligarchic rule. As mentioned previously, each continued as leader of a defensive group of allies. Sparta headed the Peloponnesian League, formed at the end of the sixth century BC by most of the autonomous city-states in that area, as a means of defense against a common enemy. Athens headed the Delian League, formed in 478 BC, combining with Athens' allies in the Aegean and northern Greece, as insurance against the possibility of continued threat by the Persians on the Greek cities of Asia Minor. While in the beginning the Delian League had only a defensive purpose, the manner by which it was constituted under Athenian leadership gradually led to their developing an imperial policy. Sparta viewed this with deepening apprehension as to how to contain Athens' expansion, that at various times threatened members of the Peloponnesian League.

Early hostilities between Athens and Sparta had already climaxed in 457 BC into a major battle they fought at Tanagra in Boiotia, north of Athens, the intensity of their antagonism toward each other resulting in great losses on both sides. Sparta was victorious, but two months later, another Athenian army reoccupied the area evacuated by the Spartan army. Animosities between the two rivals continued, further aggravated when some Athenian allies felt oppressed and rebelled, calling on Sparta for help. Clearly, Athens was converting the Delian League into an Athenian empire. Hostilities continued over the next decade with victories and defeats on both sides. Finally, in 445 BC, Athens and Sparta grew weary of the stalemate and, fearing each other, negotiated and signed the "Thirty Years Truce." The peace was broken in the fourteenth year.

Much of our knowledge about the events of this period comes from the *History of the Peloponnesian War* written by the Athenian General Thukydides (c.450-400 BC), who wrote extensively about it in this highly regarded and well-researched book. (His treatise ends with the description of events in 411 BC, as Thukydides died before he could finish it.) He himself commanded Athenian troops in the conflict and was sent to Thrace in 424 BC, where his army was defeated by the Spartans. For this he was exiled and returned to Athens only after the War, in 404 BC. Although it is popularly called a "war," the conflict was not a continuous war at all, but many separate actions between the

Athens and the Delian League

Sparta and the Peloponnesian League

Neutral

Major Naval Battles 411-405 BC

MAP. 3.0
PELOPONNESIAN WAR (431-404 BC)

Athens and Sparta were the principal Greek city-states. Though they were allies during the wars with the Persians, the end of that threat magnified their rivalry and resulted in a number of major battles between them over a thirty year period, weakening both.

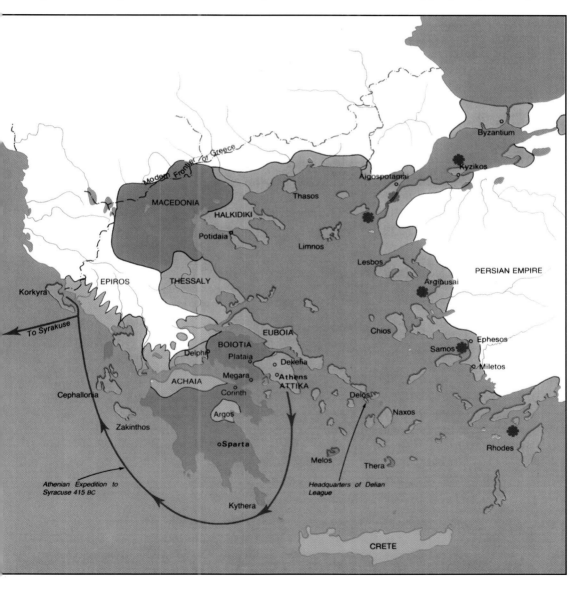

protagonists over a long period of time. The principal conflicts were the Archidamian War between 431 and 421 BC, named after the Spartan King Archidamos; the period 421 to 413 BC, during a part of which Athens also allowed herself to be tempted into what turned out to be a disastrous war with Syrakuse when Sparta came to the aid of that city; and the Ionian, or Dekelean, War of btween 413 and 404 BC, fought almost entirely at sea.

The Archidamian War
(431-421 BC)

Corinth, a member of the Peloponnesian League, was an important commercial rival of Athens. For some time, Athens had been taking actions to restrict its rival's freedom of trade. Their relationship was further aggravated in 434-433 BC when Athens came to the aid of Korkyra (Corfu), a colony of Corinth that had rebelled. Other incidents also were indicative of Athens' intent to achieve commercial supremacy. Athens placed a trade embargo on the city of Megara nearby, also a member of the Peloponnesian League, and blockaded Potidea, another colony of Corinth, located on the western coast of the Chalkidiki Peninsula. Corinth therefore declared that the Thirty Years Truce had been violated and called on Sparta as chief of the Peloponnesian League, to assemble its members and declare war on Athens. Sparta was slow to take this action, and first made demands on Athens to further provoke her. It was at this time (March, 431 BC) that the city of Thebes, itself head of the relatively minor Boiotian League allied with the Peloponnesians, attacked Plataia, an ally of Athens, believing it could bring it over to its side. Athens coming to the aid of Plataia tipped the delicate balance of affairs, and war was begun.

The Spartan King Archidamos marched into the Attika peninsula in the summer of 431 BC and again in 430, the population fleeing to Athens. The overcrowding which resulted helped the spread of the dreadful plague that lasted more than two years and caused the death of about a third of the people there (including that of Perikles himself, in 429 BC), as we saw earlier.

Many other actions took place during the ten year period since war was begun, but the results were inconclusive, Athens' gains came largely from her superior navy and Sparta's from her strong land forces. Finally, in 421 BC, the two sides agreed to another truce, the "Peace of Nikias," named after a famous Athenian statesman and general. But Sparta's allies were dissatisfied with the terms and refused to be bound by them. This change of relationships among the Peloponnesians virtually isolated Sparta.

421-413 BC

Not only was a truce signed between Athens and Sparta but the two city-states also concluded a defensive alliance. There followed a period when the Peloponnesians, unhappy and feeling insecure at this turn of events, rallied around Argos as leader, and both Sparta and Athens alternating as friend and foe of that city-state. But by 415 BC, Athenian attention turned toward Sicily. The Greek city of Syrakuse was pursuing a course of dominating other nearby Greek cities on the island, which called on Athens for assistance. Despite its own nearer problems, Athens was tempted by this opportunity to gain influence on if not control of the western Mediterranean. She responded with a great force of nearly 30,000 men transported on 134 large warships. By the summer of 414 BC, Athens' superior naval forces had blockaded Syrakuse, and the two antagonists settled down to a long siege that was likely to eventually find the Athenians victorious. The threat of an Athens dominant in the east and now in the west spurred Sparta into coming to the aid of Syrakuse, and she sent a strong relief force that landed at Himera, in north Sicily, and marched its way across the large island to enter Syrakuse from the west. The scales had now tipped against Athens. A great naval battle in the large bay of Syrakuse destroyed half the Athenian fleet, the rest landing their men on the south shore away from the city. But the Syrakusans had prepared well, blocking escape routes, and caught them at a river edge. Many thousands were slaughtered and the rest were taken in slavery. The Athenian top generals were executed by the Syrakusans as well.

The Ionian, or Dekelean, War
(413-404 BC)

Athens might have sent a reserve army to aid her forces in Syrakuse, but about the same time King Agis of Sparta fortified Dekelea, only 15 miles (25 kilometers) from Athens, and raided the nearby area from this garrison. Also at this time, another dire development for Athens took place, as the Ionian cities in Asia Minor began to revolt and to join Sparta. The Persians decided to support this trend and signed a treaty with Sparta in 411 BC, providing her with considerable financial support. But Athenian naval victories forced Sparta to sue for peace by summer of 410 BC.

The condition was temporary; the fortunes of war were turned once more against a weary Athens by the Spartan admiral Lysander. Athens won a major naval victory in 406 BC at Arginusai, her last of the war, but the Spartan fleet was victorious at Aigos Potamoi (Gallipoli) in 405, which virtually destroyed the Athenian fleet. Piraeus was now blockaded by the Peloponnesian navy, and their armies surrounded Athens. Negotiations for the final settlement resulted in Athens being forced to remove its "long walls" defenses from Athens to Piraeus; giving up its remaining fleet except for a few vessels; and returning its citizens from all colonies. The peace treaty of April 404 BC reduced the defeated and exhausted Athens to being just another member of the Peloponnesian League.

XENOPHON AND THE MARCH OF THE TEN THOUSAND
(401 to 400 BC)

Thukydides' *History of the Peloponnesian War* breaks off in mid-sentence, describing the events of 411 BC. Another author of those times begins his *Hellenika* ("A History of My Times"), completing that sentence of Thukydides. This was an Athenian, Xenophon (c.430-355 BC), who continued the history of the period, covering the years 411 to 362 BC in seven books (chapters), of which the first two cover the period to the end of the Peloponnesian War. Xenophon was not a historian, and he did not have the experience and impartiality of Thukidides. He was strongly prejudiced in favor of the Spartans that he admired, and who had sponsored him after he was banished by Athens in 394 BC when he sided with Sparta against his native city. Nevertheless, his clear and well-written accounts are about the only complete contemporary descriptions of the period to have come down to our times.

The narration of Greek history in this volume is interrupted briefly to describe an event relative to activities that took place in Persia at this time, about which Xenophon was to write in detail in another book, based on his own first-hand experiences. This event has popularly come to be known as the "March of the Ten Thousand," with Xenophon describing how a large force of Greek mercenary soldiers proceeded to Persia in the spring of 401 BC, and what happened to them there. The significance of this event is that this was the first time a Greek army penetrated into the vast Persian interior. Xenophon had joined this army and wrote about his experiences more than two decades later, between 379 and 371 BC, and his book evoked an image of Greek capability against a massive foe in their own (the Persian) terrain. The book was said to be among Alexander's favorites, he who was to conquer Persia starting 336 BC.

But the experience was also the beginning of a series of events which were to have a major impact on Sparta's leadership of the Greeks, a role she inherited after having finally defeated Athens in 404 BC, ending the Peloponnesian War.

Xenophon's book, the *Anabasis of Cyrus* (the "March Upcountry of Cyrus"), relates how, at the end of three decades of Peloponnesian War, many veteran soldiers were without work, their possessions gone, and the cities of some of them in ruins. Knowing nothing but soldiering, they were willing to hire themselves out as mercenaries to any bidder. There were many opportunities to bear arms as small outbreaks continued, and most of the city-states did not keep standing armies. But the largest single use of these mercenaries occurred outside of the Greek peninsula when Cyrus the Younger sought to oust his brother Artaxerxes II from the Persian throne. Cyrus hired more than 13,000 of these Greek veterans, many of them Spartans and fellow Peloponnesians, along with a Spartan general who led them. They were transported across the Aegean and marched east from the Asia Minor coast to assemble at Sardis. Cyrus had been satrap there, and the Greeks joined 30,000 of his native troops. One of the Greek volunteers was Xenophon, who elected a life of adventure over his disappointment with the political atmosphere at Athens.

The plan was to march after Artaxerxes, and the large force proceeded

MAP 3.1 MARCH OF THE TEN THOUSAND (401-400 BC)

Over ten thousand Greek mercenaries accompanied Persian Prince Cyrus the Younger, who claimed the Persian throne from his brother Artaxerxes II. The death of Cyrus in battle left the Greeks without a sponsor to fight their way out of a hostile interior.

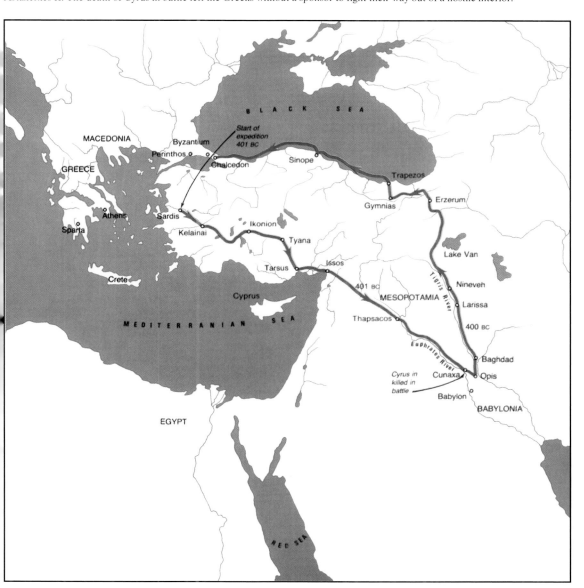

east with few incidents. In skirmishes along the way, the Persians were very impressed by the Greek fighting style. Cyrus' forces finally caught up with those of Artaxerxes several months later, at Cunaxa, near Babylon. In the great battle that ensued, Cyrus was killed. Suddenly the Greeks found themselves without a patron and a purpose, hundreds of miles in the Persian interior. At first, Cyrus' native troops confirmed their unity with the Greeks; but soon they joined their fellow Persians under King Artaxerxes. The Greeks were now alone in a hostile land and having to find a way of returning home to Greece by the quickest and safest route. The Persians also wanted them away with the least damage to the countryside and people, and they negotiated a safe passage with the Greeks, pursuading them to take a northerly route. It was shorter overland, they suggested, to where the Greeks would find Greek cities on the Black Sea coast and boats to transport them the rest of the way. And besides, they had already come through from the west; the new route would give them a chance to find food supplies in an area which had not been ravaged by a passing army. The Greeks agreed, and the Persian forces marched with them at a safe distance to keep an eye on them. But some days later at a point south of Larissa, along the Tigris River, the Persians received a group of senior Greek officers that had come to parley, and treacherously killed them all. If their thought had been that the Greek forces would be confused and disburse now that their leaders were gone, the Persians were mistaken. New officers were elected, and Xenophon was chosen to lead them to safety.

The march up-country occupies little more than one-quarter of *Anabasis*; the remainder details the arduous and dangerous journey of the Greek army seeking their way back to their homeland. Unknown to the Greeks, they were soon out of the area controlled by the Persians and they had to proceed into the mountains of Kurdestan and Armenia, fighting off the fierce tribes along the way and foraging in the bleak countryside for food. By now it was winter, too, and they had snow and bitter cold to contend with, as well. It took them five months to reach Trapezos, a Greek colony on the Black Sea. Xenophon reports that only 8,600 of the original 13,000 managed to arrive there. Most of the rest of the voyage was made by sea.

Xenophon returned to Athens only to find that the political atmosphere was even worse than before he left it, the city-state torn apart in the dissensions between the democratic leaders and the oligarchs. His teacher as a youth had been Sokrates, the great philosopher, with whom he had maintained contact for two decades. Now Sokrates became one of the victims of the political conditions in Athens. In 399 BC, he was falsely accused* and chose to drink the juice of poison hemlock from which he died rather than bend to the will of the Athenian leaders. The loss of his teacher and friend permanently estranged Xenophon. He left his native city for Sparta, and even fought at the side of the Spartan king

---

*Sokrates was declared the wisest man in Greece by the Dephic oracle, and many considered him so, though he denied this, his philosophical style being that he made himself look modest and ignorant, supposedly. While he was officially accused of religious heresies and of corrupting his students by his philosophies, in fact his accusers based their prejudices on complex political issues of the day related to their enemies whom Sokrates had befriended. Given the opportunity by the judges to save his life, he declared that he could not break the laws and elected to die instead.

against Athens. For this he was eventually banished by Athens, but for his services on behalf of the Spartan king, he was provided with a comfortable estate at Skillos, in Ellis, near Olympia. There he wrote his many treatises.

FROM THE END OF THE PELOPONNESIAN WAR TO THE AGE OF PHILIP II
(404-359 BC)

The defeat of Athens in the last major conflict of the Peloponnesian War, in 404 BC, left a power vacuum in the Greek world that was only partially filled by Sparta, the victor, since the war had also left that city-state in a weakened condition. Persia had financed Sparta in order to destroy Athens, and part of the price was to be the future subjugation of the Greek cities in Asia Minor — all of them former allies of Athens in the Delian League. Anticipating victory by Sparta, as early as 412-411 BC, Persia had concluded a formal agreement with her. Knowing that Sparta would again busy herself with the leadership and control of the city-states in Greece, Persia thereby bought eventual control of the Greek Asia Minor cities. When the War ended in 404 BC, Sparta was soon to find that she would be drawn to Asia once again, and that she was not going to be able to free herself from Persian influence. Sparta's troubled hegemony (from the Greek word meaning "leadership") over the Greek peninsula was to last only three decades or so.

Though Sparta was thrust into a leadership role of the Greeks, it became obvious that the Greek city-states were still not prepared, politically or philosophically, to accept a single leader. Nor did Sparta's authoritarian, oligarchical, and military style gain the cooperation and loyalty of many of the others. Numerous skirmishes and battles marked their unwillingness to be controlled by Sparta. In 379 BC, the Boiotions at their prinicipal city of Thebes, were able to break away from the Spartans and began to build a hegemony of their own, but it was not to last. If one of the important elements lacking to be able to achieve unity was the right kind of leader, such person was finally to appear in Macedonia in 359 BC. Philip II (c. 383-336 BC), began to forge the city-states, either by conquest or alliance, into a single country, Greece. Although Philip never succeeded entirely, he did manage to hold together a very large part of the country, as may be seen in Map 3.2. To understand this period, we must briefly examine the events before Philip II.

Spartan Hegemony
(404-371 BC)

When the "Ten Thousand" Greek mercenaries departed from the Persian interior in 400 BC, the Persian King Artaxerxes II sent his satrap Tissaphernes to subjugate the Greek city-states on the Asia Minor coast.

MAP 3.2 GREECE BEFORE ALEXANDER

Macedonia produced a dynamic, visionary Greek monarch, Philip II, the father of Alexander the Great. For the first time, Philip wa
able to combine a large part of the independent Greek city-states under his leadership either by subjugation or alliance.

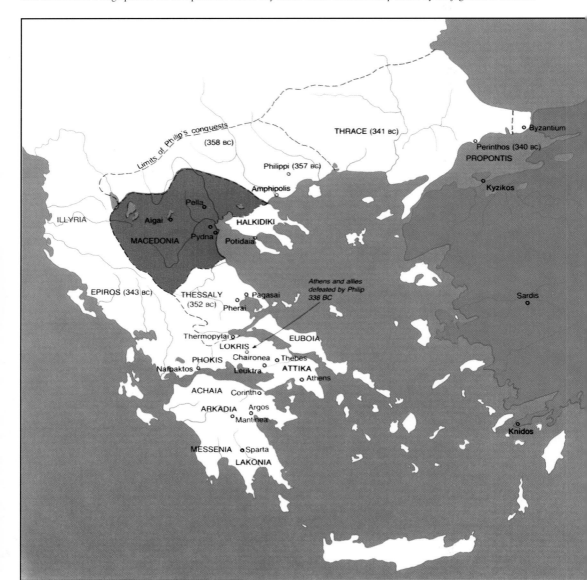

Limits of Philip's conquests
(358 BC)

THRACE (341 BC)

Byzantium

Perinthos (340 BC)

PROPONTIS

Philippi (357 BC)

Kyzikos

Amphipolis

Pella

ILLYRIA

Aigai

HALKIDIKI

MACEDONIA   Pydna

Potidaia

EPIROS (343 BC)

THESSALY
(352 BC)   Pagasai
Pherai

Athens and allies
defeated by Philip
338 BC

Sardis

Thermopylai

EUBOIA

LOKRIS

PHOKIS   Chaironea   Thebes

Nafpaktos   Leuktra   ATTIKA

Athens

ACHAIA   Corinth

ARKADIA   Argos
Mantinea

Knidos

MESSENIA   Sparta

LAKONIA

These soon appealed to Sparta, as the supreme power of the Greeks, to come and free them. Despite Sparta's formal agreement of 411 BC with the Persians, releasing these cities to them, Sparta's leadership role on behalf of the Greeks now compelled her to come to their aid. The army she sent to Asia was augmented by contingents from the experienced Ten Thousand Greek mercenaries that had remained in northwestern Asia Minor with no home to go to and forced to be living off the land. Now they had a purpose again. The Persians chose not to face this formidable army head-on, and resorted to better strategy.

Advised by a Greek traveller to the region that the Persians were preparing a large invasion fleet, in 396 BC, the Spartans sent another army to Persia. So urgent did they view the situation that the force was led by the Spartan King Agesilaos II himself. He won many victories on land, and soon converted this into a general invasion of the interior of Persia. But, according to Xenophon's *History*, the Persians sent agents to spread some gold around in the largest Greek cities on the Greek peninsula that were resentful of Spartan leadership, to induce them to take the offensive against Sparta. Not that they needed much persuasion. Boiotia, Corinth, Argos and Athens became such a threat to Sparta that Agesilaos was ordered home with his army. About the same time, in August 394 BC, the Persian fleet under the command of Konon, an able Athenian admiral employed by the Persians, as were many experienced Athenian seamen, met and destroyed the Spartan fleet off Knidos, a Greek city at the southwestern corner of Asia Minor. Agesilaos and his army were compelled to make the long march home overland.

The war between Corinth and Sparta was to continue for eight years, to 387 BC; Thebes and Athens put aside old hostilities and combined their forces against Sparta; and Corinth and Argos took the unique step to declare a political union to join their resources and efforts to the same end. Some of the Asian Greek cities rejoined their old ally, Athens. As it suited Persia to weaken both sides, she supported one or the other at various times. No one was winning, and the economy of the Greeks was in a very bad state after these many years of war. An effort for a "general peace" among the Greeks, was not conclusive. Finally, in 387 BC, Spartan King Antalkidas made the long journey to Susa, the Persian capital in the interior, to confer with Persian King Artaxerxes II on peace terms. It was obvious that without Persian participation and concurrence, peace among the Greeks could not be achieved. All the parties sent representatives to Sardis in 386, and they concluded "The King's Peace." It was generally accepted that the "king" referred to Artaxerxes; but the Greeks preferred to think it was Antalkidas. The peace terms were in fact an edict from the Persian king, served on all the others, to the effect that he would help those cities that kept the peace and make war on those that did not.

This virtually sealed the fate of the Greek city-state as an independent unit. Even Sparta was reduced to being a Persian puppet, though its hegemony lasted for a few more years and covered most of Greece. The break-up of Spartan power began when the Spartans attacked Thebes in 379 BC, and installed pro-Spartan Theban leaders. But the unprovoked attack was to reverse Spartan fortunes from this zenith of their power over the Greek cities.

The Rise of Thebes
(371-362 BC)

The anti-Spartan leaders of Thebes escaped to Athens in 379 BC, where they plotted their return to power. Finally, by the end of the year, with the help of Athens, they manged to organize a Theban force that retook their city from Spartan and pro-Spartan control. Although Athens and Thebes had little sympathy for between them and had always been distrustful of each other, they now managed a formal alliance together against Sparta. The Boiotian League of the cities in that area, was also resurrected.

Athens had also begun to organize a defensive league of cities — this time not on the imperial basis of the former Delian League she had organized about a century earlier against the Persians. Still, some seventy member-states had joined this league by 377 BC.

In Thessaly, too, from an area north of Boiotia, a strong personality emerged in 374 BC, who forcefully combined the city-states in his region under his leadership, making his capital at Pherai. This person was named Jason, and he organized and commanded large land forces and a sizable navy.

These activities kept Sparta on the defensive, even though there was little unity between the leagues and even less loyalty. A brilliant new general, Epaminondas, who arose in Thebes, emboldened that city-state to go on the offensive against neighboring cities, allies of other leagues. After a number of successes, in 375-374 BC, an alarmed Athens led the Greek city-states to seek another "general peace" agreement. But Sparta would not join in. She finally moved for a confrontation with Thebes, their forces meeting in 371 BC, at Leuktra, a few miles west of Thebes itself. The smaller Theban army was led by the able Epaminondas, and with the application of clever tactics, he destroyed the formerly invincible Spartan hoplite-phalanx.* When the Spartan leaders quickly mobilized the rest of their army and marched it to Boiotia, they arrived to find Jason waiting for them with his large Thessalian forces. Outnumbered, the Spartans were forced to agree to peace, and the Thebans were advised by Jason to do the same.

The fallen Spartan leadership was never to be resurrected to anything like its former self. If another strong leader was to emerge, it was not to come from Thessaly, either. A year later, in 370 BC, Jason of Pherai was assassinated, and Thessaly was neutralized by internal strife. Other regional leagues began to be formed, the need for unity now amply apparent, there being little safety for a city-state alone. But it was Thebes that began to conclude alliances with other city-states and leagues, in order to finish off what was left of Spartan power and to fill the vacuum that would result. These expedient alliances included Macedonia and Thessaly to the north, Phokis to the west, and Achaia and Arkadia on the Peloponnese. Even so, these allies would not remain faithful to each other for long.

Thebes and her supporters were now strong enough to invade the Peloponnese and attack Sparta itself. During the period 370 to 362 BC, several such invasions took place, all the armies allied with Thebes led by Epaminondas.

---

*A formation of heavily-armed infantry.

Each attack diminished Sparta, but none destroyed her power completely. The last major battle, that took place in 362 BC at Mantinea in Arkadian territory north of Sparta, pitted Thebes and her allies against Sparta and her confederates, including Athens. The two sides thoroughly mauled each other, and the superior tactics of Epaminondas again broke the Spartan lines. But Epaminondas was killed during the battle, and both adversaries were forced to accept peace rather than to continue the slaughter.

The description of the battle of Mantinea ends Xenophon's *History of My Times*. The terrible battle was inconclusive except for one overall result. It ended Spartan power as well as the rise of Thebes, and the Greek city-states were left fragmented once again, which left Persia as the only beneficiary after all these years of destruction between the Greeks. The city-states were to remain without the leadership of any one of them until the rise of Philip II in Macedonia in 359 BC.

THE ASCENDANCY OF PHILIP II
359-336 BC

The fame of Alexander the Great is such that it has eclipsed that of his father, King Philip II. Discoveries in 1977 of untouched rich royal tombs at Aigai (Vergina) in Macedonia, believed also to include that of Philip himself, has brought about renewed interest in Philip, his court and the Macedonia of the 4th century BC (See Map 3.2). Philip is a figure of great historical importance, a man of action, imagination, and a lover of culture in spite of his own rough manners and barbaric ways. (The suave Athenians saw all these northern kings and their hill tribe people as barbarians.) Alexander's impressive accomplishments were in no small way made possible by those of his father. The two together and their Macedonian successors affected the history of nearly all of the Greek world for the next five centuries, and of a geographical area that included that of the Greeks as well as that of other peoples north to the Danube, east to include all of Asia Minor, Persia and a vast part of Asia to India, and south to include Egypt.

Some historians say that the Macedonians were not true Greeks and that these people emanated from non-Greek northern tribes. The area did include some non-Greek tribes, but the ancient Macedonians were predominantly of Doric stock who are considered the first true Greeks. Furthermore, their language, religion, art and culture in general confirm beyond any doubt the Greekness of Philip's kingdom. The Macedonian royal family itself traced its roots to the seventh century BC, and from the beginning of the fifth century BC claimed its descendancy from the kings of Argos, a Greek city-state in the northeastern Peloponnese.

Philip was the son of the Macedonian King Amyntas III who reigned c. 393 to 369 BC. Philip's two eldest brothers, each of whom inherited the throne in turn, were both assassinated, and another brother who was the next heir later died in battle. At age 23 (359 BC), Philip was named regent to the next in line, his brother's son, then a child. The kingdom was in political disarray and would need a strong leader. Philip had inadvertently begun to be trained early for the future role events would cause him to assume. When he was only 15 years old (367 BC) he had been sent as a hostage to insure peace with Thebes, then the leading power in Greece. The three years spent there allowed him ample time and opportunity to observe the development of the formidable military techniques and tactics created by the noted Theban general Epaminondas, by means of which he had defeated the formerly invincible Spartan forces. These lessons were not wasted on the aggressive Philip, who would later use them with great success on behalf of his own Macedonia. So, as regent, Philip set about on the prodigious task to unify the kingdom, calm or checkmate its foreign enemies, and dispose of other claimants to the throne. He defeated the Illyrians, a strong non-Greek tribe in the west, in a great battle near Herakleia, to prevent their having control of key passes to the west. His victory led to his being elected king instead of his young nephew. Philip's many personal talents suited the needs of Macedonia at this time.

Philip set about to reorganize and train the Macedonian army and cavalry that was to become the most fearsome and relentless military force of the time. The basis, of course, was to expand and improve on what he had learned a few years earlier in Thebes. But military victories were not the only means employed by Philip to achieve his aims. He was a shrewd strategist and negotiator and an expert at intrigue and duplicity. Some of his diplomatic successes were to be achieved through his marriages with daughters of other rulers with whom he desired treaties and good relations. Polygamy was accepted for the ruling family in Macedonia, and Philip was to marry seven or eight times, although only one of these wives was to have great importance on the history of the Greeks. In 357 BC, he married Olympias, the daughter of the king of Epiros in the west, who was a forceful woman and had a reputation as a mystic. She bore their first child, a son who was named Alexander, in 356 BC.

By 354, Philip had enlarged the area of Macedonia, and had taken Amphipolis from Athens (a town just to the east of the Chalkidiki peninsula), which contained an area of important gold and silver mines. This greatly helped Philip finance his further political and military exploits. By 352 BC, he had won a large part of Thessaly, and nearby Phokis lost a major battle to him at Pegasai. Philip then turned his attention north to Chalkidiki and Thrace, and his campaigns forced them into submitting. For the next ten years this brilliant and restless man continued to forge alliances and create dependencies, and to take outright possession by force of arms — his imperialist aims becoming more and more apparent. Not one to stay back in leading his armies, he suffered numerous wounds, becoming blind in one eye and lame in one leg.

Athens had become a strong power by that time and was greatly disturbed by the actions of Philip that provoked her continuously. Beginning well over a century earlier, Macedonia was of great importance to Athens as a source of timber for ship-building and for precious metals discovered in the area. But Philip not only took Amphipolis from Athens, gaining its mines, he also took Methone, a colony of Athens in Macedonia which had been in its possession about a century, and was a key base to insure its presence in the area. With these and other acts, there existed a virtual if not a *de facto* state of war between Athens and Macedonia, from 357 BC. One of the most vociferous enemies of Philip was the great Athenian orator, Demosthenes (384-322 BC), who delivered many impressive speeches against the perils that Philip represented. Demosthenes became leader of Athens in 340 BC, and when Philip attacked the strategic cities of Perinthos and Byzantium on the Propontis (Sea of Marmara), seizing also 230 Athenian vessels loaded with grain, they finally declared war on him in the early fall. Although animosities between Athens and Thebes had previously prevented them from acting together, they now forced themselves into an alliance for what was rapidly drawing to a test of strength with Macedonia. Philip spent the next few months fighting his way down to the Gulf of Corinth to Nafpaktos, then turned east to face his opponents.

The final great battle between Athens and Thebes against Macedonia and her allies took place on August 2, 338 BC, near Chaironeia, on the Phokis-Theban border. The importance of this event may be seen by the fact that about 35,000 men took part on each side, a very large number for those times. Raised in the military tradition as befits a future Macedonian king, eighteen-year-old Alexander was appointed leader of the Macedonian cavalry, his specialty. Using the tactics devised by Philip with the main army feigning an orderly retreat drawing their enemy nearer, Alexander charged his cavalry into the gap created, and wiped out the elite "Sacred Band" of the Thebans. The disciplined Macedonians then charged into the trapped foe and won the battle, Philip wisely refraining from slaughtering the fleeing Greek allies. Besides, he needed the Athenian fleet, and had a greater goal which required a united Greece.

Philip began to achieve this goal at the end of 338 BC by negotiating a "common peace" agreement in Corinth with the representatives of what must have been nearly all of the mainland Greek city-states and the islands. Again, Sparta would not take part, even though she could see clearly that her enemies were thus being unified under the powerful Philip. Nevertheless, for the first time in nearly a century, wars between the city-states came to an end. Most of them were overjoyed with the prospect of peace, and others went along only out of fear of Philip. The result was a virtual end to the city-state as an independent unit in favor of a national monarchy known as the Hellenic League of Corinth, led by Philip. This alliance would now give Philip the time and the means to undertake what some have come to call a Hellenic crusade against Persia, to liberate the Greek Asia Minor cities and join them into the coalition. Something more would be undertaken too: exacting revenge for the Greeks having suffered from the Persian invasions and interference beginning more than a century-and-a-half earlier, and to add some additional territory to the east as a buffer to protect the Greek cities on the coast.

For some years, the Persians had been following Philip's progress and the rapid expansion of his empire. As early as 342 BC, Philip had begun to plan to invade the Persian Empire itself. What originally influenced him to dream of ambitious conquests beyond Greek borders is not clear. We know that the noted Greek orator Isokrates (436-338 BC) had developed and widely expounded a theory that the constantly warring Greek city-states would solve their many economic, social, and political problems if they would unite in a great campaign to invade their archenemy, Persia, which had so long interfered in Greek affairs. Isokrates wrote long open letters to many of the prominent Greek leaders about this idea, including several to Philip. Whether inspired by this idea or for a variety of reasons, Philip's leadership of a now substantially unified Greece a few years later converted the theory into reality.

In the spring of 337 BC, Philip sent a vanguard of 10,000 Macedonians and some other Greeks plus a large fleet to begin the liberation campaign. They divided their forces between the Asia Minor Greek cities of Kyzikos on the Propontis, and Ephesos on the Aegean coast, being warmly received in both cities. They were to continue their march to the other Greek cities in the area.

But, in July 336 BC, Philip was assassinated at his daughter's wedding by one of his own bodyguards. Many theories for the motive were later advanced, but none were proven; in any case, the perpetrator was killed while fleeing.

At the time of Philip's death in 336 BC, the army of several thousand Macedonians and other Greeks was camped in Asia Minor awaiting further instructions, having freed from Persian control the Greek cities in that area. Philip was to have followed them shortly on his campaign to invade Persia. Someone else would now have to carry these plans forward. That someone would be his young son Alexander.

ALEXANDER'S KINGDOM
(336-323 BC)

Alexander was born in Pella in 356 BC, three years after his father Philip II ascended to the Macedonian throne. He grew up in a world marked by his father's military, political and diplomatic successes throughout Greece. Even as a boy, Alexander developed a passion for Homer and other heroic stories of the Greeks at war. But, in addition to his physical training, his mind was not neglected either. Among other able tutors, in 343 BC Philip even brought the great philosopher Aristotle to Pella to teach Alexander, which lasted for three years. They were to remain friends and in close touch through Alexander's lifetime, despite the long distances that separated them.

The strong and able character of his father Philip and that of his spirited mother Olympias were not wasted on Alexander. His own military talents and leadership qualities were revealed at an early age. He trained well in the tradition established during the period when Philip was organizing the Macedonian army and cavalry into the formidable force that it became. At age sixteen, when Philip appointed him regent during one of his long absences, Alexander first showed his decisiveness and prowess by leading a military troop that put down a rebellion of tribes on Macedonia's northern border. At eighteen, as already mentioned, he commanded the cavalry unit that broke the Greek lines at Chaironeia.

Alexander by this time had gained the respect and loyalty of his military peers. This loyalty became all important when Philip was assassinated. Suspicion even fell on him and his mother Olympias, because Philip a year before had repudiated Olympias and had taken a young new bride, Kleopatra, of a prominent Macedonian family. She bore him a son who became the direct heir, Olympias being an Epirote princess and not a native Macedonian. But, though he was only twenty years of age, Alexander acted decisively in a style that was to typify his future actions. He had the army recognize him as its leader, he eliminated the new heir and other rivals from the Macedonian royal family for the throne. Local revolts and other attacks from the barbarian tribes in the north also threatened the stability of Macedonia and Greece. Alexander again acted quickly. He appeared before the Hellenic League that had been established at Corinth by Philip, which acknowledged Alexander's leadership, and he proved that trust by immediately attacking the northern tribes. For good measure he proceeded as far north as the Danube River, even crossing an army to the other side where he destroyed a settlement, an act more symbolic than of any other value. But shortly later, Thebes revolted with the aid of Athens, and Alexander quick-marched his army directly there. As the Thebans had taken up arms, the Macedonians attacked and soon took the city. Alexander saw to it that the Thebans paid dearly for their disloyalty. Their city was destroyed and the people were sold into slavery. The harshness of his act insured that no other city would dare to revolt.

His base secure, Alexander was now free to pursue his destiny, the conquest of Persia. His leadership and the campaign were confirmed by the Hellenic League, but it was essentially a Macedonian undertaking with some participation by other Greeks.

In the spring of 334 BC, Alexander proceeded from Pella with nearly 40,000 men and 6,000 cavalry, crossing the Hellespont to Asia at Arisbe. As Alexander's ship leading the invasion fleet neared the shore, he pitched his spear forward piercing the beach, as a symbol of his intent to conquer. His next act was to proceed to the ancient Greek city of Troy, where he sought out the tomb of Achilles, the Greeks' greatest warrior according to the Homeric epic. The eager locals were pleased to show him this site, and find for him at his request the buried shield Achilles had carried into battle. Alexander stripped naked, and after oiling his body in the manner of the Homeric heroes, ran around Achilles' tomb carrying the shield. He was to have the shield carried near him the thousands of miles of his entire campaign in Asia.

Many adventures awaited Alexander and they were carefully recorded by his scribes. For the sake of brevity and ease of understanding by the reader, they are described in numbered paragraphs below, the numbers corresponding to those locations shown on Map 3.3.

1. In his first great battle, Alexander defeated a Persian army waiting for him on the banks of the river Granikos. He appointed a Macedonian officer to be in charge of the area conquered, a pattern established as the conquests continued.

2. Sardis, the Persian capital of the western empire, fell without a struggle. Most of the coastal Greek cities readily joined Alexander's forces as their Persian garrisons fled. However, Miletos surrendered only after battle, and Halikarnassos required a long siege. It seems that Alexander's liberation campaign of these cities met with some resistance on their part; they wanted freedom and not to be under another conqueror, even one that was Greek. He continued along the coast as far as Side.

3. The schedule to winter in Gordion was met without difficulty. This was the location of one of the first of many legends about Alexander. A fine chariot that had belonged to King Gordios, the founder, was on display, dedicated to Zeus. Its yoke was tied to the yoke-pole of the chariot with a wood-bark rope having a complicated knot. An oracle was said to have declared that whoever should untie the elaborate knot would rule Asia. Alexander allegedly solved the problem by slashing it through with his sword.

4. Alexander now decided to secure the entire Mediterranean coast and proceeded to Tarsos in November, 333 BC. He continued east to Issos and on to Myriandros, where his scouts informed him that a great Persian army had marched behind him to Issos, led by the Persian King Darius III himself. Alexander turned his men back and fought a great battle along the Pinaros River. Though greatly outnumbered, the Greek army, using superior tactics, destroyed the Persians once again. Darius sent Alexander an offer to partition Persia with him, but Alexander refused; he would take what he wanted.

5. The cities of Arados, Byblos, and Sidon surrendered without a fight, but Tyre required a siege that lasted seven months. When the city finally fell, an angry Alexander took his revenge again as a lesson to all who would resist him: he put 8,000 Tyrians to death and sold 30,000 into slavery.

6. Gaza, nearby, also chose to resist and held out two months, suffering a similar fate.

7. Egypt now lay before Alexander. The area had been occupied by the Persians in 343 BC, and the Egyptians were eager to be liberated from them. Alexander visited Memphis, where he was welcomed and crowned Pharaoh of Upper and Lower Egypt; he also founded on the Mediterranean the first of what were to be 17 cities in the east to be called Alexandria. He proceeded to the shrine of Zeus Ammon at Ammonion, entering alone, where he was hailed by the priest there as the son of the god. Upon the completion of the appropriate religious ceremonies he then returned to Memphis.

8. Alexander left Egypt in the spring of 331 BC and continued the march into the heartland of Persia. At Gaugamela (near modern-day Mosul), a vast Persian army awaited him in September. Darius prepared his battle plan well and had a vastly larger army. But it did not help. Alexander's superior tactics applied by his veterans were victorious again, and Darius fled once more, with his remaining forces trailing after him.

9. The march now led to Babylon, then to the summer palace at Susa, and finally to Persepolis, the royal city. Although the tribes along the way had to be fought, the cities offered no resistance. They also yielded up vast fortunes in gold and silver and many other valuables. Alexander ordered the royal palace at Persepolis to be burned as a symbolic gesture of revenge for the acts of destruction against the Greek cities by Xerxes 150 years before.

10. In the spring of 330 BC, Alexander's pursuit of Darius took him through Ekbatana, where more royal treasure was seized by the Macedonians. It was here that Alexander declared that the revenge on the Persians for the harm they caused the Greeks had now been accomplished; from now on he no longer campaigned on behalf of the Hellenic League but for himself and Macedonia. The non-Macedonian Greek troops were discharged but were told they could stay on as mercenaries if they desired, and many did so. The hot chase after Darius continued, but at Hekatompylos, not far from the Caspian Sea, Darius was stabbed to death by his cousin Bessos and other Persian nobles, and Alexander arrived to find a corpse. Bessos had taken this opportunity to murder Darius in order to declare himself king of Baktria and Sogdiana, where he had been satrap. Respecting the murdered king, Alexander covered the corpse with his own cloak.

11. The Macedonians carried the body of Darius to Persepolis, where he was buried with full royal honors by Alexander. He now regarded himself as Darius' successor, and he was determined to punish Bessos and his followers. On the way, Alexander turned south to the Persian highlands in central Asia; the fighting of tribes in that area was the fiercest yet.

More and more, Alexander had begun to adopt a number of Persian royal ways. He wore Persian royal dress, his royal guards also wearing the royal colors, and others of Alexander's court dressed according to rank, in the Persian manner. It was no longer possible for soldiers and officers to freely approach and talk to the king as the Macedonians were accustomed to doing, and this distancing greatly troubled them. In addition to the ceaseless fighting, it began to be obvious to them that Alexander was not planning to return to Macedonia. At Prophthasia (Farah), the army's discontent resulted in a plot against his life. The accused were discovered before they had a chance to carry their plan forward and they were put to death. But the discontent was to grow.

12. The pursuit of Bessos ended in the spring of 328 BC near Sogdiana on the banks of the Oxos River. Bessos was deserted by his followers and was caught by Ptolemy, one of Alexander's generals. He was sent to Ekbatana, where he was executed cruelly after his nose and ears were cut off, in the

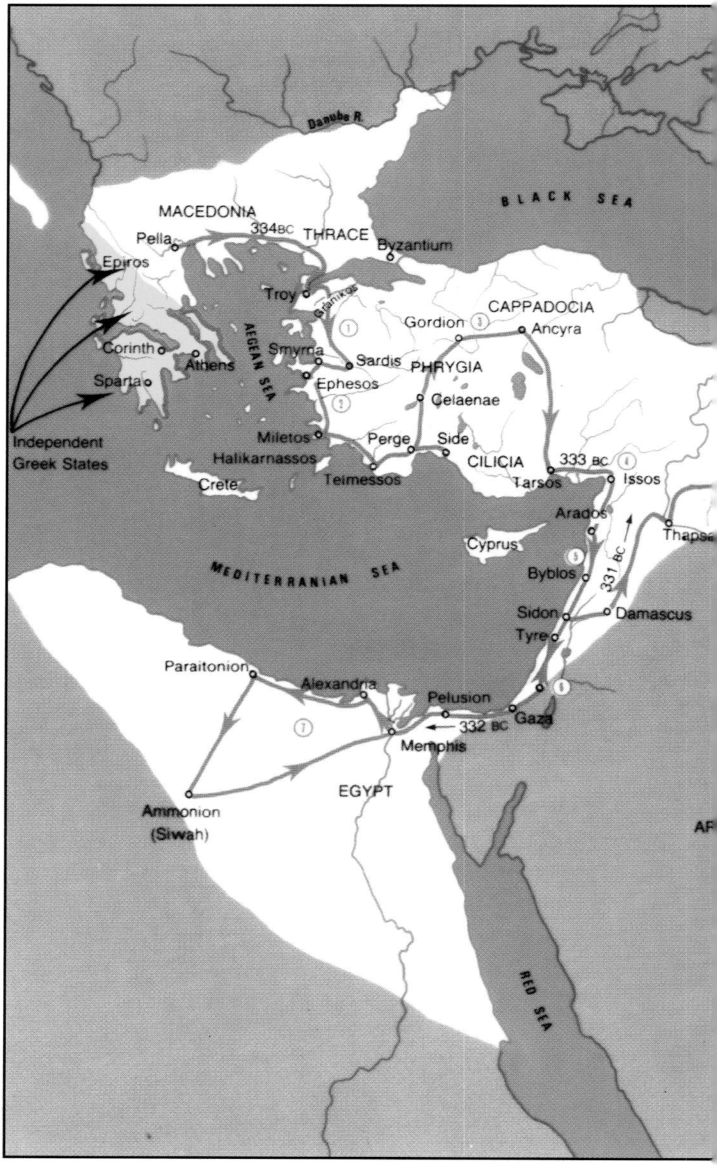

MAP 3.3
CONQUESTS OF ALEXANDER
(334-323 BC)
In a twelve-year period, beginning in 334 BC, Alexander conquered a vast territory that extended from Asia Minor to India, and Egypt. The protests of his loyal Macedonians at Alexander continuing east without end finally caused him to turn back. He died in Babylon of wounds and fever while he was planning to circumnavigate the Arabian Peninsula.

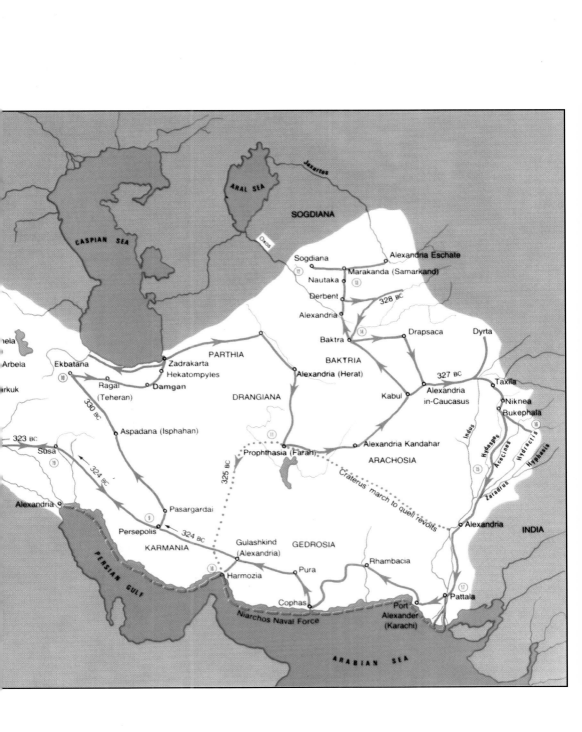

Persian manner for such rebels and traitors. Alexander spent the next year putting down revolts in the area.

13. The endless campaigning and the foreign atmosphere continued to have its toll. In Marakanda (Samarkand), Alexander, drunk, struck dead with a spear his closest friend, Kleitos, during a hot argument. Another incident revealing discontent between Alexander and his close companions involved Kallisthenes, a nephew of Aristotle who had accompanied Alexander as a historian. He refused to prostrate himself before the king (the *proskynesis*) in the Persian manner — over which they argued bitterly. Kallisthenes was later implicated in another plot, the "Conspiracy of the Pages," and he was put to death when they arrived in India. In still another incident, a trusted officer, Philotas, was told of a plot against Alexander. Philotas did not take the matter seriously enough to report it. When the plot was reported by another officer, Philotas was tried and put to death, and in accordance with the Macedonian law of treason, his father Parmenio was also killed, though he was one of Alexander's wise and loyal generals, stationed in Ekbatana, far away. Meanwhile, the spring of 327 BC was spent subduing the wild tribes in Baktria and Sogdiana, in the northeast corner of the empire.

14. It was during this same period that Alexander married Roxana, daughter of a Sogdiana chief, whom he had taken prisoner with others in one of the battles.

15. In the summer of 327 BC, the Macedonians arrived in India, where Alexander was fascinated by the local customs, religions, and philosophies. Ambi, the Indian rajah of Taxila, chose to accept Alexander's overlordship rather than do battle with him, and he proved very helpful as Alexander proceeded into Indian territory. Some regions submitted and others had to be won by fierce battles. But in the summer of 326 BC, at the river Hydaspes (Jhelum), they reached the kingdom of Poros, an enemy of Ambi, and were confronted by his huge army assembled in battle array on the eastern bank. The ensuing bloody engagement was won by the Macedonians, again by applying clever tactics and discipline in battle. Poros had proved an admirable leader, and Alexander showed his respect for him by granting him the right to retain his kingdom. But he left Ambi there, too, to neutralize each other. It was here that Alexander's famous warhorse, Bukephalas, died. In his memory, Alexander founded a town on the spot, which he named Bukephala.

16. The Macedonians continued eastward fighting hostile tribes, and when they reached the Hyphasis (Beas) River, they finally had enough; they mutinied and refused to go on. The years of fighting, the accumulation of their share in the spoils, and the relentless drive eastward away from home, finally got to them. Alexander acceded to their wishes for the first time in his life, and he gave up and turned back. How far would he have gone if they had not mutinied? (Though it should be mentioned that at various times during the years of campaigning, contingents of the Greeks departed for home, and others were sent out to take their place and to replace those that had been lost.)

17. Returning to the Hydaspes River again, Alexander had his forces build an enormous fleet, and they sailed the long distance south to the city of Pattala, on the Indus River. The journey took them nine months, fighting more tribes whenever they landed. The fleet was placed under Niarchos, who was to sail to the mouth of the Indus and west along the coast to the Euphrates River. Meanwhile, part of the army, under Krateros, was dispatched to return through central Persia, to quell revolts. Alexander led the remaining troops to explore a more southerly route on their return to the west.

18. The two Macedonian armies met in Karmania, north of the modern Straits of Hormuz, and the fleet reported having reached the Persian Gulf. They continued their journeys, the combined army arriving at Pasargadai and Persepolis in the beginning of 324 BC. Alexander now occupied himself with the problems of administering his vast conquests and combatting corruption by the Greeks and Persians left in charge of the various areas.

19. At Susa, in the spring of 324 BC, Alexander, under his policy of fusing the Greek and Persian peoples, held a mass marriage festival where he and his officers, and large numbers of Macedonian soldiers, took Persian wives. This did not suit many of the men, however, and the army again mutinied against what they considered to be a violation of their Macedonian traditions. Alexander dismissed them all in disgust. The Macedonians could not bear to lose the respect of their commander with whom they had fought for so long, and they repented and again swore their loyalty to him.

20. In the spring of 323 BC, Alexander and the army arrived at Babylon at last, from where they had departed eight years before. There Alexander decided to explore the route around Arabia to Egypt and made preparations for this enormous undertaking that would require hundreds of ships. But he had suffered a number of wounds during these years of fighting and some just before this time, and he was in pain and exhausted. By June, he contracted a fever (malaria? pneumonia?) and he died within the month at the age of 32.*

Alexander's efforts did not die with him, and rule of Persia by Greeks was to last until Roman times nearly three centuries later. His accomplishments have been matched by few people in history, although a number of later conquerors also fought their way through the vast Asian spaces. His achievements may have glorified Alexander and his political heirs, but they had little long-term affect on the welfare of Greece or the Greeks themselves at home, which fell on hard times during his long absence.

---

*Alexander lay feverish and seriously ill for ten days while his alarmed doctors tried in vain to cure his increasinbly weakening condition. Some historians have presented theories that he may have been poisoned to death by his own generals, but this is not proven.

Four

The
Hellenistic
Age
(c.600-323 BC)

T HE YEARS BETWEEN THE DEATH OF ALEXANDER THE Great in 323 BC, and the death of Cleopatra, the last Greek qheen of Egypt, in 30 BC, have been called the Hellenistic Age.

ALEXANDER'S SUCCESSORS
(323-306 BC)

W hen Alexander died in Babylon in 323 BC, his principal officers met to determine what to do with the vast empire. There were eight successors (in Greek *diadochi*) as follows: **Perdikkas** (probably in his mid-40's), the second-in-command to Alexander; **Eumenes** (39), a Thracian Greek and the only non-Macedonian among the leaders, secretary to Alexander and before that to Philip II, and later an able military commander; **Antipater** (75), a general of Philip II and the viceroy Alexander had left behind in Macedonia when he went off to the Persian campaign; **Krateros** (about 35), trusted and close officer of Alexander; **Lysimachos** (37) another close friend and officer; **Ptolemy** (44) a trusted general of Alexander; **Antigonos** Monophthalmos, the One-Eyed (59), another of Philip's generals who accompanied Alexander on his Asiatic expedition; and **Seleukos** (33), a high officer who distinguished himself in the Indian campaign. Two other figures were to become prominent in this period: **Demetrios,** son of Antigonos, who while only 13 years old in 323, soon grew to brilliant maturity under the tutelage of an aggressive and able father. He was to become Demetrios I Poliorketes (the Besieger). The other was **Kassander,** son of the aged but shrewd Antipater, who was 35 years old in 323 and who also proved worthy of his heritage.

The consequences of their decisions, and eventually, actions, plots and battles against each other over the next forty years, would result in some of the successors and their heirs ruling large portions of the empire as independent Hellenistic kingdoms for the next two to three hundred years.

Kingdoms by 303 BC

- ◼ Kassander
- ◼ Lysimachos
- ◼ Antigonus
- ◻ Ptolemy
- ◼ Seleukos

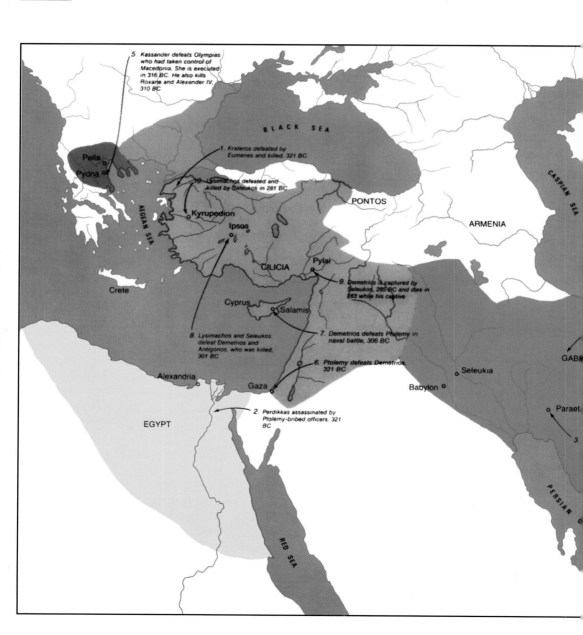

BLACK SEA

5. Kassander defeats Olympias who had taken control of Macedonia. She is executed in 316 BC. He also kills Roxane and Alexander IV, 310 BC

Pella

Pydna

1. Krateros defeated by Eumenes and killed, 321 BC

10. Lysimachos defeated and killed by Seleukos in 281 BC

Kyrupedion

PONTOS

ARMENIA

CASPIAN SEA

AEGEAN SEA

Ipsos

Crete

CILICIA

Pylai

9. Demetrios is captured by Seleukos, 285 BC and dies in 283 while his captive

Cyprus

Salamis

8. Lysimachos and Seleukos defeat Demetrios and Antigonos, who was killed, 301 BC

7. Demetrios defeats Ptolemy in naval battle, 306 BC

Alexandria

Gaza

6. Ptolemy defeats Demetrios, 321 BC

Seleukia

Babylon

GAB

Paraet

2. Perdikkas assassinated by Ptolemy-bribed officers, 321 BC

EGYPT

RED SEA

PERSIAN

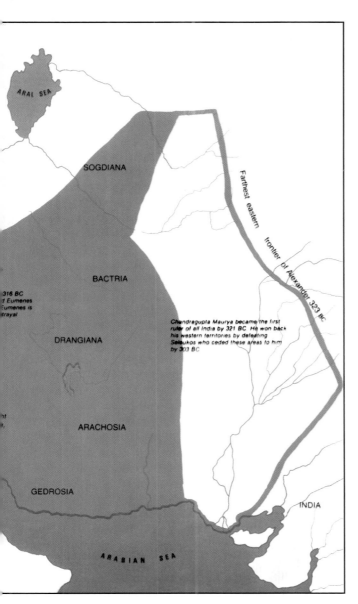

ARAL SEA

SOGDIANA

BACTRIA

316 BC
d Eumenes
Eumenes is
trayal

DRANGIANA

Chandragupta Maurya became the first
ruler of all India by 321 BC. He won back
his western territories by defeating
Seleukos who ceded these areas to him
by 303 BC

ARACHOSIA

GEDROSIA

INDIA

ht
r,

Farthest eastern frontier of Alexander 323 BC

ARABIAN SEA

MAP 4.0
THE ALEXANDER
SUCCESSORS

Alexander's generals divided up the empire
following his death, ostensibly to govern for
Macedonia. Their personal rivalries and
ambitions reduced their number in many conflicts
against each other. Finally claiming personal
rule over the areas they occupied resulted in
several large, independent Hellenistic kingdoms
which were to last for centuries.

Perdikkas, the second-in-command, had been appointed regent by the dying Alexander. Though he became too weak to speak, Alexander signified his choice by handing his signet ring to Perdikkas in front of the assembled officers. In the Macedonian tradition, shortly after Alexander died the army convened to elect a new king. The infantry respected the Macedonian direct line of royal ascendency and preferred Philip Arridaios, then 35, the only other son of Philip II, born of Meda, a Thracian girl, even though he was feeble-minded. The high officers and elite Macedonian cavalry, preferred to wait until Alexander's Persian wife Roxane, then pregnant, gave birth, which she did a few weeks later. It was a boy and he was also named Alexander; they chose him to be their king. The conflict between the two groups was intense and threatened civil war until a compromise was finally reached whereby the two would rule jointly as Philip III and Alexander IV. But a feeble-minded adult king coruling with a half-Persian days-old infant did not augur well for the future.

Decisions were also made between the successors as to where they would each be assigned throughout the empire. The election of their joint kings decided, they departed to assume their commands of the areas assigned to each of them. But the competition for power between them was already beginning to be apparent now that their beloved and respected Alexander was dead and the quality of the future traditional Macedonian monarchy very much in question.

The events that began to take place form a sad epilogue to the Philip-Alexander story. Perdikkas as regent tried to hold the empire together for Macedonia, supported by Eumenes. But the others rejected his authority, and the battles between them began. (See Map 4.0.) Antipater, back in Macedonia, became a center for the dissident diadochi against Perdikkas, and he was supported by Krateros (his son-in-law), Ptolemy, and Antigonos. By 321 BC, Krateros and Eumenes fought near the Hellespont, and Krateros was killed. In the same year, Ptolemy managed to take possession of the funeral cortège conducting the body of Alexander for burial in Macedonia, and diverted it to Egypt, where Alexander's remains would be interred temporarily in Memphis, in his own domain.* This act greatly enhanced Ptolemy's reputation but gained the enmity of Perdikkas. He decided to punish Ptolemy and marched his own army into Egypt to confront him, but before he could cross the Nile River, Ptolemy bribed some officers of Perdikkas who assassinated him.

In Macedonia, the aged Antipater died of natural causes in 319 BC, having put forward as regent in his place a Macedonian general, Polyperchon, who had well served both Philip II and Alexander the Great. This decision of Antipater embittered his own ambitious son Kassander, who began to plot against the new regent, putting into motion another series of actions in that already troubled atmosphere. Kassander was supported by the high-born Eurydike, wife of the feeble-minded Philip III Arridaios. She was another strong-minded Macedonian, and politically ambitious, able to take advantage of her husband's mental infirmity and his position as joint king. In response,

---

*Alexander's tomb was later moved to Alexandria, and placed in a cemetary prepared as the royal burial grounds of the Ptolemaic line, but these tombs have disappeared from modern Alexandria.

Polyperchon invited Olympias (Alexander's mother) back from her self-exile in her homeland of Epiros. She arrived with an Epirote army, and when the Macedonian forces came over to her side, she took over the rule of Macedonia, aided by Polyperchon. Kassander fled. Olympias promptly had Philip III executed and arranged the death of his wife Eurydike and that of others who had sided with Kassander. Inevitably, Kassander invaded with a powerful army from the east, and succeeded in defeating Olympias' forces at Pydna. After a summary trial by his army, she was executed in 316 BC. Kassander then took over the rule of Macedonia and most of Greece. In 310 BC, he killed Alexander's wife Roxane and thirteen-year-old Alexander IV, the last remaining direct heir to the Macedonian throne.

Meanwhile in the east, the most ambitious of the successors to try to keep the empire together (for his own sake as it would become apparent) was Antigonos. The principal enemy who stood in the way of his ambitions was Eumenes, who had been an ally of Perdikkas in support of the Macedonian throne. Their armies battled in 317 and again in 316 BC, at which time Eumenes was taken prisoner, betrayed by his own men who had been bribed by Antigonos. Eumenes was brought to trial and he was executed, Antigonos taking over his terrains.

Antigonos would now have to occupy the areas he claimed. Assisted by his son Demetrios, he proceeded east to Babylonia, forcing Seleukos to retreat. The remaining diadochi combined against the aggressive father and son; Ptolemy, Kassander, Seleukos, and Lysimachos fought against them for the next ten years. Attempts at peace were short-lived. While Antigonos fought in the east, Demetrios invaded Greece then under Kassander, taking a portion that included Athens in 307 BC. Ptolemy had earlier attacked the relatively inexperienced young Demetrios defeating him at Gaza in 312 BC; now their naval forces met in a huge battle off Salamis in Cyprus in 306 BC. Ptolemy's navy was utterly defeated and his possession Cyprus was taken over by Demetrios.

Having secured an area that stretched from Greece to Armenia, Antigonos (now 76 years old) and Demetrios (now 30), ambitiously declared themselves joint kings of the entire Alexandrian empire. However, Ptolemy, Kassander, Lysimachos, and Seleukos promptly also declared themselves kings of the areas they occupied. The eastern empire now took the form of independent Greek kingdoms with no political ties back to the Macedonia from where all these strong leaders had originated.

Near the end of the century, summing up the status of the remaining diadochi after twenty years of wars: Antigonos was consolidating his domains in the near east; Demetrios was continuing his successes in Greece; Kassander still ruled in Macedonia; Ptolemy remained without a fleet in Egypt; Lysimachos held sway in Thrace: and Seleukos ruled the vast area between Armenia and the Indian kingdoms.

In his continuing quest to claim the empire of Alexander, Antigonos had attacked Ptolemy in Egypt, but without success. This well-despised enemy of the rest had to be stopped. Lysimachos, Kassander and Seleukos now joined forces against Antigonos, and they proceeded into the heart of his domains. Antigonos hurriedly recalled Demetrios from Greece to assist him, and the opposing armies met in 301 BC in a huge battle at Ipsos, in Phrygia, central Asia Minor. At age 81, the irrepressible Antigonos was in the thick of the fighting where he was cut down. Demetrios also suffered great losses and fled west, his remaining forces so weakened that even his dominion of Athens dared to refuse to accept him.

The resourceful Demetrios recovered his territories in Greece by 294 BC, including Athens. Kassander had died of dropsy in 297 BC (aged 61), his son inheriting the throne of Macedonia. But in 294, Demetrios arranged the murder of the heir and declared himself king of Macedonia, adding this territory to his holdings of nearly all the rest of the Greek peninsula. This must have rankled the other diadochi, not wanting a member of the hated Antigonos-Demetrios clan to rule Macedonia. After only six years, in 288 BC Demetrios was ousted by the combined forces of Lysimachos, Seleukos, aided by the neighboring king of Epiros to the west of Macedonia. Rootless but still leading a strong army, Demetrios proceeded east, fighting a number of battles against Lysimachos and Seleukos, without result. Finally captured by Seleukos in 287 BC, Demetrios was imprisoned by him and he died four years later in captivity, but not ill-treated, it is said, aged only 54.

Lysimachos' prize for participating in the victory against Antigonos earlier was to acquire most of his territories in Asia Minor. He never ceased attempting to expand his domains, and also married a daughter of Ptolemy to maintain peaceful relations with him. After taking part in the deposing of Demetrios from Macedonia, he ousted the Epirote king who had taken possession of Macedonia for his pains, and took the throne himself in 285 BC. But the aging Lysimachos began to be hated by those around him, and he was beset by murderous family feuds, even commiting the onerous deed of putting his own son to death as a result. The son's widow fled to the court of Seleukos in the east and persuaded him to attack Lysimachos. In 281 BC, their armies met in a great battle at Korupedion, in Asia Minor, where Lysimachos was killed, aged 74.

Seleukos was now the king of all of the empire of Alexander with the exception of Ptolemy's Egypt. He proceeded to occupy Lysimachos' territories of Thrace and Macedonia. But another Ptolemy was to cause his downfall. This was to be at the hands of the eldest son of Ptolemy I, Ptolemy Keraunos ("Thunderbolt"), who was passed over by his father when he named his younger son, Ptolemy II Philadelphos, his coruler in 285 BC. Keraunos' mother was Eurydike, daughter of the successor Antipator (this was another Eurydike, not the wife of Philip III Arridaios), and she had been the first wife of Ptolemy I. As he subsequently repudiated her, the next-in-line for the throne became Keraunos' younger brother of another mother. Keraunos, of strong character, first fled to the court of Lysimachos in Macedonia. When Seleukos defeated Lysimachos, Keraunos saw his opportunity and managed to have Seleukos murdered just when he had crossed the Hellespont into Europe (281 BC). This enabled the ambitious Ptolemy Keraunos to take the Macedonian throne, but he was killed in the invasions of the Gauls from the north a year later.

The heirs of Seleukos I continued to reign to 65 BC. Though the territories of the Seleucids at their greatest extent comprised a substantial part of those of

Alexander, after the first 100 years they gradually shrank because of the rise of the Parthian empire in the east, and the loss to other rulers of Macedonia and other parts of Greece and most of Asia Minor.

After a full and productive life, Ptolemy I died peacefully at his capital of Alexandria in 283 BC, at the age of 84. As already described, two years earlier he had already picked the next heir to the Egyptian throne, his able son Ptolemy II Philadelphos. The Ptolemaic dynasty went through a number of ruling sons to Ptolemy XIV, as well as a number of ruling daughters, the last being Cleopatra VII of Julius Ceasar and Mark Antony fame, who committed suicide in 30 BC rather than submit to the Romans, ending about three centuries of Greek rule of that area. (See *Cleopatra*, p.118).

HELLENISTIC CIVILIZATION

The Hellenization begun by Alexander's conquests followed by the successor kingdoms in the east was to have a profound influence on a large part of this vast area for eighteen centuries, through Byzantine times. This very long period would also affect the history of Europe. We have seen that this Hellenization was the continuation of a process that had begun several hundred years earlier, when Greek settlers established many colonies on the Asia Minor and Black Sea coasts. (See Chapter Two, *Greek Settlements Abroad*). By the time of the conquests of Alexander the Great (334-323 BC), many of these settlements had grown into prominent Greek city-states with large populations. The principal ones included, among many others, Heraklia Pontika on the Black Sea; Byzantion (Byzantium) on the Bosporus; Kyzikos and Lampsakos on the Sea of Marmara; and Ephesos, Miletos, and Halikarnassos on the Aegean coast.

The successor kingdoms lasted up to three centuries and, starting from Macedonia itself, covered an area (see Map 4.0) comprising Thrace; Asia Minor; the Middle East, between and south of the Black Sea and the Caspian down to the Persian Gulf; Egypt and a stretch of North Africa to Kyrene (Cyrenaica); and Cyprus. During the successor period many new Greek cities were also established, along with those already there from centuries earlier. The Greek language and culture were now widely in use.

In addition to the cities settled and developed entirely by Greeks, some other settlements such as Smyrna and Magnesia, which had already been established by others, were gradually absorbed by the Greeks. Other settlements and towns, particularly in the interior, managed to preserve their own cultures, which represented a mixture forged mainly from Hittite, Babylonian, and Persian heritages. Through their travels, the Greek sholars and others came in contact with many of these people, and they introduced their culture to them, often under the sponsorship of the native rulers. Greek arts, medicine, military science, architecture and building, philosophy, poetry and literature, and religion, were widely appreciated. The Greek language became a common tongue, or *lingua franca*, among a vast array of native middle eastern peoples who spoke many tongues. After all, this was the key to enjoying the richness of Greek culture. Greek victories over the invading Persians had already shown the Greeks to be hardy, intelligent, imaginative, and energetic, a people to be reckoned with, as Alexander's own conquests were also to confirm. Greek pagan religion was adopted by many, and Homer was widely read.

Alexander had absorbed the Greek cities of the east and pushed the Greek frontier to India. Having achieved his remarkable conquests in only twelve years before he died in Babylon in 323 BC, he had barely begun to introduce the Greeks into the greatly expanded area. The Hellenization process was carried on and greatly accelerated by his successors, who settled a large number of Greeks in their domains. While the successors had rejected any political ties to the Macedonia from which they had come, and their kingdoms were independent of each other, Greek culture prevailed uniformly in the royal courts and among the educated classes. The scholars and teachers were largely Greeks, and the classic Greek authors and philosophers were read in their original language.

The Romans began to conquer the area beginning in 133 BC, and spread ever eastward from the Asia Minor coast. (See Chapter Five, *The Roman Period*). But Hellenism had become so widespread and entrenched in this area that it was never replaced by the Latin culture of the Roman Empire, itself awed and influenced by the Greek.* The Roman poet Horace wrote around 20 BC, *Graecia capta ferum victorem cepit et artes intulit agresti Latio.* ("Greece, taken captive, captured her savage conqueror and brought the arts to rustic Latium.") This was to become increasingly true in the east.

CULTURE AND THE AGE OF REALISM

For many casual readers of Greek history, the "Golden Age" of the Classical Period with its prominent architecture, beautiful sculptures, other arts, and its philosophers, playwrights, and poets, leave such an impression on them that they may not be able to separate from these the explosive accomplishments of the Hellenistic Age that began a hundred years or so later, and continued for centuries. But they were two distinct periods.

Even before Alexander, Greek kings sponsored not only the arts, but also scholarship in the natural sciences, what little there was. This grew to become a royal fascination during Hellenistic times, starting late in the fourth century BC, as the great thinkers began to search for and to discover greater knowledge of everything in the physical world in which they lived and the limitless universe beyond. We have seen that Aristotle (384-322 BC), himself a pupil of Plato, was invited by Philip II of Macedon around 343 BC to tutor his gifted son Alexander. Though this lasted only three years, the influence was profound and their friendship remained. Alexander continued to support Aristotle when he

---

* This is no different than the dominance of English culture in North America or the Spanish in Latin America.

went on to establish his own school in Athens in 335 BC. It became known as the Peripatetic Lykeion, from the Greek words for "Promenade School," from the style of teaching and lecturing sometimes while strolling along.

It was indicative of the intellectual ferment of the times that the Peripatetic School of Aristotle was more than just a place of learning. It was also a research center involved in studies in a broad range of fields including mathematics, astronomy, botany, zoology, biology, physics and metaphysics, music, politics, and poetry. (All Greek words, by the way.) The mysteries of nature were examined and analyzed by the logic and thought processes of sharp Greek minds. A large library was also organized by Aristotle at his school, for by this time literary works and knowledge were preserved in writing on papyrus scrolls. If the work of Aristotle and his Lykeion (Lyceum, in Latin) ushered in the era, a number of his prominent students and many others continued the search for greater knowledge of the nature of the world and everything on it.

Among a number of other libraries organized by rulers in the Greek cities the most famous was the Library and Museum* founded in 307 BC by one of the successors of Alexander, Ptolemy I Soter, ruler of Egypt, and greatly enlarged during the reign of his son Ptolemy II Philadelphos. These two institutions became the greatest centers of study and learning in the Hellenistic Age, lasting until the fourth century AD. The Ptolemys invited noted scholars to come live and work at these facilities in ideal surroundings. At its peak, the library was said to contain up to 700,000 volumes (papyrus rolls).

It has been reported by many historians that in 48 BC the library was burned down accidently. This is disputed by modern historians, and the details are of parenthetical interest. At that time Julius Caesar was visiting Alexandria (see *Cleopatra*, p.118), and his taking up with Cleopatra led to a battle between Egyptian forces and Caesar's Roman legion. Greatly outnumbered, Caesar ordered his soldiers to set fire to the Egyptian ships crowding the narrow harbor in their attack. As the library was located at the eastern end of the city not far from the waterfront, the fire is supposed to have spread and burned down the library as well. More careful research has disclosed, rather, that some books of the library had been presented to Caesar by Cleopatra to be carted off to Rome. These documents are likely to have been stored on the quay awaiting shipment, and it has been concluded that these were burned in the conflagration and not the entire library itself.**

Alexandria was not the only prominent center of learning in the Hellenistic world. Second after Alexandria, and strongly supported by its rulers, the Attalids, were the library and museum at Pergamos (Pergamum, in Latin) in western Asia Minor, an independent Greek kingdom ruled by the heirs of Eumenes, another of the Alexander successors. So zealously did the Attalids try to rival the library of Alexandria, that the Ptolemys prohibited to them the export of papyrus, virtually an Egyptian monopoly. The Pergamese were forced to make use of their own resource: animal skins, cured and made into parchment (a word derived

---

* From the Greek word *museion*, derived from the mythical Muses, the nine Greek goddesses who presided over literature, music, the arts and sciences. Hence, a center of learning.
** See *The Vanished Library,* by Luciano Canfora, University of California Press, Los Angeles, 1989.

from its place of origin), which also led to the development of leafed books instead of scrolls, thus resulting in a great convenience to the reader.

Some years later Mark Antony allegedly tried to compensate the library at Alexandria for the books that were lost in the harbor fire during Caesar's time. As ruler of the eastern Roman Empire, which included Pergamos, Antony arranged to make a gift to his lover Cleopatra of a large part of the Pergamos library. But it has not been possible to confirm if these books ever arrived in Alexandria.

As in Alexandria, many prominent scholars were attracted to Pergamos, and the arts were strongly supported. Evidence of this may be seen in the remains of the opulent fully sculptured huge altar to Zeus now housed in the Pergamum Museum, in Berlin, Germany. Another example is the gracefulness and emotion depicted by the "Dying Gaul" figure, one of a group of twelve sculptured at the direction of Attalus I to celebrate his victory over the Gauls. (An impressive marble copy may be seen at the Capitolino Museum in Rome.)

So great was the knowledge brought forth by these and other centers of the Hellenistic period that Professor Michael Grant, eminent English historian of the Mediterranean world, writes that these studies "showed greater progress during the first Hellenistic century and a half than in any other comparable period until the birth of modern science."* Among numerous others, Euclid (*Eukleides* in Greek) developed his theories of geometry at Alexandria (c.300 BC). The Syrakusan Archimedes (287-212 BC) studied there as well, and developed his many outanding mathematical theories, including the theory of specific gravity; Archimedes also either invented or expanded on the use of primary mechanical devices, among the many, the lever, the screw, compound pulleys, and catapults. Aristarchos of Samos (320-250 BC), a mathematician and astronomer, startled his peers who held that the earth was the center of the universe, when he presented his heliocentric theory (that the sun, "*helios*", in Greek, was the center of the universe). Erastothenes of Kyrene in North Africa (c. 275-194 BC), who headed the Alexandria Library for 40 years, was a many-talented thinker. A mathematical geographer, he measured the circumference of the world with great accuracy. Hipparchos of Nikaia in Asia Minor (c. 161-127 BC), also worked at the Alexandria Library, compiling a comprehensive list of over 1000 stars by name and inventing the concept of latitude and longitude.

Also established at the Alexandria Museum was an important school of medicine. Herophilos of Chalkedon (331-250 BC), a city opposite Byzantium, studied in the school in the first half of the third century BC, perfecting by dissection his extensive work on anatomy. Continuing this work and greatly adding to it was a colleague or possibly a pupil of Herophilos, Erasistratos of the island of Kea just east of the Attika peninsula (305-240 BC), who is considered the father of physiology as well as psychiatry.

Support of the arts by the royal patrons also produced some much-admired works. Already mentioned above are the group of figures at Pergamos, which included the "Dying Gaul" and the superb altar to Zeus. Sculpture

---

* Grant, Michael, *From Alexander to Cleopatra*, (Scribner's, New York, 1982)

achieved a very high degree of perfection in the quest for realism. Two others out of the many outstanding examples of the period, both by unknown sculptors, are the Winged Victory found on the island of Samothrace and the Aphrodite (Venus, in Latin) found on the island of Melos. Both are at the Louvre Museum in Paris. Thus for many centuries beginning in the fourth century BC, royal patronage and support led to great progress in all the arts and sciences. As the Greek world then occupied a large part of Asia Minor and the east as well as Egypt, mixing with those other cultures helped contribute to the prodigious development of knowledge.

THE SCHOOLS OF PHILOSOPHY

A number of schools of philosophy became prominent during the Hellenistic period. It is easy to see that a search for understanding reality and a need for spiritual consolation as well as for peace of mind became necessary in a Greek world that had grown explosively — geographically, politically, culturally, and intellectually. The schools were based on the idea expressed by the Greek word *ataraxia*, or "imperturbability," or the quest for inner tranquility. Many of these philosophies evolved into religions, and the existence and influence of these schools lasted for very long times. The Stoics, for example, formally existed for five centuries. So prominent did these schools become that their names were eventually passed into our own language, even though the details of what they believed in and how they applied it evolved in different ways over their long existences. The principal schools are described.

The Cynics (*Kunikoi*, in Greek). This school was founded by Diogenes of Sinope (400-325 BC) on the southern Black Sea coast. He taught in Athens and Corinth. The Cynics sought peace of mind by living naturally, without conventions or inhibitions; they believed in self-discipline and liberty, owning nothing, and rejecting all learning. The name is derived from the ancient Greek word kyon meaning "dog," because people called them dogs on account of their unconventional and sometimes uncouth behavior. The Cynics adopted the dog as the symbol of their philosophy, saying that the dog guarded their beliefs and frightened off the nonbelievers. The Cynics moved from place to place teaching their philosophy, settling nowhere. Legends abound about Diogenes: in that well-known story, it was he who walked around with a lantern in daylight looking for an honest man. Alexander the Great is supposed to have visited him in Corinth where he found him living in a large earthenware pot. Asking him if there was a wish he could grant him, Diogenes was said to have asked Alexander if he could move over for he was blocking the sunshine. According to the modern dictionary meaning, a cynic is one who is violently critical of social customs and current philosophies, hence contemptuously distrustful of human nature.

The Stoics. This school was founded by Zeno of Citium (335-263 BC) (*Kítion*, in Greek) in Cyprus as a result of his disillusionment with the philosophy of the Cynics. The name came from the Stoa Poikile (Painted Portico) in Athens, where he taught. The essence of the Stoic philosophy was not to fight providence, to be temperate, and to accept nature with wisdom and with an absence of feeling in order to achieve peace of mind. Thus, according to the dictionary, a stoic is one who is passive and indifferent to passion or pleasure.

The Epicurians. This school was founded by Epicuros of Samos (340-271 BC) in the eastern Aegean. The Epicurians brought their philosophy to Athens about 307 BC. They believed that a sense of wellbeing was the means to peace of mind, and this peace was to be achieved by respecting law, being among like-minded friends, rejecting emotions and fears. They also believed gods did not exist, as they were indifferent to man's fortunes. The school's enemies accused them of loving pleasure and luxury. According to the dictionary, an epicurian is one who is a sensualist in food and drink, but a more contemporary meaning is that an epicurian is regarded as having refined and fastidious taste, hence is a connoisseur.

The Skeptics. This philosophy was founded by Pyrrho of Elis (c.365-c.275 BC) near Olympia, in the western Peloponnese. He travelled in the east with Alexander the Great and met Indian philosophers who inspired and influenced him. The Skeptics took their name from the Greek word *skepsis*, or "thought, consideration, reflection." Their goal was to achieve peace of mind by avoiding strong judgements or opinions, which could only lead one to being affected and disturbed; they also believed that *ataraxia* could be achieved by being indifferent and unconcerned. (They even believed in not having strong opinions about not having strong opinions.) The Skeptics believed that things just happen naturally and that they did not need knowledge or beliefs; for this reason they had no written dogmas. The dictionary defines a skeptic as someone who doubts or denies fundamental beliefs in religion, providence, freedom, or revelation, and considers that knowledge is uncertain.

THE ARGONAUTS AND THE GOLDEN FLEECE

While Appolonios was head of the Alexandria Library, about 250 BC he wrote his *Argonautika*, another well-known epic poem that has survived from those times. The material is based on legend embellished by the author's imagination, and it was deliberately written in the Homeric style, though there was a span of five centuries between the two authors. Apollonios even dated his tale close to that of the *Iliad* of Homer in describing how Peleus, one of the Argonauts, was bade farewell by his wife as he was departing, raising up their infant son Achilles for him to see. We may remember that Achilles was the great warrior hero of the *Iliad*, a young man in his prime. This would place the story of the Argonauts about twenty years before the start of the Trojan War as described in the *Iliad*; that is, during the 13th century BC.

Homer's geographical references were impressive enough for the eighth century BC when he had been writing. Those of Apollonios are remarkable and amply illustrate how much knowledge about geography the Greeks had developed by this time. Indeed, geography was one of the formal fields of learning of those that studied at the Alexandria Library. Even so, that part of Apollonios' description of the Argonauts' journey west through the Danube River into the Po and the Rhône is very imaginative, even though it is not physically possible to actually achieve this passage.

The *Argonautika*

The Kingdom of Iolkos, located in eastern Thessaly, had been usurped by Pelias, the younger brother of Aison, the rightful heir. Aison had a son, Jason, who was hidden away from harm when he was still a baby. When Aison died and Jason was grown to young manhood, it came time for him to claim from Pelias the throne of Iolkos, his birthright. The shrewd king declared he was willing to give up his throne if Jason would first bring him back from Kolchis, at the far end of the Euxine (Black) Sea, the Golden Fleece, a ram skin of pure gold — fully expecting that Jason would not return from the perils of the long voyage. Jason accepted the challenge. He collected fifty brave men for the journey from throughout Greece, including Herakles, Odysseus, Peleus, Orpheus (who had an enchanting singing voice), and other sons of gods and kings. A special rowing vessel was built for the journey, the Argo.

Though several of the men died braving the perils of the voyage, Jason was able to return with the Golden Fleece with the help of Medea, daughter of King Aietes of Kolchis, who also became his wife. Medea was a popular character in Greek mythology, written about repeatedly by the ancient tragedians. The best known play about her, *Medea*, was written by Euripides in 431 BC, well before Apollonios' day.

The adventures of the Argonauts are described in the following paragraphs, numbered to correspond with those on Map 4.1.

1. Departure from Pagasai, harbor of Iolkos.

2. The Argonauts arrive at the island of Limnos, where they stay for some time with the women of the island. These women were without men for they had killed them in revenge for bringing back women from a war in Thrace.

3. The Argonauts proceed to the Island of Samothrace where at Orpheus' suggestion, they are initiated into the local secret rites and mysteries.

4. In the land of the friendly king Kyzikos, they deliver him from his deadly foes, the six-armed giants. Soon after departing, however, adverse winds bring them back during the night, when they are mistaken for enemies. In the confusion a battle ensues and Kyzikos is killed; his wife Kleite kills herself in grief.

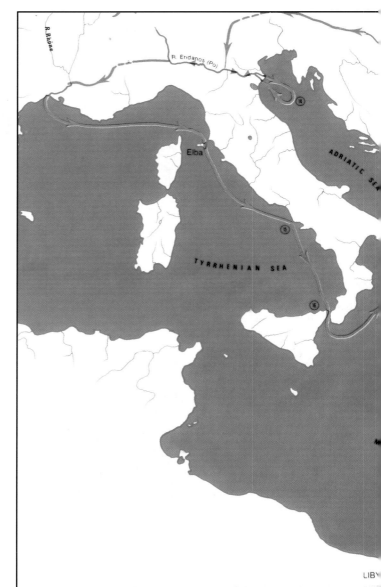

MAP 4.1
THE ARGONAUTS

Jason claimed the throne of Iolkos, his birthright, from a usurper who was willing to give up the kingdom if Jason would bring back the Golden Fleece from Kolchis at the eastern end of the Euxine (Black) Sea. Apollonios, author of this myth, describes the many adventures of Jason and his men.

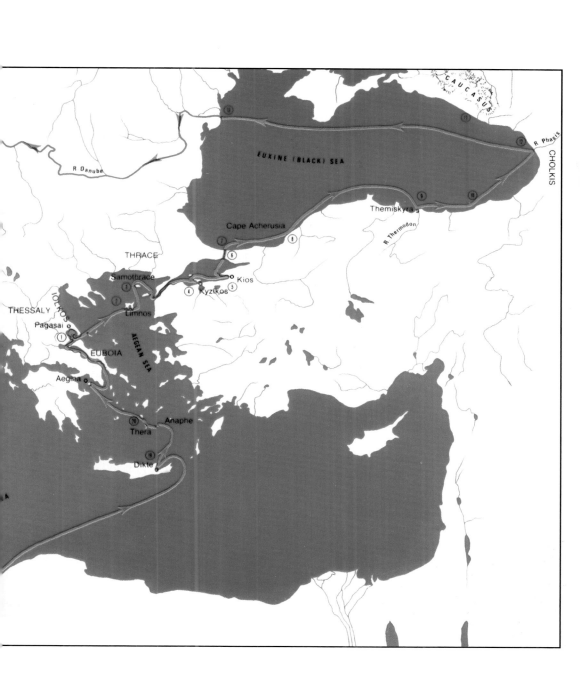

5. They put in at Kios, where the Argonaut Hylas, comrade of Herakles, goes in search of water. He finds a well, and the nymphs dwelling there draw him into the water to be their companion. Herakles goes to search for him, and the Argonauts are forced to depart, leaving both of them behind.

6. They stop on the Bosphorus, where King Amykos, a son of Poseidon, ruler of the savage Bebrykos people there, insists on a boxing match. The Argonaut Polydeukes, an Olympian boxer, boxes with him, killing him with a hard blow. As a result, the Argonauts are attacked by the Bebrykos and have to fight them, finally defeating them, following which they celebrate their victory.

7. Waves force them to land on the opposite shore of the Bosphorus (the European side), where the blind old King Phineus rules. They find that his food is being snatched away by evil and vile birds called the Harpies. The birds are chased away by Argonauts Zetes and Kalais, sons of Boreas, the North Wind. The grateful Phineus tells them how to get through the Symplegades (Clashing) Rocks just ahead. But first, he tests their chances for success by sending through a dove, which just makes it through having only its tail feathers clipped by the Rocks. They row the Argo through, losing only the mascot on its stern as the Rocks clash together behind them.

8. Tiphys, the able helmsman, dies from natural causes; and Idmon is killed by a wild boar.

9. The Argo makes a landing but casts off again to avoid encounters with the war-like Amazon women who dwell along the Thermidon River.

10. The Argonauts are attacked by birds, which drop plumes like arrows. They escape harm by making a roof over their heads with their interlocked shields.

11. Continuing their way east, they see the great Caucasus Mountains and catch sight of Prometheus, chained to a rock, where his liver is devoured every day, the liver growing back every night. This terrible punishment was ordered by Zeus because Prometheus had stolen the sacred fire from Mount Olympos and given it to man.

12. Turning into the Phasis River, they at last arrive at Kolchis where King Aietes receives the Argonauts badly and requires that they undergo some impossible and dangerous tests if they are to have the Fleece. But his daughter, Medea, herself a priestess, is made to fall in love with Jason by the goddess Aphrodite, and with her help they take the Fleece and escape, Medea accompanying them.

13. They speed west again, chased by Medea's brother, Prince Apsyrtos, with the Kolchian war fleet. At the mouth of the Danube River, they battle, and Jason kills Apsyrtos. The Argonauts flee up the Danube while the grieving Kolchians attend to the burial of their fallen leader.

14. They continue west to the river Eridanos (Po), and follow it south into the Adriatic Sea, but adverse winds drive them north again. They reenter the Eridanos and follow it west until they arrive at the Rhône River, which they follow into the Mediterranean. Turning east, they make their way toward the island of Elba and follow the coast along the Tyrrhenian Sea.

15. They escape the wrath of Circe, a witch and sister of King Aietes, an aunt to Medea. They sail past the place where the Sirens tempt them with their bewitching song, but Orpheus outsings them; they lose only one man who fell to the temptation and swam ashore.

16. Approaching new dangers, the Argo arrives at the Straits of Messina between the whirlpool of Skylla and the hideous six-headed monster of Charybdis, which they manage to avoid with the help of some nymphs.

17. Arriving at last at the island of Korkyra (Corfu), they are met by the Kolchian fleet, which has caught up with them and now demands the return of Medea. King Alkinous of Korkyra decides they cannot be separated if Jason and Medea should be man and wife. So they marry and their marriage bed is the Golden Fleece.

18. As they depart, a fierce wind drives the Argo south across the Mediterranean to the Syrtian Gulf, off the coast of Libya, and through shoals into the interior of the arid land thereabouts. The gods again come to their rescue, and the Argonauts carry their ship out of the desert on their shoulders. They lose Mopsos, their seer, bitten by a snake.

19. They proceed north to Crete and land at the foot of Mount Dikte. Medea's magic enables them to overcome Talos, the bronze giant.

20. They stop briefly at Anaphe, a Greek island. To help speed them on their way they had been given a clod of earth by Triton, a sea-god son of Poseidon, wich they now throw into the sea, creating the island of Thera.

With a last stop at the island of Aegina, they continue north with no further troubles and arrive at their starting point, the harbor of Pagasai.

As may be seen, Apollonios borrowed heavily from Homer. But this style of heroic story was always popular with the Greeks, blending as it did the adventures of men and their relations with their many gods and halfgods, monsters, and other mythological figures. Neverthless, some of Apollonios' colleagues at the Library in Alexandria, objected to the archaic style of his work. So acrimonious was the literary and intellectual atmosphere in Alexandria over that *Argonautika* that Apollonios finally left his native city to live on the island of Rhodes, where his book had been well received. Given the freedom ("the keys," as we say today) of the city for his work, he was also honored by becoming known as Apollonios of Rhodes.

THE SEVEN WONDERS OF THE ANCIENT WORLD

A number of ancient writers referred to several architectural works of antiquity as being "wonders" of concept and beauty and daring construction because of their large size. The identification of seven of these "wonders" was based on the belief from ancient times by many civilizations that this number seven was a magical or lucky number. Also, it was said that the "seven wonders" named in Hellenistic times was intended to honor the world of Alexander the Great in that all of them were located in Greece and in the areas that he had conquered. However, none of them were built at his direction, some had already perished before his lifetime, and some of them were built after his death. A well circulated small volume on the subject was written in 146 BC by Philon, a Greek mathematician and architect-engineer from Byzantion, in which he described "The Seven Wonders of the World." During Hellenistic times, a number of other writers also made up their lists of the "seven," and compilers agreed on the original list that is described below. It is perhaps not a "wonder" that five of these were Greek, but then, they were builders of phenominal imagination, experience and capability in those times, even if other daring builders preceded and followed them. The practice of listing "seven wonders" continued to later times, with other impressive structures.

The Statue of Zeus. This seated figure of Zeus stood nearly 45 feet high (13 meters) and was located in the main temple at Olympia, in the western Peloponnese, where the ancient ritualistic athletic games were held. Sculpted by Pheidias around 432 BC, its flesh areas were made of ivory and all other surfaces were covered with heavy gold plate. The statue remained intact until AD 426. As mentioned earlier, it was carted off to Constantinople by the Romans, the Olympic Games having already been banned as being pagan by the Roman Christian Emperor Theodosius I in AD 393. In AD 463, the statue was lost in a conflagration that also destroyed a large part of Constantinople.

The Temple of Artemis. This enormous shrine to the goddess of the hunt was built at Ephesos on the west coast of Asia Minor, in 290 BC. Four previous temples to the goddesss built in the same spot had been destroyed by invaders. Chersiphron of Knossos in Crete was the architect-builder. Elaborately sculpted, this was the largest temple ever built by the Greeks. Its ten foot high stepped marble base measured about 240 by 420 feet (74 x 129 meters), with 127 columns each 60 feet tall (18 meters) carrying its triangular marble roof. The overall height of this prodigious temple is estimated at 110 feet (34 meters). The structure lasted nearly six centuries, until it was destroyed by the Goths during an invasion in AD 262.

The Tomb of Mausolos. Located at Halikarnassos, in southwestern Asia Minor (modern Budrum), this elaborate marble temple was ordered to be built by Queen Artemis in 353 BC to honor her dead husband, King Mausolos. It was127 by 108 feet (40 x 35 meters) and 140 feet (43 meters) high. A tall base supported 36 columns that carried a stepped pyramidal roof upon which rested a marble carriage drawn by four marble horses. The carriage carried two standing ten-foot-tall figures, depicting the King and Queen. The structure suffered from invasions and earthquakes over a period of centuries. Around AD 1500 or so, the temple began to be plundered as a source of building material. The Knights of St. John finished the job in 1522, using the sculpted parts to decorate their castles and the rest in the fortifications. Nothing remains now on the spot, but the word "mausoleum" was coined from this ancient monument.

The Kolossos of Rhodes. Providing yet another word coined into Latin and other languages, this colossal (it is obvious from where this word is derived) statue of Apollo was about 120 feet high (37 meters) and stood on a thirty-foot-high marble pedestal built at the end of a short jetty in the main harbor of the island of Rhodes; however, the statue did not straddle the harbor as many believe. It was made of bronze sheets riveted together and supported inside by iron bars attached to stone columns. The Kolossos was sculptered by Charos of Lindos (a city in Rhodes), and was built around 290 BC to commemorate the victory of the Rhodians supporting Ptolemy I of Egypt against Demetrios, son of Antigonos (a rival of Ptolemy, both of whom were Alexander's successors). The statue had a spiked headress depicting the sun's rays, its right hand was raised shading his eyes gazing east, and its left arm carried a cloak that reached to the ground. The Kolossos did not remain standing for long. In 227 BC, it was toppled by an earthquake, which broke it off at the thighs. It remained in this condition nearly nine centuries, until AD 656, when the Saracens, Arab conquerors of Rhodes, sold the statue for scrap. It was said 1000 camels were needed to carry off the remains to Syria.

The Alexandria Lighthouse. On an island called Pharos off the port of Alexandria, a first lighthouse in the world was completed in 280 BC. It was incredible 400 feet high (125 meters), with a large fire burning at the top, its smoke guiding shipping to the port even before the lighthouse was in sight. At night the fire served the same purpose, its light intensified by some sort of a large reflector. It was largely intact despite suffering several earthquakes until AD 1165, having lasted thirteen centuries. But by the fifteenth century, little of it remained. So many legends were circulated about its destruction that it is not possible to separate fact from fiction. It was completely destroyed in modern times when some of its building material was used to construct a large building called the Qait Bey Fort which now occupies the site. But the name of the island called Pharos was adopted into many languages to mean "lighthouse."

The two remaining "wonders" were: the Great Pyramid at Giza, near Cairo in Egypt, completed around 2700 BC during the reign of Pharoah Cheops. It is the only "wonder" still standing. The other was the "Hanging Gardens" of Babylon, built around 600 BC by King Nebuchadnezzer to please his Queen Semiramis, who hankered for the coolness of mountains and greenery of her own birthplace in this hot, flat desert area. The gardens were not hanging at all, but were built on a huge square palace made of brick and carried on massive brick arched supports; the extensive elevated gardens in the interior were watered by a unique mechanical system. Some traces of the original brick arches were found by archeologists in the beginning of this century in the center of the old city of Babylon.

Five

The
Roman
Period

ROMAN RULE OF THE GREEK WORLD
(146 BC- AD 324)

I T TOOK ROME MANY CENTURIES TO EXPAND FROM A SMALL rural community to a great power that controlled the whole of Italy either by domination or alliance. But Rome was not alone in the Mediterranean world. She shared this role with Phoenician Carthage in North Africa (at present-day Tunis) which controlled the North African coast west of Cyrenaica (in Greek, *Kyrenaika*) to Gibraltar, the southern Spanish coast, and the large islands in the central Mediterranean. The other strong power in the area was the Greek Macedonian kingdom ruling over most of the Greek peninsula and the islands surrounding it. Farther east, other powerful Greek kingdoms continued to be ruled by the descendants of the Macedonian successors of Alexander the Great: the Seleucids controlled Asia Minor and Syria; and the Ptolemys ruled over Egypt. (See Map 5.0.)

Rome and Carthage had been friendly with each other, but as Roman strength grew and enemies were disposed of, these two powerful states began to compete. Between them lay Sicily. The western tip of this large and strategic island had been settled by Carthage, and the rest of the island contained a number of independent city-states settled by Greek colonists since the middle of the eighth century BC, Syrakuse being the largest city at this time. In 284 BC, a group of mercenaries from the Italian mainland called Mamertines (sons of Mars) took possession of Messana at the northeast corner of Sicily (a town settled by Greeks from Kyme [Cumae] around 700 BC and called Zankle originally, renamed Messana two centuries later, and known as Messina today). As the Mamertines began to expand their hold on the area, the king of Syrakuse, Hieron II, moved against them. The Mamertines called on both Carthage and Rome to come to their aid. The location of Messana being most strategic, both responded and found themselves at war. The Syrakusans sided with the Carthaginians, and the Romans defeated them both in this first conflict. The importance of Roman control of Sicily thus became emphasized to the Roman senate, but both the Greeks and the Carthaginians were determined to prevent this possibility.

The Punic Wars

However, by 264 BC, the first of three Punic (Carthaginian) Wars broke out over the possession of Sicily. The Sicilian Greeks first opposed Rome fearing her growing imperialism but later concluded a treaty with her, hoping to fend off subjugation. From then on, the war was between Rome and Carthage. Though it took more than twenty years, Rome finally drove out the Carthaginians from western Sicily. Shortly later, Rome also occupied the Carthaginian islands of Corsica (241 BC) and Sardinia (238 BC). Her victories against Carthage caused Rome to begin her expansionist movement beyond the Italian mainland. But Carthage was far from defeated.

A number of incidents during the next twenty years culminated in another major conflict between these two powers. Having lost naval control of the central Mediterranean, Carthage began settling across the Straits of Gibraltar into the Spanish peninsula in 237 BC. She gradually spread this hold east to the Ebro River less than 60 miles (100 kilometers) from the foothills of the Pyrenees. This land base secured by an able father, Hamilcar Barca ("Lightning"), gave his brilliant son Hannibal, who assumed military leadership of the Carthaginian forces, the means to march his way overland and over the Alps —an incredible feat for the times— to attack Italy itself. This approach had become necessary since Rome now controlled the seas, and Hannibal's daring tactics were wholly unexpected. But this second Punic War (218-202 BC), during which time Hannibal went from one brilliant success to another over all of Italy, did not defeat Rome. Delaying tactics by her military leaders gradually wore down Hannibal's forces; and Rome's limitless manpower, despite her losses, finally weighed against the Carthaginians, who were systematically prevented from obtaining adequate reserves. Finally, the daring and competent Roman military commander Scipio attacked and defeated the Carthaginians at their bases in Spain, and was victorious over Hannibal himself at the Carthaginian city of Zama in North Africa. Scipio had won the war.* Although an anxious peace followed that lasted nearly half a century, the third Punic War of 153-146 BC ended with the Romans storming the capital city of Carthage, resulting in a final victory for them.

Relations with the Greeks

During the earlier part of these years relations between the Macedonian Greeks (in northern Greece) and Romans had been relatively cordial. In a number of exchanges, the Greeks welcomed the friendship of the Romans who were busy subduing the Macedonians' traditional enemies in the Mediterranean, the Carthaginians. But when the Romans occupied the

---

* Scipio was greatly honored for his victories by the Roman Senate and given the title of "Africanus." Hannibal lived through his defeat and ruled Carthage under the Romans, until his enemies drove him out in 195 BC. He took refuge first with the Seleucid King Attalos III in Asia Minor and later with the Bithnian king nearby. When the Romans insisted he be surrendered to them, he took poison and died in 182 BC.

Rome

Carthage

Greek

MAP 5.0 CONQUESTS OF ROME

Rome had consolidated its hold on most of Italy by 264 BC. Battles won against the Carthaginians soon gave them control of the western Mediterranean, and they also dominated many prominent independent Greek cities. A number of events a few decades later led them to occupy the Greek Peninsula and Asia Minor.

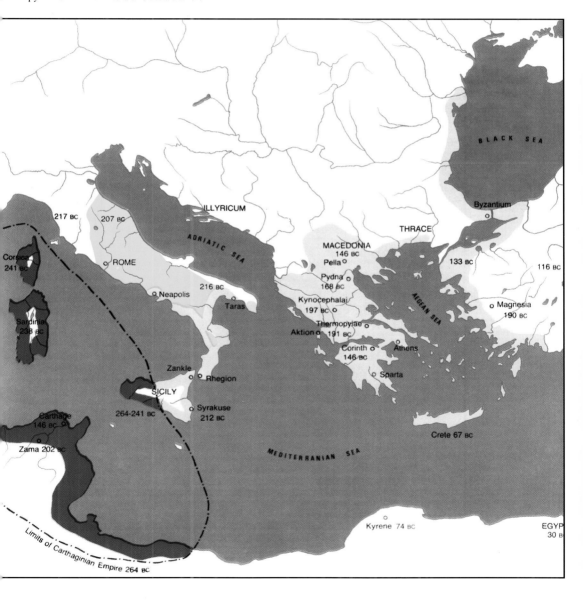

BLACK SEA

ILLYRICUM

217 BC   207 BC

Byzantium

THRACE

ADRIATIC SEA

MACEDONIA
146 BC
Pella

133 BC   116 BC

Corsica
241 BC

ROME

216 BC

Pydna
168 BC

Neapolis

Kynocephalai
197 BC

Taras

Magnesia
190 BC

AEGEAN SEA

Sardinia
238 BC

Thermopylae
Aktion 191 BC

Corinth
146 BC

Athens

Zankle

Rhegion

Sparta

SICILY

Carthage
146 BC

264-241 BC

Syrakuse
212 BC

Zama 202 BC

Crete 67 BC

MEDITERRANEAN SEA

Kyrene 74 BC

EGYPT
30 B

Limits of Carthaginian Empire 264 BC

Illyrian coast to stop pirate raids in the Adriatic Sea, Philip V, the capable king of Macedonia, felt threatened. By 215 BC, he concluded an alliance with Hannibal, who was then at the height of his victories against Rome. A few years later, in 211 BC, the Aitolian League, a confederacy of city-states in western Greece, called on Rome to help them against Macedonian aggression. As Hannibal's fortunes began to turn to losses, Philip was led into making another alliance against Rome, this time with the Antiochos III, who ruled the vast Seleucid empire in the east. It did not escape the attention of Rome either that in 204 BC Philip also had entered into a pact with Antiochos, prompted by the death of Ptolemy IV that same year, which had left Ptolemy's five-year-old son heir to the Egyptian throne. Philip and Antiochos agreed that they would invade Egypt together and divide it between them. These pacts now threatened the small independent Greek kingdoms in Asia Minor, and they called on Rome for support against the Macedonian-Seleucid alliance. By 202 BC Rome, which had little interest then in either Greece or the Asian and Egyptian kingdoms, was being inexorably drawn to the East.

Philip was also seen as a threat by the smaller Greek states and leagues on the Greek peninsula. Now that they found a power that might be able to help them against him, by 200 BC they too were calling on Rome for help. In 197 BC, at Kynoskephalai, in central Greece, two Roman legions finally met in battle the Macedonian phalanx. But the terrain did not favor the phalanx manoeuvers of the Macedonians. The ensuing battle resulted in a large-scale slaughter of Greek troops by the Roman army. Philip had no choice now but to become Rome's restless ally.

Antiochos did not hesitate at what he saw as an opportunity to gain territory, and in 197 BC, he moved his men west, invading Asia Minor and Thrace. He then marched them down into the Greek mainland. In 191 BC, the Romans, aided by Philip, finally met the Seleucid army at Thermopylai and soundly defeated them. A year later, the Romans, again with the help of Greek allies, moved aggressively into Asia Minor, and the two armies met in a major battle at Magnesia, in Ionia. The Seleucid army was decimated. The Seleucid Empire, which had eventually taken over an important part of what had been Alexander's, began to come to an end, though it would take a number of decades for the Romans to take it over completely.

It would be interesting to speculate on what would have been the result of more friendly relationships between Rome and the Greeks. The opposite eventually brought Roman domination of the Greeks for over thirteen centuries.

Meanwhile, Macedonia continued its aggressive ways under Perseus, son of Philip V who had died in 179 BC. This led to war and over the period 171 to168 BC, the Romans defeated the Macedonians in a series of battles. To end the Macedonian problem they abolished the monarchy and divided the area into four autonomous republics for better control. As this eventually proved inadequate to quell Macedonian rebellion, in 148 BC the Romans finally moved in and annexed it outright.

Resistance grew throughout the remaining city-states of the Greek peninsula, and many battles were fought against the Romans. Corinth, as leader of the

Achaian League of Greek cities, was enjoying political and commercial success and became strongly anti-Roman. The Romans made a brutal example of Corinth: when they defeated the Corinthians in battle, the men were put to death, the rest of the population sold in slavery, and the town was completely sacked and razed. The Greek cities were thus harshly warned, and soon the rest of Greece came under Roman rule except for Athens and Sparta, already Roman allies that were given relative freedom. Crete remained a free island of separate provinces until annexed in turn by Rome, in 67 BC, because of pirate activities on ships trading directly between Italy and the East. However, the Romans' style of government was to allow Greek self-rule of many of their cities under a Roman consul governing from Macedonia. With the end of the wars, the Greek spirit blossomed again, at least in terms of material benefits.

TROUBLES IN ASIA MINOR AFFECT THE GREEKS

When Attalos III, a Greek descendant of the Alexander successor Eumenes, died in 133 BC, he bequeathed to Rome his kingdom of Pergamos (in Latin, Pergamum), in western Asia Minor. His subjects made a number of attempts over the years to revolt, but Rome put them down each time and made Pergamos into a province that the Romans called Asia. Over the years, Rome settled a large Italian population in the area.

The Greek peninsula was now to be affected by another eastern event. Revolts against the Romans within Italy in 89 to 88 BC, gave the ambitious and vigorous King Mithridates VI Eupator of Pontos, an independent kingdom along the southern Black Sea coast, the inspiration to move into Asia Minor and against Roman rule in the area. Mithradates was of Persian birth but educated in the Greek tradition. Either way, he saw the Romans as invaders in the East, and his action was prompted by his hatred of the Romans who had aided his enemies. On his instigation a general massacre of Italians took place (it is said that as many as 80,000 died) in many parts of Roman Asia Minor. It was not difficult to incite a local population who had been exploited by Roman governors, tax-collectors, other officials and other Italians. He then swept west through the Aegean, and Athens as well as other Greek cities revolted from the Romans and joined him. Mithridates freed most of southern Greece, and another of his armies proceeded west across Thrace and into Macedonia. In 87 to 86 BC, the Roman general Sulla arrived in Greece with a large army to stop this brash eastern king. In revenge for disloyalty he first attacked and burned Athens and Piraeus. He then proceeded north to the Boiotian city of Chaironeia, where his army met and defeated Mithridates' forces. Soon afterwards another battle with another Mithridatic army at Orchomenos nearby resulted in a final victory for Sulla. An avenging Roman army now ravaged the Greek cities from Boiotia south, and Sulla also required them to pay a huge sum in reparations, that he would use to finance his ongoing campaigns. He also denuded the Greek shrines at Olympia, Delphi, and

Epidauros of their sculptures and many other valuables. In the end, the Greeks paid dearly for their revolt.

THE GREEK PENINSULA AND THE ROMANS

Thehe next fifty years were uniformly bad throughout the Greek peninsula. The area was now merely a small subjugated corner of the vast Roman Empire, without specific borders. Roman trade with the east was now direct, and the former trading advantage of Greece's geographical location was lost, with the obvious impact on its economy. Advantage was taken by Roman officials on the local administrations and populace, and the weakened economy of the Greeks declined further. Little protection was provided by the Romans against frequent pirate raids on the extensive Greek coastline and islands, and the Greeks did not have the means to defend themselves.

Rivalries between strong Roman leaders were to lead to civil wars in Italy that would eventually involve the Greek peninsula, as a victim rather than as a participant. The struggle for supremacy between Caesar and Pompey in the 50's BC brought their respective armies into Greece for the decisive battle, pillaging the countryside during their winter lay-up in Epiros and Macedonia and on their march across Greece. On August 9, 49 BC, on a plain west of Pharsalos in Thessaly, north of Thermopylai, Pompey's larger army was outmaneuvred, a large number were killed, and Caesar was victorious. Pompey fled to Egypt to whose ruler Ptolemy XII Auletes he had some years earlier been helpful politically and financially; he now planned to seek help to organize another army in the struggle against Caesar. But Auletes had died and his heirs, his children, Cleopatra VII and Ptolemy XIII, were themselves engaged in a civil war, Cleopatra having temporarily fled the country. Pompey's plans to involve Egypt would compromise her interests, and in any event young Ptolemy's royal counsellors (he was only 13 years old at the time) did not believe Pompey was likely to succeed. On September 28th, the situation was handled permanently, in the style of the times. Pompey arrived on his ship to meet with Ptolemy XIII, who was camped near Mount Kassios east of the Nile. A Roman officer from a dissident group who accompanied the small party in the boat sent out to meet Pompey, stabbed him to death before they reached the shore. (See *Cleopatra* p.118)

Six months later, on March 15, 44 BC, Caesar was himself assassinated by his political enemies on entering the Roman senate. Two years later, the armies of Ceasar's adopted son Octavian and his close companion and supporter Mark Antony arrived at Philippi on the border between eastern Macedonia and Thrace. They had at last caught up with Brutus and Cassius, the ringleaders of the plot that had resulted in the death of Caesar in Rome. Antony's forces defeated those of Cassius, who committed suicide. Octavian's army fought against that of Brutus, and Octavian was victorious, Brutus also taking his own life in defeat. The Roman Empire was now divided between Octavian, who assumed control of Rome and the west, and Antony assumed the rule of the eastern provinces. Antony made Athens his capital and he bled the already impoverished country to finance his administration and campaigns.

But again there was a cultural rennaissance: Greek civilization found a home among the awestruck Romans. Many aristocratic families sent their sons to study in Greece; among them were Horace, Cicero and Atticus (Attikos). Greek knowledge was held in such high esteem that Greek universities were endowed by the Imperial Treasury. Many of the early emperors had a special fondness for things Greek, among others, Nero, who was a devoted philhellene and who lavished many privileges on the Greek cities. He also began a project to cut a canal through the Isthmus of Corinth, but before much progress had been made, the costly and difficult project was abandoned by the Romans after Nero's early suicide.* Roman Emperor Hadrian built many impressive public projects the remains of which may still be seen in central Athens. Many beautiful public works were also constructed at the direction and personal cost of the philanthropist Herodes Attikos, of a Greek family that rose to prominence and wealth in high positions in the Roman government. Until the beginning of the third century AD, the Greeks generally enjoyed a privileged status under Roman rule.

THE BARBARIAN INVASIONS
(Third to Sixth centuries AD)

When discussing the barbarian invasions of Europe a number of clarifications are needed. First, who were the barbarians and from where did they come? Second, to where did they go? What was their impact, principally in the Balkan areas and western Europe? Finally, how did they affect Greece?

The origin of the word "barbarians," as already mentioned, is in the Greek word *várvari*, so-called by the Greeks because these people were uneducated and uncultured, and moreover, they did not speak Greek, but in unintelligible tongues "var, var, var...." The barbarians were a fierce and hardy nomadic people emanating from regions in central Asia (not Roman Asia, but the modern Asia of the Middle and Far East). Those that reached and affected central and western Europe were the Avars, Huns, Goths, Vandals, and a number of others. The men were fearless horse warriors, experts at hit-and-run tactics with the bow and spears. War was their way of life (and death), and their women and children and other supporters followed behind them in large numbers. It is estimated that an average of as many as four followed a single horseman.

On their restless treks, they proceeded across the vast reaches of the Asian continent, for the most part north of the Aral, Caspian, and Black Seas, where there was little population. Successive waves of barbarians pushed the previous

---

* The Corinth canal, as a project, was not to be resumed again until eighteen centuries later.

waves ever westwards, for neither were they friendly to each other. Areas of good pasture and water attracted them to settle for longer periods, such as in the central Balkans, and this led to exploring farther south towards the Mediterranean. Finding communities or cities and armed resistance, they were inclined to battle and loot.

In the second half of the third century AD, the Goths, a warlike Germanic tribe* migrating from the northwestern Black Sea coast, raided northern Asia Minor and the Aegean coast. They arrived on the Greek peninsula from Thrace, denuding the countryside and raiding and burning Athens, Corinth, Argos, and as far south as Sparta. The Greeks had no military forces, and the Roman armies were mostly occupied protecting the far-flung reaches or more important parts of the empire, or sometimes they were pitted against each other supporting internal rival factions. But a number of battles were fought between the Romans and the barbarian hordes on or near Greek soil. Some of these Roman victories provided long periods of respite from the invaders for the Greeks. The Romans finally stopped the Goths in AD 269, slaughtering large numbers in battles in the area of present-day Bulgaria as they attempted to retreat to their own region in the central Balkans.

But they returned again, migrating and gathering in large numbers in an area both north and south of the Danube where frequent conflicts were put down by Roman armies under Theodosius I (379-395) and his generals. In order to keep watch on the Goths, he made Thessaloniki the capital of Roman Illyricum, which included the Greek peninsula. These events did not prevent this able but harsh emperor being as cruel to the Thessalonikans as the barbarians had been before. When the populace of that city rioted against the Roman state in 390 because of the high taxes and other abuses, they were invited to the city's hippodrome, where on Theodosius' orders 7,000 citizens were slaughtered.

Shortly after the death of Roman Emperor Theodosius in 395, the Visigoths (western Goths) under a dynamic leader, Alaric, penetrated the Greek peninsula once more, beginning their raids in Thrace and moving south to Athens and Sparta and up the western side of Greece to Epiros. Large numbers of the Greeks were taken prisoner and sold into slavery. Later, in 410, Alaric's armies attacked and sacked Rome itself. Out of central Asia came the Huns under Attila, also raiding from Thrace to Thermopylai in 442 to 450, before heading west into Italy. The Vandals (Scandinavian-Germanic tribes), had earlier fought their way west into Gaul (France) and Spain and across the Straits to North Africa. They had established themselves in the old Phoenician capital of Carthage by 439. From this vantage point they raided the Mediterranean at will, bringing back plunder from Corsica and Sardinia, Italy, Sicily, western Greece, and the islands nearby. In 455, the Vandals also sacked Rome. This calamity was followed by a series of successive power struggles among political factions of Roman leaders. These were brought to an end with yet another barbarian invasion of Italy, this time by the Ostrogoths (eastern Goths) under Theodoric ("the Great"). By 493, his success resulted

---

* These various people in modern times are generally referred to as being "Germanic," but their orgins were in the east and they migrated westward and south over a long period. They finally settled in the Scandinavian areas and north-central Europe, beginning in the seventh century BC.

in his being proclaimed king of this area, and with his reign the Western Roman Empire came to an end.

Most important to our history is that the collapse of the western empire at the hands of the barbarians was to lead to the development of the brilliant Graeco-Roman civilization centered on Constantinople (Byzantium). Not less important but beyond the scope of this volume, the arrival of these barbarians in the west would also eventually lead to the establishment of their own barbarian kingdoms in northern and western Europe that would themselves slowly evolve into the northern European nations we know today.

FROM ROME TO BYZANTIUM

We must go back again a little in time to describe another important event that also contributed to the creation of the Graeco-Roman world. When Diocletian became the emperor in Rome in AD 284, it became obvious to him that the public administration of the empire would have to be shared to be able to effectively rule the vast domain. He appointed a second emperor to serve with him (that is, there were now to be two Augusti), one for each half of the empire, as well as two Caesars (vice-emperors). The emperors would concern themselves with the administration of their respective halves of the empire, with the two caesars each taking responsibility for military affairs under them. It was also implicit that the caesars would eventually replace the Augusti, and appoint two new Caesars to take their place. But illness forced Diocletian to retire in 305, and the several ambitious strong personalities that emerged, with their respective armies, led to a period of serious political confusion and strife. Constantine (that is, Constantinus, a high-born military leader) emerged as victor, ending the so-called "Tetrarchy" and he became the sole ruler starting AD 306. Most likely in recognition of the political reality of the rising prominence of the eastern empire, he decided to build a new city in the east on the site of the ancient Greek city of Byzantium, to be named New Rome, but the people called it Constantinople (that is, *Constantinoupolis* in Greek, or the *polis*, or city of Constantine). Built between AD 324 and 330, it became the capital of the Eastern Roman Empire. The western empire having now been lost to the invasions of the Germanic tribes, as mentioned above, by 493 only the eastern empire remained, with its strong Hellenic tradition.

Although it is the purpose of this volume to trace the history of Greece rather than to relate the history of the Roman Empire, except as it affects the Greek, a brief reference must be added concerning the events following the loss of the western empire. A century later, in AD 527, the ambitious Justinian I became Roman emperor in Constantinople. Aided by his wife, the dynamic and controversial empress Theodora, and his most able general Belisarius, he began a series of conquests to recover the lost western empire. Italy was recovered from the Vandals and the Ostrogoths between 536 to 563, and southern Spain in 554, as well as North Africa and the large islands in the western Mediterranean. His western conquests reached their greatest extent by about 563, but never equalled those of the empire at its height. Over the next several decades, the territories of the western empire that had been won back were nibbled away again by various conquerors. The Persians had taken Egypt, Spain was again lost to the Visigoths, and Italy was once more under havy attack from Germanic tribes from the north. The Roman Empire was again to consist substantially of the Greek peninsula and Asia Minor: that is, the Greek or Greek-influenced territories.

With the creation of Constantinople and the rise of Christianity in the East began a decline in the importance of Athens. As Christianity grew in strength and polytheism was surpressed and finally officially forbidden by the Roman state, the philosophical schools that heretofore had flourished in Athens, also declined, as they were considered pagan teaching. The process began under Emperor Theodosius I (379-383) who also put an end to the Oracles and the Olympic and other athletic games at various sites throughout the Greek peninsula, that were all considered pagan rites. The schools were finally closed altogether by Justinian in 529.

The eastern empire had in the meantime adopted the culture of the Greeks, which had been created through the Hellenization process already described in Chapter Four. During the reign of Heraklios (AD 610-641), the eastern empire became increasingly Greek in character, even to the point of adopting Greek as its official language. Not only had the language been learned by the aristocratic and educated classes of every ethnic background, but it had also become the *lingua franca* of the area among this multiracial population.

At the end of the sixth century, incursions from the north over a very long period largely depopulated the interior of the Greek peninsula. People moved to fortified coastal towns, which prospered by the trade the area's strategic geographical location made possible, and they farmed the plains near their port towns. A steady and for the most part peaceful penetration of nomadic Slavic peoples from the central Balkans took place in the Greek peninsula down to the southern coast of the Peloponnese. They were a hardy agricultural people busy trying to wring a living from the rough terrain and thin soil. They learned the Greek language and were gradually assimilated by mixing with the Greeks and other local populations.

CLEOPATRA: THE LAST GREEK QUEEN OF THE HELLENISTIC AGE

Cleopatra VII was the last Greek ruler of Egypt. She has always been a fascinating figure in history, but her image has been greatly distorted in modern times by the several films and plays purporting to portray her. In Roman times she received a "bad press" because she was certainly controversial from a Roman point of view. This brief summary of the life and times of this historically interesting figure will explain the reasons for these reactions, by describing her true purposes and character. With her passing, Greek rule of Egypt came to an end after nearly three centuries.

Alexander liberated Egypt from Persian occupation in 332 BC. Upon his death in 323 BC, the vast territory his forces conquered was divided among his successors on behalf of their mother country, Macedonia, and his general Ptolemy was made governor of Egypt. But this division of the empire was followed by murderous competition for power and territory among his successors, for years. By 306 to 305 BC, those who were left alive declared the areas they occupied to be their personal kingdoms, Ptolemy being one of these. (See Chapter Four - *Alexander's Successors* p.87)

From Ptolemy I Soter to Cleopatra VII were eighteen reigns of the Ptolemaic Dynasty. The rulers married within the royal family for the most part, or sometimes with other Greek Macedonians. They also adopted the ancient Egyptian tradition of the king and queen being brother-sister corulers as well as husbands-wives, especially as queens were not permitted to rule without coruling with a male member of the royal house. But the language and traditions of their Greek origin were continuously maintained in the royal court for almost three centuries.

Cleopatra lived up to her Macedonian heritage, being dynamic, intelligent, and strong-minded. It is said that she spoke all the many languages of her domains and other countries nearby. In 51 BC, her father, Ptolemy XII Auletes, appointed her co-ruler with him when she was eighteen years old. When he died in the same year, she became queen ruling jointly with her ten-year-old brother, Ptolemy XIII. Two years later internal strife in the royal court found her powerless, and she was compelled to flee from the country over the eastern border. She was subsequently deposed by her brother upon the instigation of his counsellors who feared her strong character.

We have already seen that in 48 BC, Pompey's army lost a major battle against that of Julius Caesar in a civil war between these two strong leaders and contenders for power over Rome, and Pompey fled to Egypt to seek help to recoup his losses. Pursuing his enemy, four days later Caesar arrived to find Pompey had been murdered on orders of Ptolemy, whose advisors saw the superiority of Caesar, and the weakness of Ptolemy. Caesar had to accept this *fait accompli* and arranged a funeral for his dead enemy. This accomplished, he now began to ponder how he could take advantage of the riches of Egypt and how to use this country to suit his own political strategy.

Cleopatra was to solve this problem for this strong Roman who could become her own ally. She managed to get herself smuggled back into her own country and to appear before Caesar and appeal to him to help her regain the throne. He quickly became impressed with her intelligence, political acumen, and considerable charms, and he decided to support her. This forced Caesar into a short but decisive war against the Ptolemy's forces which he won, even though his own army was greatly outnumbered. Ptolemy XIII was drowned in the Nile when he fell from an overcrowded boat fleeing the battle.

Caesar and Cleopatra became lovers: he was 52 and she 21, and she would bear him a son a year later whom she named Ptolemy Caesar, and the Egyptians called "Caesarion" (Little Caesar). After a stay in Egypt of some months, Caesar finally went back to his duties in Rome, now as virtual dictator.

He was compelled to fight a number of battles against various external and internal dangers, and he was victorious in all of them. Ceasar returned to Rome in triumph, and Cleopatra shortly later joined him there together with their son, in celebration of his triumphs. She was accompanied also by her thirteen-year-old younger brother-husband, Ptolemy XIV. She and her retinue resided at a guest palace of his while in Rome, where she maintained a lavish and flamboyant court . Her relationship with Caesar was commonly known and gossiped about, which must have been an embarrassment to Calpurnia, Caesar's legal wife, of a noble Roman family. The controversy of Caesar's political dictatorship was not helped by his relationship with this excessively visible foreign queen, and this also strengthened the determination of his enemies.

This curious idyll suddenly came to an end on March 15, 44 BC, when Caesar was assassinated by his political opponents. A short while later, Cleopatra and her entourage returned to Egypt. Ptolemy XIV barely made it there. It was alleged he was killed by poison either at the hand or on the orders of Cleopatra, to whom it must have been obvious what the benefits could be of the heir to the throne being her infant son, Ptolemy Caesar. She promptly named him her co-ruler.

On Caesar's death the rule of the Roman empire was divided between his youthful adopted son Octavian, who became the ruler in Rome and the West, and his close friend Mark Antony, a strong military leader, who became ruler in the East, making his headquarters in Athens.

Needing funds to make war against the Parthians in the east, and Egypt then being the wealthiest country in the world, in the summer of 41 BC, Antony summoned Cleopatra to come to him at Tarsus (Tarsos) in Cilicia, Asia Minor. Having been close to Ceasar, Antony had known Cleopatra when she was in Rome. But now Antony was the ruler of the eastern Roman empire. In order to show his superiority over her he had her come to him instead of visiting Alexandria himself. Not intimidated in the least, Cleopatra and her courtiers arrived in Tarsus by ship from Egypt, with great pomp. She also needed the support of Antony in order to protect and keep her throne, just as she had needed Caesar. It did not take much time before they also became lovers, and after her departure Antony soon followed her to Alexandria, where he spent the winter. But events at the eastern border of his kingdom with Parthia, and the deterioration of his already poor relationship with Octavian in Rome, compelled him to leave Cleopatra's side. By the autumn of 40 BC, Cleopatra gave birth to his twins, who were named Alexander and Cleopatra; later they received a second name in accordance with Egyptian tradition: Helios and Selene, respectively, the Sun and the Moon. But Antony's serious political problems would prevent him from seeing Cleopatra again for nearly four years.

Political rivalry had always plagued the relationship between Antony and Octavian, and various attempts were made over these years to reach a lasting accord. Some compromises were political treaties; another was Octavian's offer for Antony to marry his beautiful sister Octavia, which took place in 40 BC. The couple lived happily in Athens, where they enjoyed its intellectual atmosphere. But relations did not improve between Antony and Octavian, and Antony continued to have serious problems with the Parthians on his eastern border.

Not able to count on support from Octavian and Rome, Antony needed Cleopatra and the wealth of Egypt. Sending Octavia back to Rome, he again summoned Cleopatra, and they met in Antioch, Syria, in 37 BC, where they took up again where they had left off. They soon returned together to Alexandria. Despite his marriage to Octavia, Antony now married Cleopatra. Another son was born to them a year later whom they named Ptolemy Philadelphos. The personal estrangement with Octavian was now nearly permanent, with Antony increasingly committed to Cleopatra and the east, and his publicly supporting Ptolemy Caesar as Caesar's heir. Antony and Cleopatra now declared their intention to create an Egypto-Roman empire with its capital in Alexandria instead of Rome. Some prominent Romans sided with Antony, but with Octavian still in power in Rome, the danger of civil war was becoming a reality. Antony's rejection of Octavian's authority was made final by his divorcing Octavia in 33 BC. In the Roman Senate, Octavian had Antony's authority cancelled reducing him to a private citizen, and Rome declared war on Cleopatra. A final conclusion to their mutual antagonisn was now imminent.

In 32 BC, Cleopatra accompanied Mark Antony, with a large fleet and military reinforcements provided and arranged by her, on his campaign to invade Italy and depose Octavian. But in the spring of 31 BC, Octavian's forces surprised them bottled up where they had stopped enroute to winter in the protected waters of the Ambracian (*Amvrakikos*) Gulf near Aktion, in western Greece. The superior Roman forces routed those of Antony, who was further weakened when many of his own Roman forces deserted him and joined those of Octavian. As agreed together with Antony, Cleopatra fled back to Egypt, but the demoralized Antony soon followed leaving behind his remaining fleet and army. He would soon have to prepare for the invasion of Egypt that was to come.

Sure of his victory, a year later Octavian's forces proceeded to Egypt. Antony had prepared valiantly to fight against them, but when the time came for battle, his fleet surrendered and his remaining Roman forces deserted to Octavian. Awaiting the consequences, Cleopatra had retired to a fortified mausoleum-treasury she had built on the waterfront of the city's great harbor. The two had agreed they would take their own lives rather than surrender to Octavian. Upon hearing a rumor that Cleopatra had already committed suicide, the completely shattered Antony decided to take his own life and mortally stabbed himself with his sword. But Cleopatra had not yet died.

Faced with a choice of being humiliated and possibly executed or taking her own life, as Octavian's forces approached Cleopatra chose to die. Despite legend and modern theatrics she most likely died by taking poison, and not very likely by snakebite, the details are not certain. Caesarion, her son by Caesar, was executed by the Romans. Her other three children by Antony survived; Selene was given in marriage by Octavian in due time, to a prince of Mauretania, Juba II. The fate of the two brothers, Helios and Philadelphos, has been lost in history.

Cleopatra's ambitions were political, and she had the courage and intelligence to try to achieve them. She was not merely motivated by hopeless love as modern playwrights and filmmakers would have us believe. She depended first on Caesar to accomplish her goals but he was assassinated, and then on Antony who weakened at the end. She had been "the Queen of Kings." With her passing in 30 BC, nearly three centuries of Greek rule in Egypt came to an end, and Egypt became a Roman province.

Six

The Greeks in the Medieval and Ottoman Periods

THE BYZANTINE PERIOD

SEVERAL NAMES HAVE BEEN USED BY HISTORIANS referring to or regarding the Eastern Roman Empire, with its capital at Constantinople (formerly Byzantium), with the result that the casual reader of Greek and Roman histories is often confused. "Graeco-Roman" civilization is a frequently used term; other historians refer to the "Greek Empire" and the "Medieval Greek World" —even more confusing names unless the history is familiar. Also, from where did the term "Byzantine Empire" come? All these names and others refer to the same area.

The reader of Greek history is also led to other questions: What exactly was the involvement of the Greeks in the Eastern Roman, or the Byzantine, Empire? To which Greeks do we refer, the Greek people of the nation we now call Greece, or Greeks that settled many centuries before in Asia Minor and the East? How does the history of the Byzantine Empire bear on that of the Greek people?

To begin with, Byzantine Empire is a relatively modern name for what was then known as the Eastern Roman Empire. The name was first used by French scholars only in the seventeenth century, to mark the historical change when the capital of the Roman Empire was transferred from Rome to the site of the old Greek colony of Byzantium (in Greek, *Byzantion*), which city lent its name to an empire just as the city of Rome had done earlier. This term has become widely used and accepted, even as other names for the area are also used. Being Greek in culture dating from the influence of Alexander the Great and the successor kingdoms over a period of three centuries, the occupation of this region by imperial Rome and the addition of its own influence, made it into the Graeco-Roman civilization.

Rome having taken possession of the eastern areas either by war or by peaceful means starting in the second century BC, it is obvious that the early eastern emperors would be Romans. This begins with Constantine I, who reigned as sole ruler of the Roman Empire (AD 324-337) and built his new city of New Rome on the site of the old Greek city of Byzantium and made it the capital of the empire instead of Rome. Starting with Theodosius I, when he was enthroned in 379, succeeding emperors came from all parts of the eastern empire; but, in spite of the strong Greek tradition, there was a consciousness of the continuity with the Roman emperors of the past. The people called themselves (in Greek) *Romaioi* — Romans, not *Graikoi* — Greeks, and never Hellenes. The Hellenes were the people of classical Greece, not the people of the empire in the east. Obviously, any reference to Byzantines is strictly modern usage. Indeed, since 212, when an edict was issued by Roman Emperor Caracalla, Roman citizenship was conferred on all free people who lived in organized communities in his vast domain. This meant that all Greeks as well as other minorities residing within the empire were considered Romans. Even so, the dominant culture of the entire eastern empire, together with its language and literature, was Greek. The Hellenization process had already transformed what was to become the Eastern Roman Empire into a Hellenized world. The process systematically continued, developed, and strengthened over the centuries. In addtition, the people of other foreign nations such as the Latins, Germans, and Russians called the people in the eastern Roman area "Greeks," because their culture and language — even their race — had dominated the area.

This Hellenization and the subsequent Christianization of the Eastern Roman, otherwise known as the Byzantine, Empire, are the keys to the Greekness of the area. This eastern Byzantine Greekness is distinct from the classical Hellenism of antiquity on the peninsula, and yet they are two halves of a whole. Whether of direct Greek heritage or not, the people of the Byzantine Empire greatly respected their classical Greek heritage, and took pride in its continuation and development. The events described should be seen as a part of the overall history of the Greek people wherever they resided independently for centuries. Yet, the efforts of the modern Greek nation to unite that heritage with the Byzantine period led to many of its problems, as described and as summarized in the Epilogos.

HELLENIZATION CONTINUES

The process of Hellenization took a giant step forward during the reign of Heraklios (AD 610-641), when he made Greek the official language of the Byzantine state. Up to now Latin was still the official language of the government, while Greek was the spoken and written common tongue. Heraklios did away with this cumbersome two-language system, and favored the language which was primary, the Greek. The church had also been a strong influence on this decision, Greek having been used as its language from its inception. The knowledge of Latin was lost within a single generation, except for some scholars.

The Shrinking of the Roman Empire

The Roman Empire had reached its maximum area from Spain to Armenia and north Africa about the beginning of the second century AD, and was able to maintain its hold on this vast territory for at least three centuries, always having to defend its borders against many attackers. During the next hundred years the empire was overwhelmed, especially in the west by Germanic tribes, and in the Balkan area by the Huns and Slavs. As we saw earlier, Emperor Justinian, installed in 527, won back the western territories of Italy and southern Spain, but these were lost again over the next century or so. In the middle of the seventh century, the conquering Arabs reduced the empire yet more in the east as well as in North Africa, and the Slavs and Bulgars invaded the western empire from the north. These were again pushed back, as were the Arabs in the east, and Crete was again recovered during the reign of the dynamic Byzantine Macedonian Dynasty (867-1057),* a house of rulers whose founder, of Armenian lineage, came from the region of Byzantine Macedonia. They were also to bring disaster to the empire near the end of nearly two centuries of their rule.

At the beginning of the eleventh century, internal power struggles in Constantinople between the bureaucrats and the military reached serious proportions. Because of this the countryside was deprived of its armies at a time when the area was being subjected to constant raids from warrior Turkic tribes attacking the eastern and northern edges of the empire. These raids gradually grew bolder, being largely unopposed, and the Turks began to take some eastern towns and cities as well, where the booty was greater. The Byzantine army had been substantially dismantled in an effort by the bureaucrats to gain power over the military. Now they had to rely on less loyal mercenary troops for protection against the growing menace, and the frequent discontent of these foreigners only added to the chaos. A number of victories against the Turks stiffened the resolve of the Byzantines, but this also led to the more orderly organization of a large army of Seljuk Turks under a very able leader, Alp Arslan ("Valiant Lion"). It was inevitable that a major battle would take place, and this occurred in August, 1071, near Manzikert, on the shores of Lake Van in eastern Anatolia. The Byzantine forces were led by a proven military leader, general Romanos Diogenes, who had shortly before been made emperor, Romanos IV. But his 100,000-man army was destroyed by the vast force led by Alp Arslan. Emperor Romanos himself was taken prisoner. Now largely unapposed, the Seljuks proceeded to conquer all of Asia Minor. As the Turks had been converted to Islam earlier, Christianity began to be suppressed in the occupied territories.

The empire was now reduced to only the Greek peninsula, the Thracian region north to the Danube River, and the area around Constantinople. Nevertheless, the period is known as one of brilliant Greek cultural blossoming and strengthening, there being little other influence on the empire, neither Latin nor eastern. It is this period especially that makes historians refer to "the Greeks in Constantinople." A significant effect of the defeat at Manzikert was that a future emperor would soon call on the west for help against the invading Muslims, leading to a series of Crusades, and yet more disaster for the empire, this time at western Christian hands. (See *The Crusades and the Final Schism*, p.132)

As for the Greek peninsula, classical Greek culture had moved east, to

---

* Not to be confused with Greek Macedonia only. Macedonia covers an area that extends from northern Greece even farther north, east, and west, to parts of present-day Bulgaria and Serbia.

MAP 6.0 ROMAN EMPIRE

This was the Roman Empire at its greatest extent, about the middle of the second century AD. For administrative reasons and for better control, it was divided about the end of the fourth century into the eastern and western empires, with capitals in Constantinople and Rome, respectively, and an Augustus and Ceasar in each.

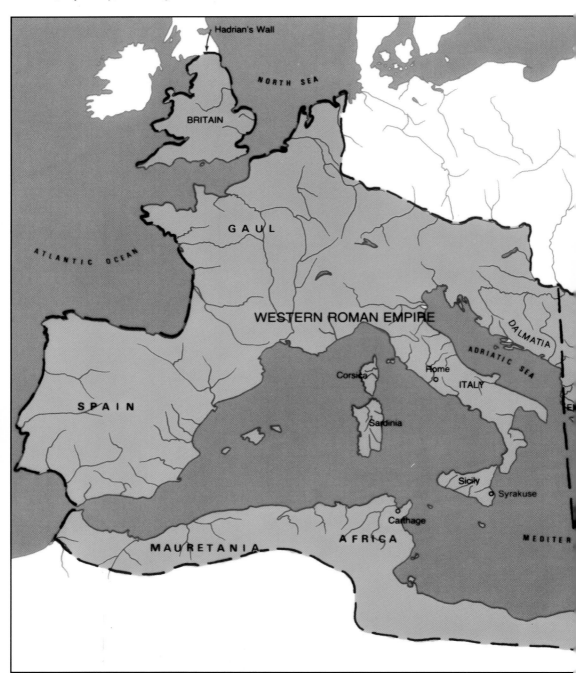

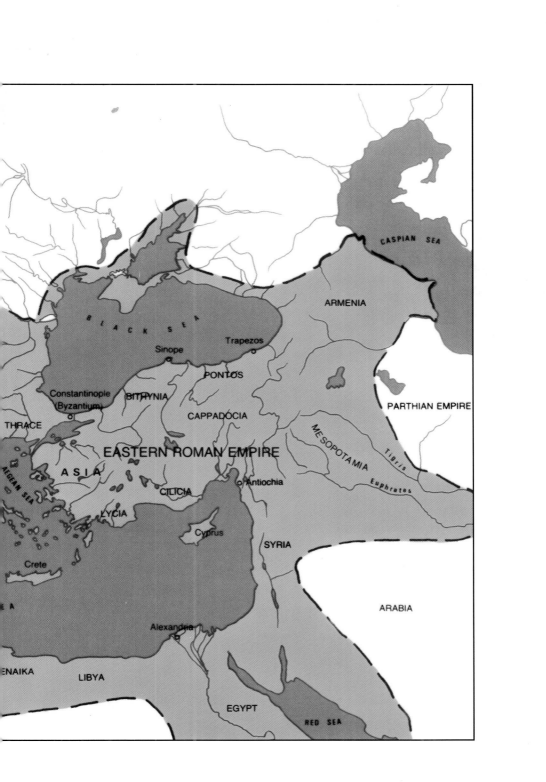

Constantinople, with its Byzantine rulers, eventually becoming a "local" Greek product after several centuries of development and use away from its place of origin. The peninsula was no longer the center of the Greek world. Among other indignities, inumerable fine sculptures and works of art from Athens and elsewhere in Greece were taken by the Roman emperors to decorate and enrich Constantinople, just as many more had earlier been taken away to Rome. The demand was so great that a sizeable industry was created to produce exact "Roman copies," many of which may now be seen in museums around the world in addition to some of the originals.

THE GREAT CHURCH

Greek religion and how it developed from polytheistic worship to Christianity is described in Chapter Nine. Two aspects of Byzantine history bear strongly on the church and must be included here: first, the integral relationship between the church and the state, and particularly in the person of the emperor; and second, the relationship of the church in the West, centered on the Pope in Rome, with that of the east, centered on the Christian Patriarchs, and the consequences of their schism.

Christian religion evolved slowly and painfully over its first several centuries of existence. It was born in the Eastern Roman Empire in Judea (Palestine); it developed its doctrines of the faith there in the first four ecumenical councils (so-called because decisions taken pertained to the universal church); it was persecuted by the imperial state, then tolerated, and then made and maintained as the only official religion by the Roman emperors; it was uniformly practiced through the medium of a single church doctrine. Through missionary work it spread to the west, north, and south — well beyond the borders of the empire.

Originally descended from Hellenistic Judaism, Christianity was gradually transformed by contemporary Greek philosophical thought and intellectualism, itself seeking a new means of finding expression by this time. Use of the Greek language by the Christians, and the New Testament and other Church documents being written in Greek, imposed an even greater Greek influence on this important new spiritual experience that was sweeping through the vast empire and beyond.

THE COUNCILS AND THE SCHISM

The acceptance of Christianity by the Roman state was a traumatic process that took about three centuries to be achieved. When the emperors ceased their antagonism and began to support the new religion, beginning with Constantine the Great, they began to embrace it themselves and associate the Roman throne with it. They convened the

Ecumenical Councils to define the doctrines of the faith and the organization of the Church, so important to the religion's systematic development and general acceptance. The first Ecumenical Council was held in Nikaia in 325, summoned by Constantine himself. Then Theodosius I convoked the second council, held in Constantinople in 381. (He was to declare Christianity the official religion of the state ion 392). Succeeding emperors called for the next five councils over a period of four centuries: Ephesos, 431; Chalkedon, 451; Constantinople II, 553; Constantinople III, 680; and Nikaia II, 787.

As Christianity grew in importance, and by this time it was growing very rapidly, the closeness of the church and the state cannot be overemphasized. The Byzantine emperor was considered God's representative on earth, responsible for the spiritual welfare of his people, as well as being their secular monarch. The church and the state were two halves of a single whole. None ruled over the other, and none ruled without the other.

At the first council, in 325, they designated three principal centers, or Apostolic "Sees" (Latin for "seats"), of Church administration and ranked them in order of honor as Rome (then the capital of the Empire and where Saints Peter and Paul were martyred), Alexandria, and Antioch. Jerusalem was also added as a See in last place, but under the Metropolitan of Ceasaria. (It was to be freed of this restriction and assume equal status at the fourth Council in 451.) Constantinople became the capital of the Eastern Roman Empire five years later, and having been founded as a Christian city, by the time of the second council it was designated as second in honor, after Rome and before Alexandria. Each of the Sees was headed by a Bishop with the title of *Patriarch*, from the Greek word meaning father + ruler, the equivalent of which in Rome was Pope. It was also decided that though the ranking of the Sees was based on political and cultural considerations and courtesies, their Patriarchs were ranked equally. The Pope at the old capital city of Rome was considered the *first among equals*.

With four of the five Holy Sees in the east (Constantinople, Alexandria, Antioch, and Jerusalem) and all Greek-speaking, there was an imbalance with the single other Latin-speaking in the west (Rome). The western empire was lost to the invading Germanic tribes, and it was recovered briefly and then lost permanently by the end of the seventh century. In spite of this, Christianity as a religion continued to grow in the west, even among peoples who were outside of the Roman Empire. But political differences contributed to religious rivalry between the east and the west. In the east, the Church and state were integral; in the west the Pope was only a religious leader. By the ninth century, the Pope nevertheless began to see himself as the supreme and absolute head of the church, which the eastern Patriarchs rejected, insisting on the principle of equality among themselves as always. It was not difficult in this atmosphere to arrive at disputes in aspects of the faith as well. The concept of the supremacy of the Pope, which the east rejected, as well as a number of interpretations of the faith, worsened an already delicate and difficult relationship.

The final schism of the church was not long in coming, which would force the Byzantine Empire further into a emphasis of its Greekness. In 1054, a strong-minded Patriarch in Constantinople, Michael Kerularios, taking issue with the western church, was met head-on by an equally uncompromising Latin, Cardinal

Humbert, sent by the Roman Pope to negotiate several important matters. It is indicative of the degree of their deteriorated relationship that when they could not agree, a Papal Bull of Excommunication against the Patriarch was placed by the cardinal on the altar of the Church of the Holy Wisdom (Haghia Sophia) during a service, and he departed from Constantinople. Although the act had not been authorized by the Pope, it was also not withdrawn by him. In retaliation, the Patriarch issued a similar edict against the Pope. Worse was to come.

THE CRUSADES AND THE FINAL SCHISM

The church might have found a way to make peace, but political events led to a permanent estrangement. The holy cities of Jerusalem, Antioch, and Alexandria had already been lost to the conquering Muslim Arabs. Now the Seljuk Turks, also Muslims, were threatening the remaining empire itself. Late in the eleventh century, Byzantine Emperor Alexios I (1081-1118) appealed to the west for military aid. The Pope in Rome, Urban II, preached a crusade and persuaded the western Christian nobles to go on a Holy War to free the holy places of Christendom. Starting in 1095 (the crusades were to continue for two centuries), crusaders from England and Europe travelled with their armies to the east. Their actions further intensified the separation between the eastern and western cultures. For the most part, the leaders of the crusader armies were belligerent, adventurous, and avaricious knights. These westerners neither knew nor understood the eastern ways of the Byzantines, and had no respect for them. Though they swore fealty to Alexios when they passed through Constantinople, their motives were otherwise. It was the holy places of Christendom they had come to free, and to keep for themselves and to Latinize, not to return them to the eastern empire. As they freed Nikaia (1097), Antioch (1098), and Jerusalem (1099), they set up Latin Patriarchs in rivalry with existing Byzantine Patriarchs. Nor were their conquests limited to war against the Muslim infidel for the holy places; other large areas of the empire were conquered by the crusaders as well. In 1204, French knights and their Venetian allies of the Fourth Crusade, ostensibly diverted to Constantinople to help restore the rightful emperor to the Byzantine throne, finally sacked the city for their own account (see *The Franks and the Venetians* p.140), desecrating churches and other holy places, taking as booty or destroying priceless Church relics. This Latin sacrilege on the east's most Holy City finalized the schism begun by the mutual excommunication of 1054.*

---

* It took until 1965 for the mutual excommunications to be lifted, primarily through the efforts of the Greek Orthodox Ecumenical Patriarch at Constantinople (Istanbul), Athenagoras I. These efforts begun a number of years before by the Patriarch, found warm receptivity in Pope John XXIII upon his election to the Papal throne in 1958. He was succeeded in 1963 by Pope Paul VI who was equally receptive to healing the nine-century-old

THE GREEK PENINSULA AT THE CROSSROADS OF THE EMPIRE

Earlier, the Holy War of Muhammad had brought new havoc to the shrinking Byzantine world (see *The Arabs and Islam* p.136). Directed north and west from Arabia starting 622, it spread rapidly, and in two decades the Arabs captured Syria and Egypt. Arab corsairs pillaged Greek coastal towns and islands. By 823, the Arabs captured Crete from the Byzantines, and the island remained in their possession until 961. A number of naval battles between the imperial fleet and the Arab pirates were won by the Byzantines. But in July 904, an attack on Thessaloniki, the second city of the Byzantine Empire, by a very large renegade Arab force from Tripoli, in North Africa, resulted in a thorough sacking and the horrible slaughter of a very large part of the population of 200,000, except for the selection of 22,000 of these who were carried off and sold in the slave markets of Arab Crete.

A period of peace and relative well-being was experienced by the Empire in the eighth and ninth centuries. By subterfuge, the Byzantines had gained the knowledge from the Chinese of the silk-making process. They established important growing, manufacturing, and exporting centers safely located at Corinth and Thebes. In other ways, too, while the geographical location of the Greek peninsula had brought about many of its problems from invaders and pirates, it also provided trade opportunities through which at least some of the Greeks prospered, showing considerable commercial flair.

The dangers from the north found yet another aggressor in the ninth and tenth centuries, the Bulgars. They penetrated south as far as the Gulf of Corinth, an area that had been invaded, occupied mostly by Slavs from two centuries earlier. The Byzantine armies were unable to dislodge the Bulgars, and their powerful Tsar Symeon (893-927) declared himself "Emperor of all the Bulgars and the Greeks." Though his empire weakened following his death, half a century later another strong Bulgarian Tsar, Samuel (976-1014) recovered his country's previous glory. The eminent and capable Byzantine Emperor Basil II (976-1025) spent twenty years stubbornly recovering the Balkan areas of the empire occupied by the Bulgars, including northern Greece. After numerous encounters in the Balkans, the final battle came in October 1014, at Belasitza, near the river Struma, in central present-day Bulgaria, when Basil's armies annihilated the Bulgar forces. According to historical sources, as many as 15,000 Bulgar prisoners were taken and systematically blinded by orders of Basil, then were sent back to Samuel in groups of one hundred each led by one of them blinded in only one eye. Samuel collapsed at the sight and died two days later. Basil earned the title *Bulgaroktonos* (the "Bulgar-Slayer").

There were Vlach penetrations into the Greek peninsula in the eleventh century, too, these being another tribe from the central Balkans. But it was the

---

schism. Finally, a joint act was prepared, issued and read to all simultaneously in both Rome and Constantinople (Istanbul) on December 7, 1965. While remaining differences in the doctrines of the two churches were recognized, the way was now open to try to resolve these in the atmosphere of mutual respect and *rapprochement*.

Normans, who had settled in southern Italy and Sicily, who were the start of a series of events that would eventually destroy the Byzantine Empire and greatly alter the course of history.

THE NORMANS

During the middle of the eleventh century, a group of Norman adventurers proceeded into the Byzantine-held south end of Italy and began to carve out a territory for themselves, ousting the last Byzantines from the area. By 1071, they were elevated to dukes by the Roman Pope. They then began the conquest of Sicily, in Saracen Arab hands by this time. By 1081, the audacious Norman leader Robert Guiscard (the "Crafty") began to plan the invasion of Constantinople itself. His forces proceeded across the Adriatic to attack Dyrrhachium (Durazzo in Italian, or Durrës in present-day Albania), a fortified port city at the European end of the ancient Via Ignatia, the Roman road leading to Constantinople more than 500 miles (850 kilometers) distant. The Byzantine Emperor Alexios I Komnenos (1081-1118), newly enthroned at a time of great weakness in the empire with the loss of nearly all of Asia Minor to the Seljuk Turks, called for the help of the Venetians. This maritime city already had a strong merchant fleet and naval force. To secure this assistance Alexios gave Venice generous trading rights along the route to the east and in Constantinople itself, thus creating another key element that would eventually contribute to the destruction of his empire. Though the Venetian fleet overwhelmed the Norman sea forces, the Normans on land defeated the Byzantine army. There followed a period when the Normans harassed the coasts and nearby areas of Epiros, Macedonia, and Thessaly. Finally, in 1085, the Venetians regained Dyrrhachium for the Byzantines. More accurately, the Venetians fought for their own interests. A Norman hold on both sides of the narrow Straits of Otranto in the Adriatic Sea would effectively plug the outlet of Venice for commerce with the east.

A few years later, Emperor Alexios' appeal to the west for military assistance against the Muslims who had overwhelmed the Holy Land had resulted in the First Crusade. On the way east, some of the crusader armies came through the Norman Italian domains in 1096. The Normans decided to join them; it was an unexpected opportunity to arrive unopposed in the Byzantine area with an army —exactly what they had been unable to do by force. It was the Normans who succeeded in regaining Antioch, but kept it for their own account. The city and surrounding area were to remain in Latin hands for two centuries despite attacks by Turks and Byzantine armies. Back in the Adriatic other Normans attacked Dyrrhachium once more, were again defeated, and spent the next several years raiding the Greek coastline in frustration.

The persisting problems of the empire continued to whet Norman appetites. In 1147, the year of the Second Crusade to the Holy Land, the Normans seized Corfu, from where they again raided the Peloponnesian coast.

MAP 6.1 BYZANTINE EMPIRE

End of the eleventh century

The Byzantine (East Roman) Empire toward the end of the eleventh century. Its extent was being reduced by attacks of its neighbors. The Normans, who had established themselves in southern Italy and Sicily, were raiding the Greek coastline at frequent intervals.

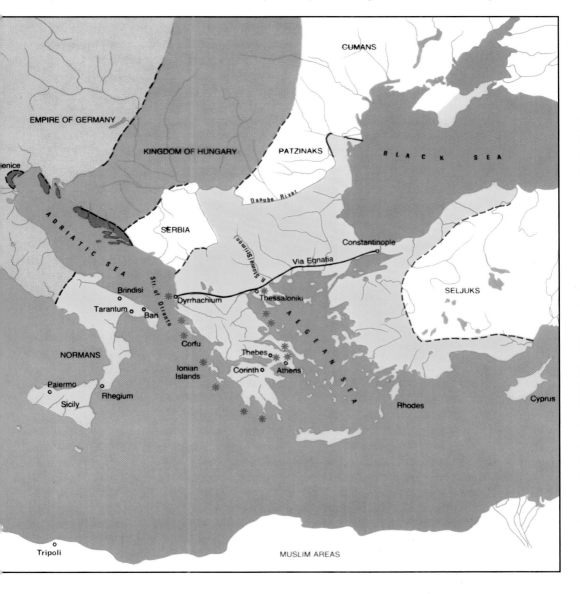

Proceeding into the Gulf of Corinth, they attacked the rich cities of Corinth and Thebes, looting the silk warehouses and carrying off the skilled silk workers and weavers, subsequently establishing their own silk industries in Sicily — an important enterprise that exists to this day.

The recovery of Corfu jointly by the Byzantines and the Venetians two years later did not prevent the Normans from renewing their piratical raids on the Greek coastline and islands. Finally, when political problems distracted Constantinople and kept their armies close to home, in 1185 the Normans sailed east with a force of 80,000 and a very large fleet. They again stormed Dyrrhachium and took it, also occupying the Greek Ionian islands to the south. They proceeded to Thessaloniki, recovered again and still the second city of the empire, and after a nine-day seige they broke in at last. Once again the city suffered untold barbarisms, with thousands of citizens killed and the city looted. So were the Orthodox churches, which were destroyed in an anti-Orthodox frenzy by these Latin invaders — expressive of the ill-will of the west at the independence of the eastern Church. Flushed with victory and loaded with loot, some of the Normans turned back to return home, others continued east on the Via Ignatia, their main objective still being Constantinople. Being now more of a rabble force than a disciplined army, they were met by the Byzantines on the banks of the river Strymon in Macedonia, where they were defeated for the last time.

THE ARABS AND ISLAM

Eleven hundred years after the Persian threat to the west, a new religious force out of Saudi Arabia led to the long process of conquest that eventually also enveloped the Byzantine Empire and Greece itself. This was born in the person of Muhammad (c.570-632), founder of the Muslim religion.

The conquering spirit of the Muslims was first applied to the Arab peninsula. Before the death of Muhammad in 632, the dissident Arab tribes had been united by force in the new spirit of Islam (the Muslim world), the believers in which had the duty to convert others or eliminate them. This *jihad*, or Holy War, also promised benefits to those who fought in the name of Allah and the Prophet Muhammad, either through the fruits of their conquests if they survived, or by assuring their place in heaven if they were vanquished.

This explosive religious force soon reached north and west. In the north, the conquerors defeated the Byzantine forces in a major victory at Yarmouk (in present-day north Jordan) in 636, and among other areas they occupied in Palestine were two of Christendom's principal holy places, Jerusalem, in 636, and Antioch, in 638. Within a few years and with stunning success, they had defeated the Persian forces and occupied Syria, Iraq, Armenia, and the rest of Persia to India, just as the forces of the Persians had done in an earlier age, followed by Alexander and then the Romans.

The Arabs also conquered Egypt, and with it Alexandria, in 642, another of the holy cities of the Christians. By the start of the eighth century, they had performed the remarkable feat of taking the entire North African coast from Egypt to Gibraltar; then they crossed the Straits and occupied most of Spain. They suffered their first defeat at Poitiers, France, in 732, against the Franks, and they finally ceased their efforts to penetrate farther into western Europe by 759, withdrawing behind the Pyrennees Mountains. In the eastern Mediterranean, they occupied Cyprus in 648, and Rhodes in 654. The greatest city of Byzantium, Constantinople itself, suffered a five-year-long siege (673 to 678), the Arab forces finally withdrawing without success. They tried again (717 to 718) with the same result. For the time being the Byzantine Empire held back the Muslim forces that eventually would overtake them. The great islands of Sardinia and Corsica fell in their turn along with Sicily. Crete was occupied, 823 to 961.* The Mediterranean had become "a Moslem lake".

The story of the Islamic religion and civilization is fascinating, but what concerns us here is their effect on Greece and the Greek people as a part of the Byzantine Empire. The principal event now came out of the steppes of central Asia in the form of nomadic warrior Turkic tribes that began to invade to the south into Persia and Iraq and to the west toward Asia Minor. As contact with the Arab Muslims was established, they were quickly converted to Islam — the warriors' religion. The idea of *jihad* fitted very well with their life-style, already filled with the glory of battle, now enriched with the spiritual satisfaction of war on the infidel and rewards in heaven, if not on earth.

The largest of these Turkic tribes, named the Seljuks after a revered leader, began to replace the now weakening Arabs in the area east of the Caspian Sea, starting the second quarter of the eleventh century. The Seljuks, accompanied by their numerous Egyptian warrior-slaves (known as *Mamluks*), became a large nomadic army. This army proceeded west, and by the middle of the eleventh century, it had raided Armenia and was continuing west. Between 1065 and 1070, Byzantine Emperor Romanos IV campaigned with a large army against the invaders who were threatening his eastern hinterland, the richest part of the empire. As we have seen, the climax took place in August 1071 with the battle at Manzikert, in which the vast Byzantine army was destroyed by Seljuk troops.

The disaster at Manzikert proved decisively what western Europe had known for a long time, that the Byzantine Empire could no longer defend itself against this fierce new enemy. In addition, Christians taking the pilgrimage to the holy places, now entirely in Turkish Muslim hands, were subjected to all manners of dangers. Pilgrimage without armed escort was becoming impossible except for those who had nothing to lose. Holy Orders sprang up about this time such as the Knights of St. John (see p.150) who offered protection to pilgrims as well as medical assistance. The Muslim threat was met by a series of crusades as already mentioned in the preceding section. Some crusader lords

---

* As the Arabs were not builders, virtually no trace of their long presence on Crete remains. Yet an interesting fact about the Greek-Arab contact with each other occurred in the ninth century, when the Arabs discovered the writings of Aristotle (384-322 BC). His theories of philosophy, logic, science, and theology greatly influenced Islamic thinking. Moreover, it was through the Arabs that Aristotelian philosophical thought was reintroduced into Western Europe, from where it had been lost.

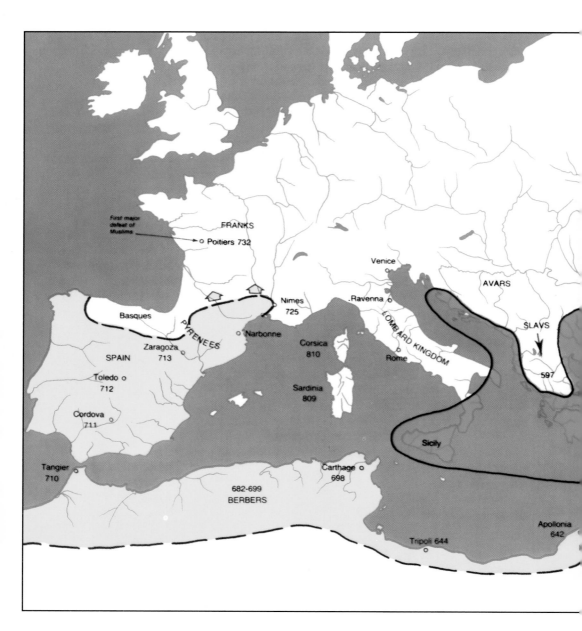

East Roman Empire

Arab Conquests 632-732

FRANKS

First major
defeat of
Muslims ——→ ○ Poitiers 732

Venice

AVARS

Nimes
725

Ravenna ○

Basques

SLAVS

PYRENEES

○ Narbonne

Corsica
810

LOMBARD KINGDOM

Rome

597

Zaragoza
713

SPAIN

Toledo ○
712

Sardinia
809

Cordova
711

Sicily

Tangier ○
710

Carthage ○
698

682-699
BERBERS

Apollonia
642

Tripoli 644 ○

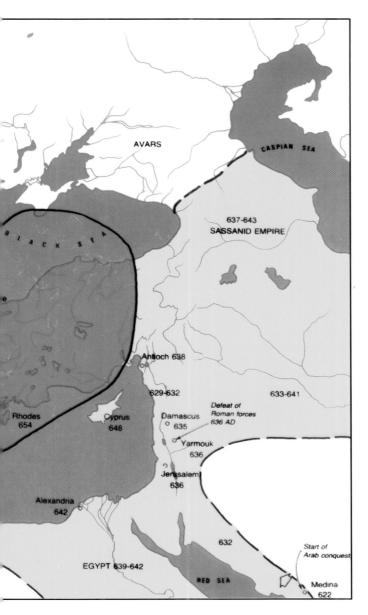

AVARS

CASPIAN SEA

637-643
SASSANID EMPIRE

BLACK SEA

Antioch 638

629-632

633-641

Defeat of
Roman forces
636 AD

Rhodes
654

Cyprus
648

Damascus
○ 635

Yarmouk
636

Jerusalem
636

Alexandria
642

632

Start of
Arab conquest

EGYPT 639-642

RED SEA

Medina
○ 622

MAP 6.2
CONQUESTS OF
ISLAM

Upon the death of Muhammad, in AD 632, at
Medina, in the Arabian Peninsula, the
conquering spirit of Islam moved east and west
with great speed. Within a hundred years they
controlled an area roughly equivalent to that
conquered by Alexander in the east as well
as North Africa and Spain to the west. The
Byzantine Empire finally stopped them from
overrunning the rest of Europe.

and their armies remained in the areas they conquered, managing to rule them as independent feudal kingdoms in spite of the hostility around them; others departed for home after their campaigns. But battles took place frequently over the area for two centuries. It now amounted to a Holy War by the Christians on the Turkish and Arab Muslims. Most important to Greek history is that these events galvanized the Christian-Muslim relationship into a rivalry that would eventually affect a large part of eastern Europe, including all of Greece, for the next several centuries.

In the decade beginning with 1080, the Greek cities of the western coast of Asia Minor and those on the islands of Lesbos, Chios, Samos, and Rhodes were occupied by the Seljuk Turks, and were again abandoned by them. As the Arabs before them, the Seljuks now began to decline, and others began to take their place. The new Muslim conquerors were another tribe of Turkic nomads from the region of Armenia, named after their leader Osman (or Othman), the Ottomans. Othman's reign began in 1288. Their story and how they came to occupy Greece for four centuries is told starting p.153.

THE FRANKS AND THE VENETIANS
(1204-1566)

The Byzantine Empire was growing weaker by the end of the 12th century under increasing pressure from the Muslims in the east. Yet its greatest disaster, which led also to another conqueror's subjugation of the Greeks in their homeland for the next seven centuries, was at the hands of the Fourth Crusade, whose leaders were predominantly northern French nobles and knights. Together with their horses, squires, foot soldiers, arms, and baggage, they arrived in Venice in August 1202 on their way to the Holy Land. But they arrived without the funds to make the down payment for the sea transport that was to be provided by the Venetians, as they had previously agreed and contracted.

The trade routes granted to Venice by Byzantine Emperor Alexios I a century earlier, had greatly helped to transform this city into a mighty trading power between the East and the West. Merchant vessels guarded by a naval fleet against the frequent piracy made at least two round trips per year between Venice and Constantinople, with Venetian trading agents established permanently at various locations en route. An even stronger hold on the sea coasts and islands along the way was very attractive to the Venetian leader, the shrewd Doge Enrico Dandolo, well over 80 years old by this time and blind or nearly blind by the time the 35,000-man crusader force camped in the area unable to pay for their voyage. He let them fret for weeks with their dilemma.

Doge Dandolo finally announced to the impatient knights that he was willing to join the Venetian forces with theirs and provide the necessary transport, as well as deferring their debt, if they would first recapture from the Hungarians the former Venetian city of Zara, on the Dalmatian coast, along the trade route to the East. The need for funds converted the crusaders into mercenaries, and, in November 1202, they attacked and took the rebel city for the Venetians. They then moved down the coast to the island of Corfu, where they camped for the winter, until May 1203. During this time, they were visited by Alexios, son of the former Byzantine Emperor Isaac II Angelos, who had been deposed by his brother, blinded, and imprisoned. Alexios offered them financial assistance if the crusaders would agree that they would first proceed to Constantinople to free Isaac Angelos and restore him to the Byzantine throne together with his son Alexios as co-rulers. The Venetians also saw this as an opportunity to enhance their trading interests with Constantinople. On July 17, 1203, they stormed the walls of Constantinople and after days of fierce fighting were able to break in at last. Emperor Alexios III was forced to flee. Isaac II Angelos and his son (now becoming Alexios IV) were enthroned as co-emperors in his place. But the victory was short-lived. In February 1204, a palace revolt suddenly toppled Isaac and his son, and they were replaced by Alexios V Dukas. The crusaders and the Venetians saw their benefactors, whom they had aided for profit, stripped from power and their financial promises vanish. They resolved to seize the empire for themselves, in no small way having been dazzled by the display of wealth around them.

The heavily fortified and defended city, the richest in the world at that time, finally fell to the assault of the crusaders and the Venetians on April 13, 1204. Three terrible days of rampage followed, destroying forever countless records, and looting priceless treasures. Even more important, the event marked the long slide into oblivion of the Byzantine Empire, which event eventually released the Turkish hordes to occupy eastern Europe for centuries.

The terms of agreement between the Frankish noblemen and the Venetians, if they should succeed in taking Constantinople, were that the Latin Emperor (agreed to be a Frank) would himself receive one-quarter of the empire, and the remaining three-quarters would be divided equally between the Franks and the Venetians, with specific emphasis on the Venetians keeping and expanding their commercial privileges, trading posts, and routes.

However, it was one thing to conquer Constantinople and agree to a division of the empire; it was quite another to actually accomplish the division and keep the territories. Some of the areas willingly pledged themselves to the new rulers, other parts were available only by conquest, and some were just too difficult to capture or hold at all. The destruction of Byzantine rule also gave opportunities for other warlike neighbors to advance their boundaries. Within a few years following the conquest of 1204, the empire was divided as shown on Map 6.3, and as summarized in the following: (See also Appendix - *Medieval Fuedal Lords of the Greek Peninsula and Islands*).

Latin Empire. Count Baldwin of Flanders was selected emperor, and his one-quarter share was the area covering most of present-day Greece and both sides of the Sea of Marmara around Constantinople, as well as most of the capital city. He awarded many fiefs, among which was the important kingdom at Thessaloniki, the second city of the empire, given to placate Boniface, Marquis of Montferrat, who had expected to be made emperor and was not. Others selected by Baldwin were able to take over their territories

MAP 6.3
THE BYZANTINE
EMPIRE TOWARD
THE END OF THE
TWELFTH CENTURY

The Christian Crusades began in 1095, when
help was requested from the Roman Pope
by the Byzantine Emperor, as his armies
were unable to stop the Muslim Seljuk Turks.
The routes of the Third and Fourth Crusades
are shown, as is the resulting dissolution of
the empire after the sacking of Constantinople
by Franks of the Fourth Crusade with their
Venetian allies.

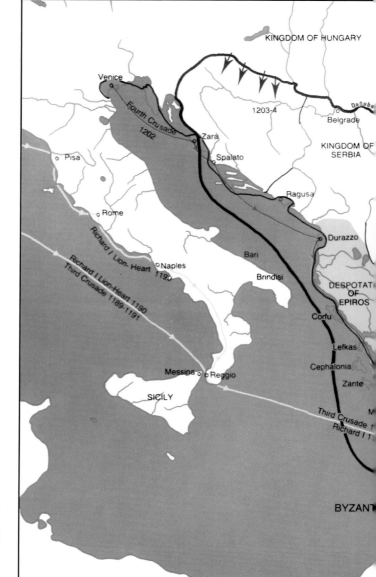

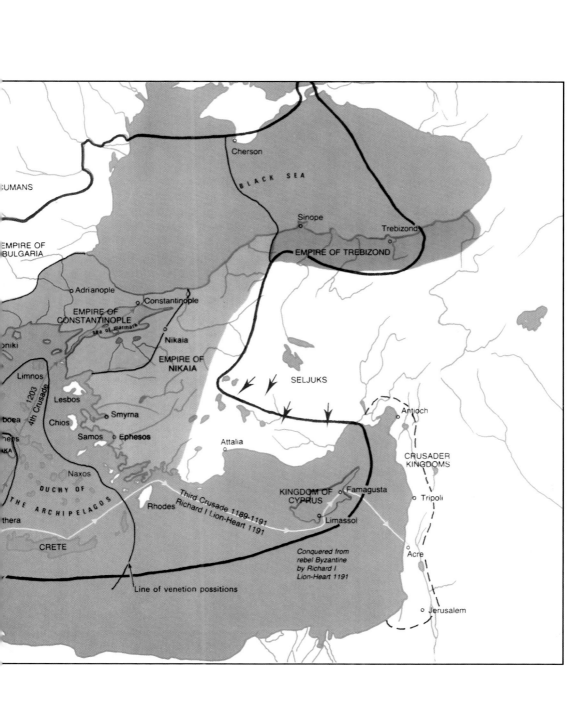

CUMANS

EMPIRE OF
BULGARIA

BLACK SEA

Cherson

Sinope

Trebizond

EMPIRE OF TREBIZOND

Adrianople

Constantinople

EMPIRE OF
CONSTANTINOPLE

Sea of marmara

oniki

Nikaia

EMPIRE OF
NIKAIA

Limnos

SELJUKS

4th Crusade 1203

Lesbos

boea

Smyrna

Chios

Samos   Ephesos

Antioch

hens

Attalia

CRUSADER
KINGDOMS

KA

Naxos

DUCHY OF

KINGDOM OF
CYPRUS

Famagusta

Tripoli

THE ARCHIPELAGOS

Third Crusade 1189-1191
Richard I Lion-Heart 1191

Rhodes

thera

Limassol

CRETE

Conquered from
rebel Byzantine
by Richard I
Lion-Heart 1191

Acre

Line of venetion possitions

Jerusalem

peacefully, and some could only take possession of them by force. Guillaume of Champlitte and Geoffroy of Villhardouin together conquered the Morea (the Peloponnese). Attica and Boiotia were taken over by Othon de la Roche of Burgundy, the area becoming known as the Duchy of Athens.

Venetian Possessions. A brief look at the territory taken over by Venice confirms their objective of preserving the trade routes to the east of this city-state. They had already won back the rebel city of Zara on the Dalmatian coast with the aid of the Frankish crusaders, as mentioned earlier; Ragussa and Durazzo were already their possessions. The Ionian islands in the Adriatic came under the Venetians in this period, as well as the two Greek cities of Modoni (present day Methoni) and Koroni on the southwesternmost tip of the Peloponnese, that they subsequently fortified. The large island of Euboia (later called Negroponte) was their principal holding on the way to the east, although during the early period the Franks also had properties there, mostly only in the interior. The nephew of Doge Enrico Dandolo, Marco Sanudo, seized the large fertile sland of Naxos, in the central Aegean, soon after the fall of Constantinople, and he gradually added the other surrounding islands, creating what was became known as "the Duchy of the Archipelago." The Venetians also occupied Limnos and other islands in the north Aegean. The strategic island of Crete was taken by the Venetians, some areas by purchase from the Franks and some by feat of arms, but they occupied it entirely from1210 to1645, and they held on to some areas as late as 1669 before they lost it entirely to the Ottomans. Finally, the terms of agreement with the Franks also gave them three-eighths of the capital city of Constantinople.

Despotate of Epiros. Albania and Epiros had been allocated to the Venetians in the division of the Byzantine Empire. However, before they could occupy these areas in 1204, Michael I Dukas Angelos Komnenos, a bastard son of the Angeli family (i.e., the Angelos dynasty of the empire), married the daughter of the Byzantine governor of Epiros and established an independent despotate there. While originally comprising an area from Dyrrhachium to the Gulf of Corinth and about halfway across the Greek peninsula to the east, by 1224 the despotate was extended by conquest to include the important Latin kingdom of Thessaloniki, along with Thessaly and most of Macedonia. In this expanded condition, its ruler prepared to assume the imperial throne by attacking Constantinople. But competitors in the form of the strong Bulgarian Empire in the north and the rival Byzantine heirs who had assumed control of Nikaia soon shattered this aspiration and reduced the despotate once again to about its original size. Nevertheless, in one form or another the despotate lasted more than 130 years.

Empire of Nikaia. The new crusader rulers of the fallen Byzantine Empire were unable to push back the Greek forces beyond Nikaia, leaving a large area from the eastern Aegean to the Black Sea organized and defended under the leadership of Theodore Laskaris, son-in-law of Alexios III, creating a buffer between the crusaders and the Seljuks. Within a few years the Laskaris also pushed the Latins entirely out of Asia. The Latin Empire of Constantinople was now reduced only to the city itself and its immediate surroundings, squeezed as it was between the Byzantine heir-kingdoms of Epiros in the west and Nikaia in the east. The two Byzantine kingdoms then competed for the imperial throne along with the Bulgars. Though the Bulgars defeated the Epiros armies, they themselves were reduced by Mongol attacks from the northeast, so the Nikaian rule was gradually enlarged without competition. The Nikaians invaded European Greece itself by 1246 and were generally recognized as the likely heirs to the Byzantine throne; indeed their actions constituted a revival of the empire and they took the initiative and crowned their ruler as Byzantiune Emperor. By 1261, they recaptured Constantinople with little trouble, when it was left temporarily defenseless by the Latins, their army off elsewhere on an expedition. Michael VIII Palaiologos, ruler of the Nikaian Empire, restored the Byzantine throne under his leadership.

Mystra. In 1249, William II of Villehardouin, heir to the Peloponnese (otherwise also called the Morea or Achaia), had a fortified castle built as his capitol on the peak of a steep hill located south of Sparta. The hill was nicknamed *Myzethra*, a Greek word referring to a soft white mound-shaped cheese made in that area, which word became "Mystra" in French. In 1259, William II was captured in battle with the Byzantines in northern Greece. He was able to secure his freedom after three years captivity by giving in ransom his castle on Mystra together with a wedge-shaped area southeast to the seacoast that included Monemvasia and the Mani peninsula. The Byzantines slowly expanded this holding over the next century, but Latins continued to retain large areas of the Peloponnese and Venetians held a number of key coastal cities. Mystra continued to be ruled by Byzantine governors, who were important members of the imperial families. But, by 1460, the Turks had taken the entire Peloponnese including Mystra. The area went through good and very bad times through the various occupiers and maurauders for four centuries.

Rhodes. This strategically placed island had previously provided trading privileges to the Venetians, but it remained independent after 1204 under its Greek Byzantine governor. By the mid-twelfth century, it was absorbed into the Empire of Nikaia. Finally, it was conquered by the Knights of St. John in whose hands it remained until 1522. (See p.146).

Cyprus. This island had already been conquered from the Byzantines by the English King Richard I "Lion Heart" by 1191, during the Third Crusade. He then sold it in 1198 to the Frankish crusaders of previous crusades who had been ousted from Jerusalem by the Arabs. It remained under Frankish rule (but never under the Franks of the Fourth Crusade) for more than 100 years.

Southern Anatolia. The weakened and defeated empire lost southern Anatolia to the Seljuk Turks by 1207. It was never won back from Muslim rule.

Trebizond. The nephews of former Emperor Andronikos I (1183-1185) proceeded to the southern coast of the Black Sea, conquering the zones between the cities of Sinope and Trebizond. The area remained in Byzantine hands for over 250 years until 1461, when the Ottomans captured this last remnant of the empire.

T he Byzantine emperors had ruled over the empire and its capital city of Constantinople nearly nine centuries (from AD 330 to 1204) until the Franks and the Venetians destroyed that continuity. But it took only 57 years (to 1261) for the Franks to lose the throne back to the Byzantines, who retained their rule over a much reduced empire another two centuries until it was lost permanently to the Turks in 1453, as we will see.

From 1261, the restored empire was subjected to major invasions from the Bulgars, Serbs, and Vlachs from the north and the Turks from the east. The rest of the area, comprising roughly present-day Greece, was the zone of continuous both peaceful and military exchanges among the Byzantines, the various Frankish rulers, the Venetians and other Europeans, and the Turks. The Venetians managed to retain most of their coastal areas and islands, although by now some of their traditional rivals (principally Genoa, Florence, Pisa, and other Italian city-states) also penetrated and occupied some areas for varying periods. The Franks were nearly gone by the end of the fourteenth century. The Venetians, Florentines, and Genoese stayed quite a bit longer. After several wars with the Turks, they departed from the Greek mainland and Aegean by 1566, except for Crete, which was finally conquered by the Ottomans between 1645 and 1669. Finally, the Venetians were forced out of the Ionian islands by 1797, which they had held stubbornly to the bitter end in defense of these stepping stones to their commercial interests, which had contibuted greatly to this foreign occupation of Greece in the first place.

THE KNIGHTS OF ST. JOHN (1291-1522)

A visit to Rhodes will reveal much evidence of the presence of the Knights of St. John. Who were these Knights, what part of Greece did they occupy, why, and for how long?

The creation of the Orders of the Knights Templar, the Teutonic Knights, and the Knights Hospitalers of St. John, came about as a result of the need to protect the European pilgrims to the Holy Land. By 1071, after the crushing defeat of the Byzantine armies by the Muslim Seljuk Turks at Manzikert, the Seljuks seized Jerusalem and the surrounding area. While pilgrimage continued without opposition from the Turks, the passage was hazardous. All of the Knights' Orders were settled in the Morea (Peloponnese) and on the Aegean islands for relatively short periods of time. However, only the Order of the Knights of St. John stayed longer and played a significant role in Greek history.

A Benedictine hospice for pilgrims was established in Jerusalem about 1080 under Brother Gérard, having as its patron saint John the Baptist. It became apparent that caring for the sick in that part of the world and at that time, also required providing armed protection. Pope Pascal II approved the creation of the (originally French) Knights in 1113, becoming a formal order caring for the sick and performing military service in 1120. They were overwhelmed and ousted from Jerusalem in 1224 by the Seljuks, and from nearby cities and castles in the area successively, until the final defeat at their last stronghold at Acre in mid-July 1291. They then moved to Cyprus, where they had estates at Limassol, Nicosia, and elsewhere on the island. They remained in Cyprus until 1310, with headquarters at Limassol.

MAP 6.4 KNIGHTS OF ST. JOHN (1291-1522)

The Knights Hospitallers of St. John were organized and established themselves in Jerusalem to protect and aid the Christian pilgrims to the Holy Land against the many hazards of the arduous journey. The course of their settlements is traced over the four centuries of their presence in the east and in Greece.

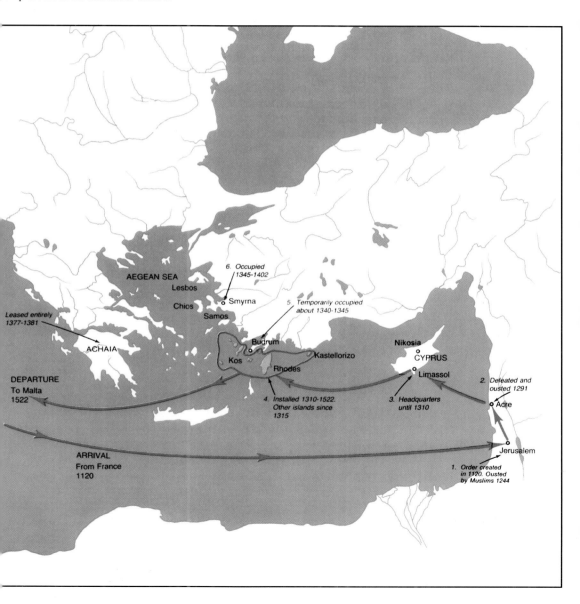

AEGEAN SEA

Lesbos

Chios

Samos

6. Occupied 1345-1402

Smyrna

5 Temporarily occupied about 1340-1345

Budrum

Kastellorizo

Nikosia

CYPRUS

Kos

Rhodes

Limassol

Leased entirely 1377-1381

ACHAIA

DEPARTURE
To Malta
1522

4. Installed 1310-1522. Other islands since 1315

3. Headquarters until 1310

2. Defeated and ousted 1291

Acre

ARRIVAL
From France
1120

Jerusalem

1. Order created in 1120. Ousted by Muslims 1244

The King of Cyprus, though himself a Latin, severely restricted the growth of the order, and the knights were feeling a loss of purpose. Obtaining an area of their own appealed to the Hospitalers, and they began to consider moving to Rhodes. Meanwhile, in 1306, a Genoese pirate and adventurer, Vignolo dei Vignoli, went to the knights claiming he had been granted a lease from the Byzantine ruler for the Greek islands of Kos and Leros north of Rhodes. He suggested that the knights should join forces with him to wrest these islands from the Greeks, Turks, Venetians, and whoever else had possession of them, and share the territory and income that could be derived as they might agree. Dei Vignoli's involvement disappears from history at this point, but the knights took possession of Rhodes by force on August 13, 1309, and they moved their headquarters there in 1310.

Over the next two centuries, the knights acquired lands in many parts of the Peloponnese (also called Morea or Achaia), and they leased it entirely for five years from its Latin feudal lord, in 1376. When the lease expired in 1381, they gave up the area as being too troublesome to keep and also unprofitable. They concentrated on Rhodes and the nearby islands and on coastal areas adjacent to these in Asia Minor. By 1315, they had taken possession of the islands of Kos, Kalymnos, Leros, Piskopi, Nisyros, Simi, Khalki, and Kastellorizo. They also settled in Budrum (ancient Halikarnassos) on the Anatolian mainland opposite. In 1345, they took Smyrna (modern Izmir), which they occupied until 1402, when they were pushed out by the invading Tartars under Timur the Lame (called "Tamerlane" in the west).

They were finally defeated by the Turks and left the area altogether by the end of 1522. In 1530, Charles V, the Emperor in Rome, granted them the island of Malta in the central Mediterranean which they made their headquarters, resulting in their becoming known as the Knights of Malta.

THE CATALAN GRAND COMPANY
(1302-1388)

Alittle-known event in the history of Greece was the arrival there of a group of Spanish mercenaries whose rule over Thebes and Athens and the surrounding area was to cover a period of close to a century.

An important influence on the presence and fortunes of the Franks in Greece was brought about by the Catalan Grand Company, a group of professional Spanish soldiers who (despite the name) consisted of Aragonese, Catalans, Navarrese and other Spanish ethnic groups. Their presence in the eastern Mediterranean was a progression that began with the Spanish *reconquista* of its own peninsula from the Moors. The mercenaries also fought under Peter III of Aragon for possession of Sicily and southern Italy against the French house of Anjou, starting in 1282.

When peace was finally declared twenty years later, in 1302, the mercenaries were without work, and most of them had little interest in returning

Byzantine Empire

Frankish Kingdom

Venice

Path of the Catalan Grand
Company from Sicily to
Constantinople and to Athens

Attacks by Admiral
Roger de Lluria in 1292

MAP 6.5 CATALAN GRAND COMPANY (1302-1388)

Spanish mercenaries hired by Byzantine Emperor Andronikos II to help him fight the Seljuk Turks, eventually attacked the Frankish occupiers of Thebes and Athens and remained there as rulers for 86 years.

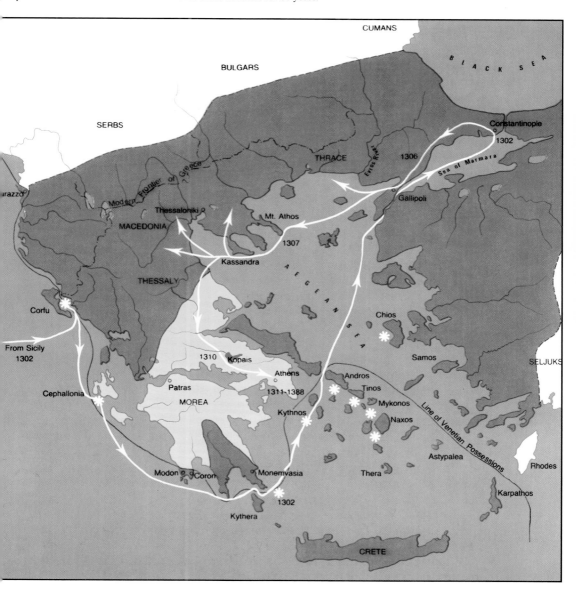

to their own country after many years away. This military group had become the most brutal professional fighting machine in the Mediterranean at that time. Keeping itself together under the dynamic leadership of Roger de Flor, the company hired out to Emperor Andronikos II (1282-1328), who was in dire need of mercenaries to fight against the Seljuk Turks.

This was not the first time the Spaniards appeared in Greek waters. In 1292, the Aragonese Admiral Roger de Lluria plundered coastal towns and islands with piratical impartiality, whether Byzantine, Latin, or Venetian. Corfu, Patras, Kephalonia, Monemvasia, Naxos, Andros, Tinos, Kythnos, and even Chios, among others, were further impoverished in his wake.

The Catalan Grand Company, on its way to join the Emperor at Constantinople in 1302, ravaged Corfu in its turn, as if by demonstration of their own style. Arriving at their destination they immediately went to work. They fought well against the Turks, but between battles with their assigned enemy, they battled everyone else as it suited them. This resulted in their losing the patronage of the emperor. But de Flor was assassinated while on a visit to the headquarters of Michael IX, co-emperor with his father Andronikos II. Enraged and murderous, the Catalans wreaked havoc and they soon moved out of Constantinople setting up their camps at Gallipoli. Now clearly on their own, from this vantage point they plundered the nearby countryside of Thrace. By 1307, they moved to the Kassandrea peninsula of Khalkidiki, raiding Mount Athos (the Holy Mountain) along the way, while they continued their actions now against Macedonia. In this new position, they threatened Thessaloniki, at this time again under Byzantine rule, as well as points south towards Athens, that was still under the Franks and the Venetians. Walter of Brienne, Duke of the Duchy of Athens, hired them (rather than fight them), and, by 1310, they had conquered most of the countryside of Thessaly. Fatally, Walter and the Catalans then argued about the permanence of their stay in the area. Meanwhile the Catalans had worked their way down into Boiotia and camped near Skripou on the banks of the Kephissos River near Lake Kopaïs.

Something would have to be done to rid the area of these troublesome renegades, once and for all. Walter of Brienne assembled the flower of Frankish chivalry, 700 knights, lords, dukes, and barons all told, plus other horsemen, and thousands of foot soldiers. They armed suitably for the final battle. But the professional Catalans also prepared themselves well; they selected the battlefield, a flat plain irresistible to the knights on their heavy chargers, but one they had earlier planted with grass over a soft swamp. On March 15, 1311, the battle took place. The 700 heavily armored knights on their armored horses led the charge across the green meadow, into which they immediately sank. They were wiped out by archers and Catalans on foot, and only a few escaped with their lives. The Franks never completely recovered from this catastrophe, and their stay in the area was permanently affected.

The Catalans marched south to Thebes, which gave up without a struggle, and continued to Athens and the surrounding duchy, which they took over and ruled for the next 76 years. Over the years the Catalans lost their fighting spirit and military organization, until at last they lost the Duchy of Athens to the Florentine Nerio Acciajuoli in 1388.

BYZANTINE LIFE AND CIVILIZATION

The continuous existence of the highly developed Byzantine civilization over a period of 1100 years requires a closer look at what it was and how it lived. Controlling a vast territory for so many centuries, how could it have come to such a disastrous and abrupt end?

If a single factor could guide the growth and destiny of the Byzantine Empire that factor was its geographical location. The empire covered southern Europe, the central to the eastern Mediterranean areas, North Africa, Asia Minor to the edge of the Persian kingdom in the east, and Egypt to the south. A uniform catalyst was the centuries-old widespread Hellenistic culture that preceded it, to be combined with Roman administration. Since 330, the capital was Constantinople, in the center of this territory, at a crossroads that gave access to all parts of the empire and beyond, by sea and by land. Caravans and merchant ships regularly plied their trade routes to and from western and northern Europe, north Africa, and as far east as China. The materials brought included silks, spices, precious metals and gemstones, wines, grains and other foodstuffs, wood, hides, base metals, and raw materials of every description. Highly organized guilds (a Roman contribution) were at the heart of her industries. The imperial court and nobility, including the church, were served by a hard-working class of artisans, merchants, assistants, and laborers.

The emperor was supreme in all matters, secular and spiritual. If he was personally above the law, Roman statutes were also in force. The intelligent Emperor Justinian I in 528 ordered an extensive codification of Roman law. The imperial court developed into a dazzling display of wealth and pomp, and frequent audiences and public functions were designed to awe the many official visitors and the people in general. Part of the vitality was that the population of Constantinople was by no means homogenious and they came to this crossroad from all parts of the far-flung empire. At its peak the city had about one million inhabitants, an enormous figure for the times.

Constantinople was located at the entire southeastern most hilly tip of Thrace, where they installed the palaces, the senate and other public buildings, parks, and elaborate churches, the Haghia Sophia Cathedral included (translated in English as the Church of the Holy Wisdom), built between 532 and 537 at the direction of Justinian I. The city itself, on a roughly snout-shaped peninsula facing east, was bounded in the south by the Sea of Marmara, and in the north and east by the Bosporus, a narrow waterway connecting to the Black Sea. Stout defense walls were built along the entire waters' edge, and Constantine had another wall built to protect the landward side, about 1 1/2 miles (2 1/2 kms) from its eastern tip. About fifty years later, this enclosed area was expanded westward another kilometer, and battlements were built in three rows of successively higher walls with towers behind a wide and deep moat. Inside this encircled area was enough space for all its inhabitants, a large water-supply, and land for agriculture. A heavy chain stretching about 1500 feet (450 meters) was located across the mouth of the Golden Horn, supported on wood floats except for a length in the middle to allow vessels to pass when tension was released by the winches on the shores This device prevented hostile ships from entering the Golden Horn waterway in times of attack, where the many gates through the wall to handle goods made this area of the city most vulnerable. Thus, Constantinople was virtually impregnable from external attack. In fact, the only times the city was taken was: in April, 1204, by the Frankish crusaders with their Venetian allies; retaken from them in 1261 by Michael VIII Palaiologos, the Nikaian emperor, who proceeded into the city unopposed when the Byzantine forces were away on an expedition, walking through an open and unguarded gate; and by the Ottoman Turks in 1453, who by that time had the use of heavy cannon to pound down and breech the stone fortifications. Considering that Constantinople was beseiged twenty-nine times, it speaks well for her defenses, as well as for her defenders.

From the reign of Constantine I beginning in 324, to Constantine XI Dragases, ending in 1453, there were 93 reigns of Byzantine rulers, including those in Nikaia when the capital had been occupied briefly by a Frankish ruler. Some emperors came into power twice. (See Appendix - *The East Roman [Byzantine] Emperors*). There were many co-emperors, usually a father and one or more sons, or two brothers, or husbands with their wives. Two sisters co-ruled (Zoë and Theodora), and only two women were ever elected to rule alone (Irene and the same Theodora). This was unusual, as women were not selected to rule, whatever power they wielded behind the throne. There was no single method by which a ruler was named. The throne was at times passed on by hereditary right, or through marriage into the imperial house, given to a military leader, or selected by other means. While the imperial court was lavish, and the emperors often came from the higher nobility, this was not always the case. There were peasant emperors, barbarians, civil servants, plain soldiers, one had been a butcher, another a ship painter (or caulker), a swineherd, and so on. Many were brilliant and high-minded, others were drunkards, incompetants, or tyrannical. Some transfers in rule took place in an orderly and peaceful manner, and others were violent. There was a degree of cruelty in the imperial court. Decapitation of a deposed ruler seems a relatively peaceful end in view that others were tortured and mutilated, bludgeoned, stabbed, buried alive, drowned, or strangled. A favorite punishment was blinding and seven rulers suffered this fate. Other rulers were exiled, imprisoned, or placed in a monastery, sometimes after suffering one of the nonfatal punishments as described. In the eastern style, the court was also served by many eunuchs. Indeed, castration was not necessarily looked down on or considered a punishment. Eunuchs served in many key posts, and not only in the women's quarters. But a eunuch could never be emperor, by imperial edict, and this kept some brilliant administrators of the Byzantine court from aspiring to that lofty office.

The arts were highly appreciated by the Byzantines, with the most lasting and impressive that have some down to us being inspired by religion. The most beautiful architecture of the period was applied to churches, such as the Haghia Sophia, still intact in Constantinople (now called Istanbul). Its spacious interior open area was made possible by a huge dome, 102 feet (over 30 meters) in diameter (the largest in the world until relatively recent times). Its interior is 180 feet (55 meters) from the floor to its highest rise. It was graced by other smaller domed areas. This multi-domed architectural style of the Haghia Sophia is still applied in the design of even simple Greek Orthodox churches. Mosaics were brought to a very high level of quality; the Byzantine taste for the lavish was applied here, too, through the use of tiny brightly colored or gold-plated glass cubes, in addition to the traditional marble chips. Handsome icons were set off with decorative and elaborate friezes, which were also used throughout other surfaces. Featured in the center of the main dome was a representation of the Christ Pantokrator ("ruler of the Universe"), and in other prominent locations, images depicting the Virgin Mary, Saint John the Baptist, and the other religious figures. Later, when the economy of the empire began to decline, this rich mosaic church decoration was replaced by paintings. Beautiful church music was also composed to be sung by choirs, much of which is still heard today in Greek Orthodox churches and elsewhere.

Whatever the level of sophistication reached within the Byzantine Empire, it was surrounded by barbarian hordes and hostile peoples: various tribes of Mongols and Tartars from the east, Arabs (Saracens) from the south, Germanic tribes from the north, and Bulgars, Slavs, Huns and others from the west. Not the least of these were the Normans out of Sicily and southern Italy, and the various crusader forces. Muslim tribes and the Latins resented the eastern church, and all were after booty and land. For the Byzantines military defense and offense was a constant necessity for the protection of the empire or to regain lost territory or to keep their enemies from becoming too strong. Much of the wealth gained out of the extensive commerce made possible by the empire's geographical position, and particularly Constantinople, went for military purposes. Diplomacy also became a weapon, and less costly than war, and it was developed to a very high degree ranging from good will to duplicity; deviousness and intrigue for them could at times be a matter of life and death.

But the internal and external problems were to culminate in disaster for the empire, brought to a focus by the rise and growing strength of the Ottoman Turks from the east. Even so, from the time they first appeared on the Byzantine eastern frontier, to the destruction of the empire was to take another 120 years.

BYZANTINE AND OTTOMAN RELATIONS

Another aggressive Turkish tribe, the Ottomans, named after their leader Osman (or Othman), now came on the scene in Asia Minor on the Byzantine eastern frontier. In 1326, Bursa was captured by Osman's armies in his expansion westwards. But he died in the same year, and his campaigns were continued by his son, Orkhan, who conquered the remaining Byzantine territory in Anatolia by 1338. His advance was mostly unopposed owing to prolonged civil wars in Constantinople between rival factions of the ruling Palaiologos family. There followed a period of twenty years without further campaigns by either the Muslims or the Byzantines, during which time the gains of the Ottomans were consolidated and their rule and armies organized and strengthened. Also during this time they created a fearsome elite troop, known as the *Yeni Tscheri* ("New Troops"), or "Janissaries," as the Europeans called them. The Janissaries were formed from a forced conscription averaging perhaps 1000 Christian boys per year, converted to the Islamic faith and subjected to rigorous training, but their benefits were also substantial. The system quickly led to the creation of a formidable instrument of war for their masters, which wreaked cruelty on their enemies — Christians for the most part. During the three centuries before the practice came to an end, several hundred thousand Janissaries had been created.

The Byzantine court was plunged further into disarray when Andronikos III died in 1341, leaving his nine-year-old son John V Palaiologos the Byzantine throne. At Adrianople, in Thrace, John Kantakuzenos, who had been the chief minister for Andronikos and named regent for John V, also proclaimed himself emperor, resulting in yet another civil war. In an unprecedented act for a Christian Byzantine ruler, in 1346 he gave his young daughter Theodora in marriage to the 61-year-old Sultan Orkhan, in order to secure his aid to try to put down his rivals for the throne. Prompted by this alliance and for the first time, the Ottomans sent an army across the Hellespont to the European side. They succeeded in helping Kantakuzenos, but they also penetrated as far as the Balkans, and the booty gained whetted their appetite for incursions westward. Meanwhile, Serbian Czar Stephan Dushan also took advantage of the general confusion to invade the Byzantine territories of Macedonia and Thrace in 1345 and then Epiros and Thessaly in 1348, adding to the chaotic situation of the weakened empire. It was at this time that Stephan proclaimed himself "Emperor of the Serbs, Greeks, Bulgarians, and Albanians". No other Serbian leader had the capability to assume this ambitious title after his death in 1355.

THE OTTOMANS' FIRST CONQUESTS IN EUROPE

The second Ottoman penetration to the European side occured in 1350, once again resulting from yet others' dissension. This time the Venetians and Genoese, intense trading competitors in the area of Constantinople, warred on each other, and self-proclaimed Emperor John VI Kantakuzenos joined the Venetian side. John V joined the Genoese as did Orkhan's Ottomans. In 1354 Orkhan's army crossed the Hellespont, where the Genoese had a trading concession, and established an Ottoman base on the Gallipoli peninsula. Expansion was tempting, and by 1358, the Ottomans had taken several towns on the European side, and the process of Ottoman occupation accelerated. Orkhan died at this time, his son Murad succeeding him. By 1361, Murad had declared holy war against the Byzantine infidels (that is, Christians), capturing Adrianople, then the second city of the empire after Constantinople, that he made his European capital. In 1363, he also took Philippopolis, and in the same year a Christian crusader force of Hungarians and Serbs sent to drive the Muslim Ottomans out of Europe was annihilated by the Turks on the banks of the Maritza River near Adrianople.

For the next twenty-five years Murad extended his conquests north and west, and no force could stop him.

Manuel Palaiologos, son of the Emperor John V, as part of yet another sort of diplomatic exchange to guarantee peace between the Byzantines and the Ottomans, had been serving in the Sultan's court at Bursa, very much a hostage despite his position and background. When John V died in 1391, Manuel left the court without permission and arrived in Constantinople to claim and assume his father's throne. The Ottoman ruler at this time was Bayezid I, "the Thunderbolt," son of Murad, who had assumed Ottoman rule in 1389. Deciding to forestall Bayezid's territorial ambitions, the Serbian, Hungarian, and armies of other Balkans joined forces and made a supreme effort to stop the Ottoman advance, but they were destroyed in a disastrous battle on the Kossovo Plain (in Serbia). Bayezid, who was to prove even more of an authoritarian and ruthless disciplinarian than his father. He now carried forward the Turks' plan to attack Constantinople, his anger increased over Manuel leaving his court. He attacked and besieged Constantinople in 1393. While his armies did not break in, the city was cut off and isolated, all surrounding lands now in Ottoman hands. The Muslim forces then invaded Macedonia and Thessaly, capturing Larissa, in 1395, and Thessaloniki, in 1397, after a three-year siege. Headed by Bayezid himself, the Ottomans continued their march southwards, virtually unopposed, taking Athens also in 1397. He proceeded farther south, occupying the Peloponnese, where "thirty thousand Greeks were removed thence by Bayezid's order, and transported to Asia; and Turkoman and Tartar colonies were settled in their stead in the classic regions of Lakonia, Messinia, Achaia, Argolis and Elis."*

At this time an event took place that was to have a major impact on the Ottomams for years, curtailing their activities in Europe. This was the rise of the Mongols and the Tartars out of central Asia under Timur the Lame, or Tamerlane, as he is known in the west. Having conquered a vast Asian territory, even greater than Alexander's, he proceeded west, capturing Armenia, Iraq, and Syria, and penetrating Anatolia by the end of the fourteenth century. Bayezid sped back to his Asian domains and met in battle with Timur in 1402, near Ankara. As historian Edward Gibbon was to write, "Timur was impatient of an equal, and Bayazet (*sic*) was ignorant of a superior".** His force of 100,000 men was wiped out by the Mongols, and he himself was taken prisoner, dying from this indignity eight months later. Timur's campaigns did not proceed farther west. Many of the Greek areas were temporarily abandoned to the former holders, Byzantines, Venetians, Franks, Florentines, and others, during the interregnum period of eleven years that followed Bayezid's death.

It took until 1421 for the Ottomans to reorganize and build up enough strength to return to their campaigns in Europe, and in 1422 they again unsuccessfully besieged Constantinople. They also proceeded west and attacked Thessaloniki once more in 1430, now protected by a garrison of Venetian troops who held out vainly. The city was taken by force and its Greek inhabitants were slaughtered or taken into slavery. Under the circumstances, Ioannina wisely

---

* Edward S. Creasey, *History of the Ottoman Turks*, 1878.
** Edward Gibbon, *The Decline and Fall of the Roman Empire*, seven volumes, London, 1900.

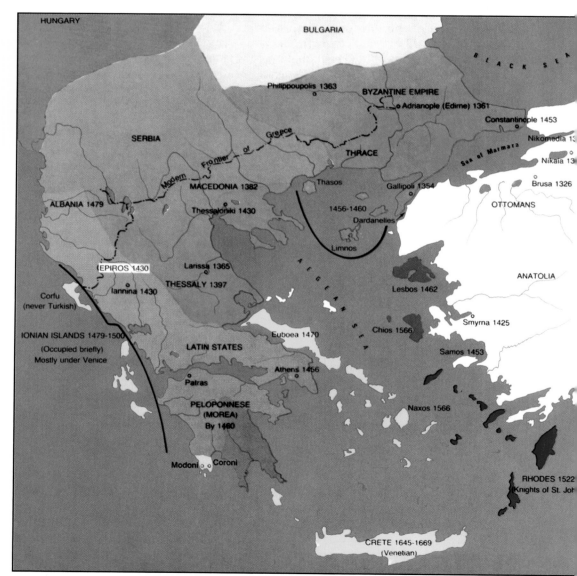

	Byzantine Empire		Latin States
	Bulgaria		Genoa
	Hungary		Venice
	Serbia		Knights of St. John

MAP 6.6 OTTOMAN CONQUEST OF GREECE (1354-1669)
The Byzantine Empire lost its dominions in Asia Minor to the Seljuk Turks. Another Turkish Muslim tribe, the Ottomans, crossed t
Hellespont and raided Thrace. This process was to continue largely unaffected by a greatly weakened Byzantine state. In the beginnin
the Ottomans did not remain in Greece, but they were back again, eventually to take and occupy the entire peninsula and much of t
Balkan area for several centuries.

HUNGARY

BULGARIA

BLACK SEA

Philippoupolis 1363

BYZANTINE EMPIRE

Adrianople (Edirne) 1361

Constantinople 1453

SERBIA

Frontier of Greece Modern

Nikomedia 1

Nikaia 13

THRACE

Sea of Marmara

MACEDONIA 1382

Thasos

Gallipoli 1354

Brusa 1326

ALBANIA 1479

Thessaloniki 1430

1456-1460

OTTOMANS

Dardanelles

Limnos

EPIROS 1430

Larissa 1365

AEGEAN SEA

ANATOLIA

Corfu
(never Turkish)

Iannina 1430

THESSALY 1397

Lesbos 1462

IONIAN ISLANDS 1479-1500
(Occupied briefly)
Mostly under Venice

LATIN STATES

Euboea 1470

Chios 1566

Smyrna 1425

Samos 1453

Athens 1456

Patras

PELOPONNESE
(MOREA)
By 1460

Naxos 1566

Modoni Coroni

RHODES 1522
Knights of St. Joh

CRETE 1645-1669
(Venetian)

surrendered in 1431. The Balkan countries again came under continuous attack from the Ottomans over the next twenty years. When peace terms were at last negotiated with them, the Turks were free to move south, by 1446 occupying the Greek peninsula down to and including the northern Peloponnese to Patras.

THE END OF THE EMPIRE

The last stage affecting the Ottoman conquests of Greece and what little was left of the Byzantine Empire now took place during the reign of Mehmed II (or Muhammad) (1451-1481), who became known as "the Conqueror." Sultan Mehmed was single-minded about taking Constantinople, now reduced to little more than a city-state in pitiful condition. He prepared well for what was to be the last siege of the Byzantine capital at the nadir of its former glory. Emperor Constantine XI Palaiologos mustered his meager remaining forces behind the city's still impressive defenses.

So desperate was Constantine that, against the wishes of his people, he appealed to the Pope in Rome to urgently send help by offering his last remaining asset, the unification of the two churches, which had always been desired by Rome (on its terms) and which had always been refused by the Byzantines. The offer was accepted this time and the union was actually proclaimed on December 12, 1452 in a special ceremony in the Haghia Sophia Cathedral. But the West was not of a mind on the price for this assistance. Most of the European leaders were determined to return Constantinople to Latin rule and not help save it for the Byzantines, notwithstanding the formal agreement to unite the two churches at last. At this late date, this church unification was more a gesture than a reality, for the Byzantine Empire was finished by this time. In the end, a contingent of only 1700 Genoese fighting men arrived before the fighting began. The Ottoman troops outnumbered the defenders by more than ten to one, and their navy five to one. The largest cannon ever made had been cast, to breach the previously impregnable walls of the city. Mehmed was fiercely determined not to fail this time. After 53 days of intense fighting on the walls and in the sea around they broke in at last and took the capital. The empire ceased to exist on May 29, 1453, as the Turkish troops rampaged without control on their customary three days of pillage; the desparate scene can hardly be imagined. The last Byzantine emperor died with his empire, fighting on the ramparts.

What parts of Greece were not already occupied by the Ottomans from earlier invasions were now fiercely attacked by Mehmed's armies. The price for daring to defend was annihilation, so that much of the remaining territory was taken by them without serious fighting on the part of either the Latin or Frankish feudal lords. But a number of areas nevertheless defended themselves with determination to equal that of the Ottomans. Rhodes under the Knights of St. John was heavily attacked in 1480 and would have been taken finally, except that Ottoman troops were denied the pillage of that island pending the arrival of the sultan, and they eventually withdrew. The knights held it for another 42 years. The Venetians in Crete were also able to resist. Nearly two centuries later in 1645, Crete was attacked again with more fierce determination. But the Venetians who had possession of it since 1204, were equally resolved to defend themselves, and it took twenty-five years for the Ottomans to capture it completely. As for Cyprus, this Greek island remained under Frankish rule until 1489, when Venice assumed control. In 1571, the Turkish armies of Selim II crushed the Greek and Venetian defenders of that last holdout, inflicting great slaughter in punishment for their resistance.

It would be of no satisfaction to the Greeks that in some ways they were to be better off under Turkish occupation than they had been under either the Franks or the various Italians, as will be seen in the pages that follow. But in fact it was another dark age for Greece and the population that remained there.

Seven

The Making
of the Modern
Greek State

THE GREEKS UNDER TURKISH RULE

AFTER THE CAPTURE OF CONSTANTINOPLE BY the Turks in 1453, nearly all the remaining areas occupied by Greeks came under Ottoman rule. The few remaining under the Venetians, Genoese, other Latins or Franks were soon to follow. Though Greek culture had captivated the vast Roman Empire and transformed it, the Muslim Turks were unmoved by it. Nor were they persuaded by Christianity. While the Ottomans did not believe in forcible conversion to Islam, and in fact their religion forbade it, Christians were treated as second-class citizens, and there were periods during which they were persecuted. Christian churches were often desecrated. But the Turks did not harm the Greek heritage of classical architecture in the occupied lands, which structures, however, had already suffered at the hands of other invaders before and the Latins more recently. The Parthenon on the hill of Akropolis, in Athens, which had already been converted by the Romans from a pagan shrine into a church in the sixth century, the Turks now converted into a mosque. The bell tower the Christians had built into one corner of the graceful temple the Turks converted into a minaret.

Greece itself is relatively barren, and very little of the terrain is arable so agricultural production was limited. Nevertheless, Greece was placed under Turkish governors whose principal duty on behalf of their government was to collect taxes. While there were many abuses and rights were few for the Greek population, for the most part if they obeyed the Ottoman laws they were left to their own devices. Under the more efficient feudal system of the Franks and the Venetians, life had been more harsh compared to the more casual, Oriental Turkish style of administration. But the Turkish government also did nothing for the people of the lands they occupied. They were rooted to the areas in which they lived and isolated from the rest of the world. Poverty was widespread, and survival was the primary goal for the great majority.

Yet some Greeks fared well under the Ottomans. While disdaining commerce themselves, the Turkish governors were still not about to discourage an increase in productivety and trade that increased their own incomes and the taxes they collected, if the Greeks had the ability to progress without any help. However, in many instances also, agricultural lands and businesses were under

Turkish ownership, using Greek labor and employees. Cotton and tobacco growing and processing in central Greece became sizable industries. A fur industry developed around Kastoria, in the north, and silk weaving in the towns of Mount Pelion (near Volos), both becoming large commercial enterprises. Activities related to the sea were largely in Greek hands, especially for those people living in the smaller, strategically placed islands relatively free from Turkish presence. Shipping combined those Greek talents of skillful boat-handling, fishing, and, especially, trade. Besides, being at sea was a chance to be out of the sight of the Turkish authorities.

Some of the Greeks who lived in the areas of Constantinople, Smyrna, and other parts of Asia Minor fared even better, especially from the eighteenth century on. The Turks found useful their commercial and diplomatic abilities and talent in languages, and many Greeks rose to prominence and wealth. It was a precarious status for them, however, since no matter how high they rose, they could be and sometimes they were summarily executed for real or imagined wrongs, and their fortunes (amassed after years of service) confiscated.

The Orthodox Church provided an important unifying element at this time, both in Greece and in Asia Minor. The Greek Patriarch in Constantinople was looked upon by the Turks as the ethnic leader of the Greeks, not just their spiritual leader. The church hierarchy, from archbishops to bishops to priests, were successive rallying centers for the Greek population, who had no other representatives or control of their destinies.

The largest part of the population in Greece considered themselves to be Greeks at least in terms of language and religion. But the Greek peninsula had gone from independent city-states in antiquity, to Roman, Franco-Venetian, Byzantine, and now Ottoman occupation — it never was a nation in the modern sense, to enable people to feel a sense of nationalism. Besides, during the nearly four centuries of Ottoman rule, many other people lived in Greece: among them, Vlachs, Serbs, Bulgars, Albanians, and Turks, and many languages were spoken in addition to Greek. It was not an atmosphere in which nationalism could easily take root and grow. Moreover, the Greeks were separated from their historic past by the very long passage of time, except for such few scholars as there were. The few architectural ruins that could be seen, dating from the Classical Period, imparted little feeling of Greek historical continuity to the viewer.

THE BATTLE OF LEPANTO

Yet, while the process of Greek national awareness took a very long time to manifest itself, there were a number of skirmishes and uprisings against Ottoman rule over the long period; however isolated, these had the effect of becoming a sporadic armed resistance to the Turkish rule. In addition, major battles on or near the Greek peninsula between the Ottomans and others, also raised Greek hopes of deliverance. One of these, the great naval battle of Lepanto (modern Nafpaktos, a small town on the Greek mainland across the bay northeast of Patras), took place on October 7, 1571. To stop Muslim Turkish ambitions in the western Mediterranean, a Holy League was formed by the Christian states of Spain, Venice, Genoa, and the Roman papacy. The combined fleet of more than 200 vessels sailed into the Gulf of Patras in Greece, and met an equal-sized Turkish navy off Lepanto. The battle resulted in the destruction of nearly all the Turkish ships and a loss of about 20,000 men, against 8,000 of the League's. While the Turks rebuilt their fleet in time, they cooled their aggressions westwards. This did not prevent them from finally conquering Crete from the Venetians, in 1669, after decades of trying. Also, Russia as the now dominent Orthodox power, was hostile to the Muslim Turks and supportive of the Orthodox Greeks, which fired their ambitions. Empress Catherine II (the Great) of Russia sent a fleet to western Greece in 1770, and her representatives induced the Greeks in the Peloponnese to mount a revolt against Turkish rule. But the meager support of Russia in manpower and arms, and Greek disorganization and lack of experience, failed against a superior Turkish army. Catherine quickly lost interest in the matter and the Greeks were abandoned to their fate. They suffered many cruel reprisals for their uprising, while the Russians were to continue their aggression against the Turks over many decades, but not in Greece.

PREPARATION FOR REVOLT

Towards the end of the eighteenth century, Ottoman rule began to weaken, for many political and economic reasons. As the Ottomans declined, the sense of Greekness strengthened even more, especially among Greek intellectuals living abroad such as Constantine Rhigas (Pheraios) and Adamantios Koraïs, themselves inspired by the French philosophers Voltaire and Rousseau. This reawakening of the spirit of nationalism from this and other sources brought on a desire for political freedom for Greece.

A coordinated effort to secure that freedom had not been previously possible. However, the movement for revolution against oppressive rule and independence from colonial dominion that began to pervade Europe and America late in the eighteenth century was not lost on the Greeks, both living in Greece and abroad. The American Revolution, with its stirring "Declaration of Independence" of 1776 and "Bill of Rights" resulted in the freedom of America from England by 1783. This was followed by the French Revolution, symbolized by the taking of the Bastille by a Paris mob July 14, 1789, and resulting in the issuance of the "Declaration of the Rights of Man and Citizen," (*Liberté, Egalité, Fraternité*). These and other movements to throw off the yoke of opression, began to even more intensify the desire for independence in Greece, too. Indeed, Napoleon's campaigns in Europe also resulted in the French occupation of the Ionian islands in 1797, ridding them of the Venetians under whose rule they had lived for nearly six centuries. While this did not exactly represent freedom, in a way this imparted a feeling that at least one part of Greece was finally being freed.*

Another group contributed strongly to the Greek revolutionary efforts to free themselves from the Turks, these being a group of distinguished Greek families known as the *Phanariotes*. A brief explanation of who they were and what they did will make this clear.

THE PHANARIOTES

The Greek Orthodox Patriarchate in Constantinople was, and still is, situated in the Phanar (meaning "lighthouse") district of the capital. Beginning in the sixteenth century, the Greeks that began to distinguish themselves in the Turkish court also had close contact with the Patriarch, who had been made ethnic leader of all the Greek people by the Turks. They began to build rich homes and settle themselves in the area surrounding the Patriarchate. They grew into a prosperous and influential aristocracy, becoming interdependent on each other by personal friendships and by means of intermarriages and mutual business interests. These Greeks became known as the "Phanariotes." Many sent their sons to study abroad, extending their usefulness and distinguishing themselves by being educated in languages, and in banking, medicine, and in other professions and services in demand at the Sultan's court. As a result, they also had the freedom to associate with and learn from other intellectuals abroad and to be exposed to the rise of awareness for political independence, applying it to their dreams for Greece.

Some Phanariotes became active in the Danubian provinces of Wallachia and Moldavia (in present-day Rumania), which was a self-governing Vlach area under Turkish suzerainty, but also of Greek Orthodox faith with the Patriarch in Constantinople as their spiritual leader. Through marriages into the royal Vlach families and investments during a century and a half, the Phanariotes exerted strong influence on these provinces. Thus, they insinuated themselves into the royal court and soon they virtually took over political and administrative leadership. This relatively free atmosphere where the Phanariote Greek rulers inherited the title of *Hospodars* (meaning Princes),** also gave them the opportunity to luxuriate in the idea of not just securing a free Greece but of reviving the Byzantine state.

Another element contributed to the independence movement both before and during the struggle that was to come. This was the redirection of the *Philiki Etairia*, or "Society of Friends," which was begun first as a social club of Greeks

---

* But real independence came hard. The French were driven out in 1800 by Russian-Turkish forces, which occupied the islands until 1807, when the French regained them. They were in turn ousted by the British in 1814, who declared the islands independent under their protection. They were ceded to Greece in 1864.

** While originally the title was hereditary, after 1730, it had to be bought at auction from the Turkish Sultans, who used this means to raise their personal income, hence the princes were deposed and new ones appointed or former ones reappointed, with great regularity.

abroad. At a meeting in 1814, in Odessa, Russia, where many prominent Greeks lived, it also became a secret revolutionary political body, with many distinguished members also dedicated to the idea of returning Greece to the "former Christian glory of Byzantium." Of course, among them were many of the Phanariotes. By the time the revolution began in 1821, the *Etairia* had spread throughout Greece, in eastern and western cities and capitals, and in Asia Minor, with thousands of members, various grades of membership, and secret signs.

None of the groups aspiring for the liberation of Greece could hope to achieve success without the help of the Greeks themselves actually living in their subjected country. A key group among these was a large number of patriots or outlaws or volunteers that had become bands of armed brigands living in the rough mountainous regions or other remote areas throughout Greece, out of sight of the Turkish authorities. They were collectively known as *klephtes* (klephts), since they stealthily preyed on rich Turks or Greek collaborators, or *armatoloi* (armed men), who had been recruited by the Turks as Greek civil guards, some of whom had turned klephts, secretly or actually. Many of their *kapetanaioi* (captains or commanders) had also been sworn into the *Philiki Etairia*. Among them were Makriyannis, Athanasios Diakos, Theodoros Kolokotronis, and Markos Botsaris. Some others ready to serve the cause were admirals Andreas Miaoulis and Konstantinos Kanaris, who were to command ships furnished principally by the islanders of Spetsai, Hydra, and Psara. By the time the revolution began in 1821, many of these Greek fighting men and leaders had been organized and armed by the *Etairia*.

The timing of the events to free Greece were greatly influenced by the attack of the Turkish army in mid-1820 against the rebellious Albanian Ali Pasha, powerful Turkish governor of the large province of Epiros who controlled all of northern Greece from the Adriatic to the Aegean Seas. A cruel, treacherous, and self-serving conniver, he actually became a member of the *Etairia* while serving Sultan Mahmoud II. No doubt he was prepared to take personal advantage whatever would be the outcome of the events. But Ali allowed himself to wage a personal vendetta against important figures of the Sultan's court, and the furious Sultan finally ordered him deposed — which was to take a major war to accomplish. The Greeks saw this as an opportunity to press their cause, with the Turkish forces withdrawn from their garrisons throughout Greece and fully engaged against the armies of Ali Pasha.

THE REVOLT AGAINST THE TURKS
(1821-1833)

Early in 1820, the *Philiki Etairia* had given the leadership of the revolution to Prince Alexander Ypsilantis, a Greek of a notable Phanariote family originally from the Turkish-ruled Danubian provinces. The Ypsilantis family leaders had been passionate to liberate Greece for three generations, for which reason they had been living in exile from Turkey in Russia. After Constantinople fell to the Ottomans, Greek Orthodox Russia had become the patron of the Orthodox Greeks. As a powerful christian country whose rulers opposed Muslim Turkey, she welcomed as residents many prominent Greeks who became exiled to escape the Sultan's displeasure, as well as many other Greeks who made their homes there. Some of these became officials in the tsar's court. Alexander Ypsilantis had become a general in the Russian army and aide-de-camp to the Tsar; his brother Dimitrios was also a high officer in the Russian army. The time had come at last when the Greeks of Russia and other countries (the Greeks of the Diaspora) had to move forward.

The first plans of the *Etairia* leaders, meeting in Russia with Alexander Ypsilantis, were to invade the Peloponnese (Morea). Altering this plan, they decided to send an invasion force led by Alexander into the Ottoman-ruled Danubian principalities, whose Vlach people were also largely Greek Orthodox, counting on an uprising of all these Christians there. At the same time, Ypsilantis' brother, Dimitrios, proceeded to organize an uprising of the Greeks in the Peloponnese, to take place if Alexander's efforts should be successful. Alexander assembled his forces of some 4,500 volunteers at Jassy, in Moldavia, near the Russian border. Since the plan was now to begin the insurrection against the Ottoman rule starting in the Danubian principalities, the volunteers consisted of Greek officers leading Moldavians, Wallachians, Serbs, Bulgars, and other Balkans, as well as about 700 Greek students. Unfortunately they were not experienced in warfare, and were poorly organized and poorly armed.

To help promote a simultaneous uprising of the Vlach and Greek populations, Alexander Ypsilantis hinted that Russia was backing his effort. In early March 1821, his volunteers proceeded south, fighting some skirmishes and raiding and killing any Turkish merchants and landowners they came across, in the anti-Turkish fanaticism of some of the volunteers. By June, his rough forces reached Dragatsani, in Wallachia, where the Turkish army had assembled (without interference from the Russians, and indeed with their knowledge) and was waiting for them, and the volunteers were massacred. Leaders of other irregular forces in the principalities were not prepared to shed blood for the Greek cause, and the populations did not rise up as Ypsilantis had expected, so this first effort to lift the Turkish yoke was nearly stillborn and was fought entirely out of Greece in present-day Rumania. Ypsilantis himself escaped to Austria where he was imprisoned by a government there that was not prepared to harbor revolutionaries against the Ottoman regime. Becoming a victim also of larger political interests, the Tsar disowned him and forbade his return to Russia. Pressured by the Sultan, even the Greek Patriarch in Constantinople excommunicated him to distance the Greek population from this catastrophe and try to save them from retribution from the Turks. (Seven years later, he was to be released at the request of another Russian tsar. He went to live in Vienna, where he died in poverty soon after at age 36.)

"LIBERTY OR DEATH"

Duduring those days of early March, the Greek Orthodox Metropolitan bishop Germanos of Patras had been ordered to report to the quarters of the Turkish governor of the Peloponnese at Tripolitsa. Stopping at Kalavrita on the way he learned about the uprising and seeing that revolt was in the air, the Metropolitan realized that there was no way that events could be reversed. On March 25, 1821, he seized the initiative, and raising the cross as a standard at the monastery of Aghia Lavra nearby, he called on all the Greeks to fight for their independence.

Early in March, when the revolt under the Alexander Ypsilantis became known in Constantinople and spies reported the unrest in the Peloponnese, the Sultan ordered the arrest of the Greek Orthodox Patriarch Gregory V as the ethnic leader of the Greeks, capturing as well two metropolitans and twelve bishops and the leading Phanariotes. Shortly later they were all hung; and many other Greeks, clerics, and private citizens alike were killed by the Turks in the wild bloodbath that took place in the Greek quarters of Constantinople, as well as in other cities in Turkey. By May, the Phanar was no more. The cruelty of the Turks was protested by world leaders.

Some 64,000 Turks were living in the Peloponnese (estimated at 16 percent of the total population) when the war broke out in 1821. Many already lived in or fled to the fortified port towns of Patras, Rion, Corinthos, Nauplia, Tripolitsa, Monemvasia, Koroni, Methoni, and Navarino. The garrison town of Kalamata was the first to fall to the Greeks. In April 1821, battles broke out everywhere. So fierce was the struggle — "Liberty or Death" was the slogan — that more than half of the Turks in the Peloponnese lost their lives in the first weeks of the war. The Turks treated the Greeks equally without mercy, and tens of thousands were killed by them. Early in 1822, in a particularly violent act of vengeance, the Turks invaded the island of Chios, in the eastern Aegean, and slaughtered about 25,000 Chiotes and took as slaves another 50,000 out of a total population of about 100,000. The event was immortalized by the French painter Eugène Delacroix in his "The Massacre of Scio" (Chios), which hangs in the Louvre Museum in Paris. The trials and suffering of the Greeks to achieve their freedom attracted sympathy and support worldwide.

The plight of the Greeks gave rise to another group called the "Philhellenes." Many of these individuals, originating from countries throughout Europe and from America, had an idealistic view of Greece based on its classical history. Some had military backgrounds and gave a measure of military leadership and organization to the hit-and-run style of the guerilla bands of the Greeks. Well known literary figures such as Lord Byron and Shelley also lent their names publicly to the cause.

Byron gave more. He arrived in Greece in January, 1824, in his romantic imagination to lead Greek fighters against the Turks. But he was also appointed to disburse funds for the cause whenever they should beome available, to be collected from English sympathizers by the newly-formed Greek Committee of London. Some of his own funds (actually sums borrowed, he was relatively broke) were made available by him. The Greek leaders anticipation of his "great wealth" made him the target of much pressure. He became exposed to the complexities of dealing with these sharp and eager Greeks, but he was never to see to the end or success of his idealistic, heroic, and romantic endeavors. He fantasized that he would give his life bravely for Greek freedom. But he was in ill health, suffering from a morbid fear of epilepsy and general hypochondria. He began to be greatly frustrated and depressed being unable to be useful and he began to uselessly expose himself to the inclement weather and tire himself unnecessarily "to harden his body." He died rather less dramatically three months later of general weakness ending with uremic poisoning, in Mesolongi, aged 36. Even the funds expected from London never arrived before his death. But his greatest contribution to the cause was that the death of this celebrated young poet brought even more world attention to the Greek struggle.

The Greeks were determined to gain their freedom with suicidal courage despite meager resources, and the Turks were equally determined to put down the revolt. The struggle was to last without let-up for eight years. For ease of understanding, the events it can be divided into three periods:

1821 to 1825: The Greeks Alone

1825 to 1827: The Egyptian Invasion

1827 to 1833: European Intervention

THE GREEKS ALONE
(1821-1825)

It was not possible for the many strong-minded Greek leaders who contributed greatly to the war effort to cooperate with each other to create a nation. There was little experience in statesmanship and public administration, and no past history of a Greek nation on which to draw. At this time, key figures included the fierce klepht captains accustomed to their autocratic ways, whose bands of loyal *palikaria* (braves) were doing much of the fighting and who expected to derive future benefits from their efforts. Also involved were a number of eminent Phanariotes who joined the cause, including the Ypsilantis brothers, Alexander and Dimitrios (mentioned above), Prince Alexander Mavrokordatos, Theodore Negris, and many others. Prominent landowners and islanders had their own cores of strength, and political prejudices. The Greek Orthodox church leaders were also participating and had their own strong views. These divergent and parochial antagonists ended up in civil war, and some important leaders retired in disgust, even while the Ottoman enemy was still to be defeated. There had been no historical precedent that might have enabled these parties to decide on a common destiny for a new country of Greece and for their roles in it.

During all these internecine problems, the Peloponnese had nevertheless been virtually liberated by the end of 1824, and the various factions tried to form

MAP 7.0 REVOLT AGAINST THE TURKS: FIRST PERIOD (1821-1825)

e revolt of the Greeks against the Turkish occupation of four centuries began in the Peloponnese on March 25, 1821. Over the
xt four years, the Greeks took nearly all of this area in bloody battles, except for a few fortified port cities.

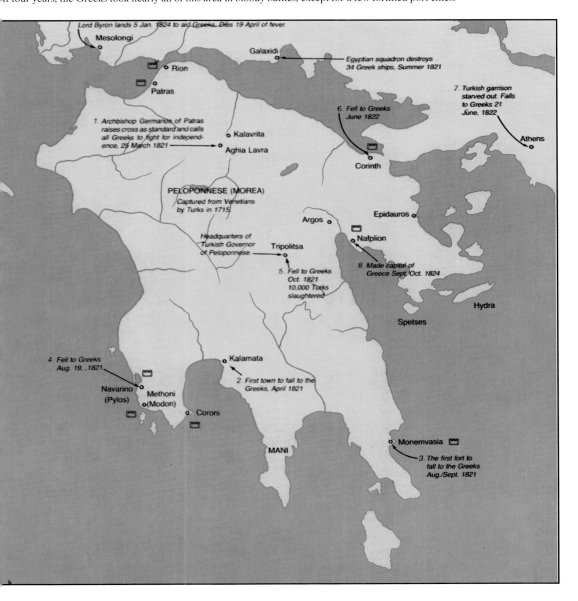

Lord Byron lands 5 Jan. 1824 to aid Greeks. Dies 19 April of fever.

Mesolongi

Galaxidi

Rion

Egyptian squadron destroys
34 Greek ships, Summer 1821

Patras

6. Fell to Greeks
June 1822

7. Turkish garrison
starved out. Falls
to Greeks 21
June, 1822

1. Archbishop Germanos of Patras
raises cross as standard and calls
all Greeks to fight for independence, 25 March 1821

Kalavrita

Aghia Lavra

Athens

Corinth

PELOPONNESE (MOREA)
Captured from Venetians
by Turks in 1715.

Argos

Epidauros

Headquarters of
Turkish Governor
of Peloponnese.

Nafplion

Tripolitsa

5. Fell to Greeks
Oct. 1821
10,000 Turks
slaughtered

8. Made capital of
Greece Sept./Oct. 1824

Hydra

Spetses

4. Fell to Greeks
Aug. 19, ,1821

Kalamata

2. First town to fall to the
Greeks, April 1821

Navarino
(Pylos)

Methoni
(Modon)

Coroni

MANI

Monemvasia

3. The first fort to
fall to the Greeks
Aug./Sept. 1821

a constitution and a central Greek government, but with no real success. Meanwhile, Sultan Mahmoud II asked Mehmet Ali, Turkish Pasha of Egypt (born in Kavala, Greece, of an Albanian father), to intervene with his fleet and powerful forces. The price for this involvement was high. Mehmet Ali was to receive the *pashalik* (province) of Crete immediately. If his forces won, he would also be given the *pashalik* of Syria for himself; and for his able son Ibrahim Pasha, who would lead the forces, all of the Morea (Peloponnese).

THE EGYPTIAN INVASION
(1825-1827)

In February, 1825, the Egyptians landed a large invasion force at Methoni, in the southwest corner of the Peloponnese, one of the few forts remaining in Turkish control. The progress of the invading Muslim forces was rapid and devastating, and within a year most of the Peloponnese was retaken by them. Mesolongi also fell in April, 1826, after a very long siege, in punishment for which the Muslims massacred 10,000 of the 12,000 inhabitants (of which only 3,000 had been combatants). To a lesser extent but no less brutal, towns in the Peloponnese, elsewhere on the mainland, and on the islands suffered "sword, smoke and slavery." Athens fell in August 1826, though the Akropolis held out a few more months. The atrocities brought more world attention to the area.

The severe plight of the Greeks, especially under the destruction wrought by Ibrahim Pasha's forces, continued to arouse the conscience of the world. Public sympathy was one thing, securing aid from governments was another. For some time, it had been obvious that however bravely the Greeks fought for Greece's independence, aided by the Philhellenes, their own factionalism and the superior Muslim forces could not be overcome without additional help from the Great Powers of Europe. Of these, England, France, and Russia were the principal countries with interests in the area, each with policies of their own and suspicious of the others' motives. While they were generally sympathetic toward the Greeks, they were by no means entirely against Turkey. They finally concurred on a first action, however, to stop the fighting. Expanding on political activities begun earlier, the Three Powers signed a treaty in London on July 6, 1827, to seek mediation with Turkey on behalf of the Greeks, and created a combined naval fleet to enforce the armistice when it came.

The fleet had specific orders to remain out of the hostilities. Ibrahim Pasha's naval force was operating out of Navarino Bay (in the western Peloponnese near modern Pylos), supplying and supporting his troops. Ibrahim was asked by the admirals of the Powers' fleet that he respect the armistice. For some reason, he failed to respond. On October 20, 1827, the European fleet sailed into Navarino Bay to confront the Turkish-Egyptian fleet anchored in a semicircle. The tense atmosphere was suddenly broken when someone on an Egyptian vessel fired on a small boat from an English warship whose occupants

MAP 7.1 REVOLT AGAINST THE TURKS: SECOND PERIOD (1825-1827)

e Turks arranged with their governor in Egypt, Mehmet Ali, to send an invasion force to retake the Peloponnese. Led by his son Ibrahim
sha, they nearly succeeded. Finally, the Egyptian fleet, assembled in the harbor at Navarino, was approached by a large British, French,
d Russian fleet, sent to assure a ceasefire. A minor incident led to general cannonfire, destroying the Egyptian fleet and ending the war.

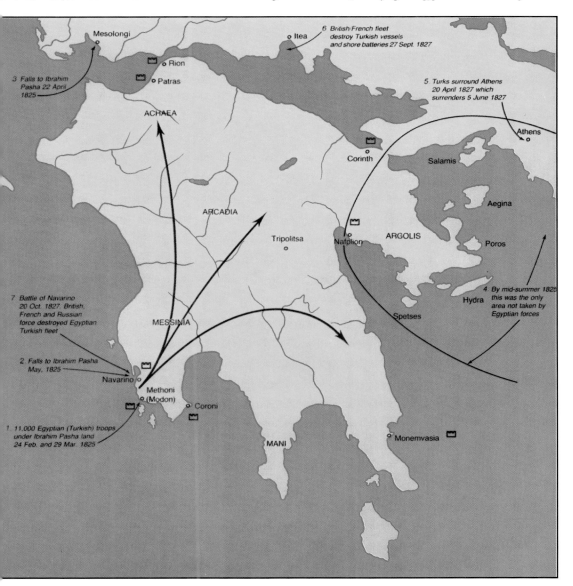

Mesolongi

o Itea

6 British/French fleet
destroy Turkish vessels
and shore batteries 27 Sept. 1827

Rion

o Patras

3 Falls to Ibrahim
Pasha 22 April
1825

ACHAEA

5 Turks surround Athens
20 April 1827 which
surrenders 5 June 1827

Athens
o

Corinth

Salamis

ARCADIA

Aegina

Tripolitsa
o

Nafplion

ARGOLIS

Poros

4 By mid-summer 1825
this was the only
area not taken by
Egyptian forces

Hydra

7 Battle of Navarino
20 Oct. 1827. British,
French and Russian
force destroyed Egyptian
Turkish fleet

MESSINIA

Spetses

2 Falls to Ibrahim Pasha
May, 1825

Navarino o

Methoni
o (Modon)

o Coroni

1. 11,000 Egyptian (Turkish) troops
under Ibrahim Pasha land
24 Feb. and 29 Mar. 1825

o Monemvasia

MANI

were sent to parley with them. General cannonfire immediately broke out that lasted for several hours. At the end of the shooting, two-thirds of the Muslim vessels had been sunk or were sinking and many thousands of their sailors killed. The Powers suffered damage but no vessels sunk and fewer than 200 of their men killed. This destruction of Muslim forces signalled that the days of the Ottoman occupation of Greece were numbered.

EUROPEAN INTERVENTION
(1827-1833)

The three European Powers in the Treaty of London of July, 1827, had agreed to seek autonomy for Greece under the Ottomans rather than outright independence. Their failure to get the Porte* to agree to an armistice, let alone autonomy, even after the battle of Navarino, led England, France, and Russia to withdraw their ambassadors from Constantinople in December, 1827. Russia went further, declaring war on Turkey in April, 1828. After suffering a number of defeats, the Turks agreed to a list of provisions favoring Russian interests in the area, but also including a basis for negotiating a peace agreement with Greece. The war ended in September, 1829.

The Navarino incident also hastened action by the Greeks to better organize themselves. In April, 1827, the various Greek factions managed to unite their interests long enough to elect as their first president for a seven-year term Count Giovanni Antonio Capo d'Istria (1776-1831, his name later Hellenized to Ioannis Kapodistrias). He hailed from an aristocratic Italian family from Istria, a Venetian region southeast of Trieste, who had settled in Corfu since 1373, where Kapodistrias was eventually born. (The title had been given to the family in 1689 by the Duke of Savoy.) Kapodistrias entered government service in Corfu at an early age, and his career finally brought him into diplomatic service first in Corfu and then in Russia at the invitation of the Russian Tsar during the time the Russians were involved with Corfu (1800-1807). He was an experienced politician, having served Tsar Alexander I of Russia as joint foreign minister for several years beginning1816. Kapoditrias had been a supporter of the Greek cause from the beginning but had not agreed with the opening strategy of Alexander Ypsilantis in the Danubian principalities. Kapodistrias now arrived in Nauplia on January 19, 1828, to take up his duties, after touring European capitals to seek assistance for Greece.

Although influential in European circles, Kapodistrias' aristocratic ways antagonized many of his own countrymen, notwithstanding his capabilities and zeal on behalf of Greece. For that matter, it is unlikely that anyone would have done better under the circumstances. Frequent disagreements among the various Greek leaders resulted in fighting that often came close to outright civil war. In

---

*In French, the *Sublime Porte*, or "High Gate," where the principal Ottoman government offices were located. Hence, "Porte" became synonymous with the government of Turkey.

MAP 7.2 REVOLT AGAINST THE TURKS: THIRD PERIOD (1827-1833)

Despite internal political dissension among the Greek leaders, the European Powers finally obtained the agreement from Turkey for the independence of a part of Greece, the freedom of which they would guarantee. Assassination of the first Greek president resulted in the Powers selecting a king to rule Greece, seventeen-year-old Prince Otto of Bavaria.

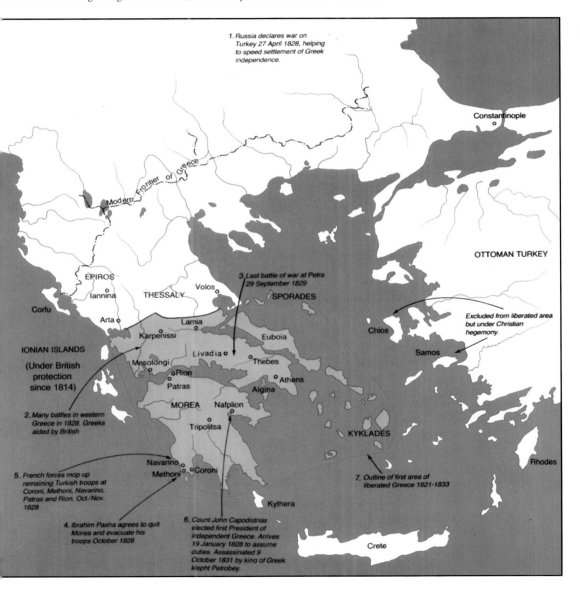

1. Russia declares war on Turkey 27 April 1828, helping to speed settlement of Greek independence.

Constantinople

Modern Frontier of Greece

OTTOMAN TURKEY

EPIROS
Iannina

Volos

3. Last battle of war at Petra 29 September 1829

THESSALY

SPORADES

Corfu

Arta

Lamia

Karpenissi

Euboia

Chios

Excluded from liberated area but under Christian hegemony.

IONIAN ISLANDS

(Under British protection since 1814)

Livadia

Mesolongi
Rion
Patras

Thebes

Athens

Samos

MOREA   Nafplion

Aigina

2. Many battles in western Greece in 1828. Greeks aided by British

Tripolitsa

KYKLADES

5. French forces mop up remaining Turkish troops at Coroni, Methoni, Navarino, Patras and Rion, Oct./Nov. 1828

Navarino
Methoni   Coroni

7. Outline of first area of liberated Greece 1821-1833

Rhodes

Kythera

4. Ibrahim Pasha agrees to quit Morea and evacuate his troops October 1828

6. Count John Capodistrias elected first President of independent Greece. Arrives 19 January 1828 to assume duties. Assassinated 9 October 1831 by king of Greek klepht Petrobey.

Crete

early 1831, Kapodistrias was compelled to order the arrest of Petrobey Mavromichalis, a guerilla leader from the Mani peninsula. As a result and under the hard mountain code of the Mani, Petrobey's brother and his own son Georgos assassinated Kapodistrias on October 9, 1831, on his way to Sunday church service. Civil war again broke out in Greece, the Ottoman enemy all but forgotten.

As a solution to the Greek political problems, the Powers had in mind for several years to appoint a neutral leader in the person of a hereditary king to rule Greece. This king would be selected from a European royal family excluding their own. Indeed, most of the Greek leaders themselves were in favor of it, with the exception of Kapodistrias, who had seen himself as already heading the Greek state as president. His death and the chaotic events that followed hastened the need to select a monarch. In mid-1832, the Powers finally agreed to give the throne to Prince Otto, the 17-year-old second son of King Ludwig I of Bavaria. He arrived in Nauplia at the end of January 1833 on a British naval frigate. The appointment of the king also carried with it the independence of Greece within borders selected by and under the protection and guarantee of the Three Powers. The Greece of 1833 would consist of the Peloponnese, an area of the mainland between and south of the Greek cities of Arta and Volos, and the islands immediately adjacent in the Aegean (see map 7.2). The Greeks wanted more territory, of course, but this was the final decision of the Powers — a decision to choose between a small Greece that would be fully independent or a larger Greece that would remain a vassal state. It would take another series of struggles and more European intervention for Greece to achieve its present boundaries.

THE FIRST DECADES OF GREEK INDEPENDENCE
(1833-1910)

Four centuries under Ottoman ocupation did not prepare the Greeks for self-government at the national level. As it turned out, nor was the leadership to come from 17-year-old Prince Otto of Bavaria, who had been selected by Britain, France, and Russia to be the King of Greece. Being inexperienced as well as underage, he was accompanied on his arrival by a regency of three senior Bavarian ministers. Conditions of civil unrest in the country were such that 3,500 Bavarian troops also arrived with the young king in early February, 1833.

It was not long before most key posts in the government were occupied by Bavarians. Naturally, Greek leaders who had fought in the war for independence were resentful. Some of the stronger Greek personalities were neutralized by being sent abroad as ambassadors. The Bavarian control and autocratic style were especially annoying to the Greek "democratic" outlook and independent character. The drawing up of a constitution was not progressed, although it had been agreed that this should be prepared at the time the king was appointed. This discontent finally erupted in a bloodless revolt in September, 1843. The Bavarian ministers were dismissed and the Bavarian officers remaining were sent home. The king was forced to form a national assembly and order the preparation of a constitution. While a major popular objective had been achieved, the resulting constitution was largely ignored by Otto to the continued discontent of his subjects. Nevertheless, a government of Greek nationals had beeen installed.

The Greece that was formed in 1833 contained a population of about 800,000. Another two million or so Greeks lived in the surrounding area under continued Ottoman domination, and others on the Ionian Islands under British control. Greek leaders dreamed of a Greece that would include all these people and the areas in which they lived: the Ionian islands, Thessaly, Epiros, Macedonia, and Thrace, the Anatolian coast, the Aegean islands and Crete. This concept became known as "The Great Idea." While strongly supported by Otto, this concept at the same time fed Greek dreams and aspirations and served to distract the populace from more difficult everyday matters.

In 1853, Russia committed yet another of its many aggressive acts against a weakening Ottoman Empire, in its desire to gain access to eastern Europe and the Black Sea. When Russia invaded Turkey's Danubian principalities ostensibly as protector of the Eastern Orthodox Christian faith, Turkey declared war and was subsequently joined by Britain and France, which now feared Russia's expansionist aims. Known as the Crimean War, this was to last until 1856. The Greeks saw this as an opportunity to liberate more territory of Greece and sent a large body of guerillas to occupy Thessaly on its northern border. Turkey reacted by breaking off relations with the Greek government, and in reprisal expelling many Greeks who had been living in Constantinople and Smyrna. Greek army units also joined the irregulars but were defeated by the Turks in two battles. To prevent Greece from declaring war on Turkey, in May, 1854, Britain and France sent troops to occupy Piraeus, remaining there until 1857.

Greek resentment against Otto continued even more strongly for his being unwilling or unable to further Greek irredentist aims and for his flagrant disregard of the 1844 constitution. This discontent manifested itself in 1861 in an attempt to assassinate Queen Amalia; and in 1862 incidents led to two revolts against the king. The second of these revolts took place when Otto and Amalia were travelling in the Peloponnese, and were prevented from returning to Athens. The National Assembly quickly met and deposed the king, and the three Protecting Powers were finally forced to advise him to step down from the Greek throne. The king and queen reluctantly returned to their native Bavaria. Otto never abdicated and continued to express his love and intense interest for Greece. He died in Bavaria five years later. He had been king for nearly three decades.

The new constitution was voted in by the Greek National Assembly in 1864 under a provisional government. It gave more power to the people within a "crowned democracy." The assembly also confirmed a new king selected by the Powers, Otto and Amalia having left no heirs. This was another 17-year-old, Prince George, the second son of a member of the Danish royal family who was later to become King of Denmark. The new king became George I, "King of the Hellenes," rather than "King of the Greeks" as Otto had been named, in respect of Turkish sensitivities about the many Ottoman Greeks who did not live in Hellas itself. In March, 1864, in a goodwill gesture, Britain ceded the Ionian islands to Greece, which had been under her protection since 1815. This added a sizeable population to Greece, which by this time had grown to over a million.

The Ottoman possessions in the Balkans and Crete continued to press for independence. Crete revolted in 1866, as it had many times in the past and would again in the future, and once more called for union with Greece. The revolt lasted until 1869, and the Ottomans treated the Cretans harshly, with the Greeks unable to help. When the Balkan provinces of Bosnia and Herzegovina revolted against the Turks in 1876, at Russian instigation the Serbs and the Montenegrins came to their aid, but they were crushed by Turkish forces. Russia then entered the war in 1877.

Efforts to Gain Thessaly

These years were an especially troubled time for Greece. She realized that Russian interests in the area were increasingly linked with those of Bulgaria. With the new Russo-Turkish war, Greece moved to advance her own national interests, and she mobilized her armies, sending irregulars into Thessaly once again. This was short-lived as Turkey and Russia agreed on an armistice in February 1878. The peace terms were clearly against Greek interests, but, fortunately, Britain and Austria also objected to an enlargement of Russian influence in the area. Another peace agreement was forced on Russia that modified the terms, reducing the original intention of giving newly-autonomous Bulgaria access to the Aegean. Most of Macedonia, Montenegro, Serbia, and Rumania now also became independent, and Britain concluded an agreement with Turkey whereby Britain would administer Cyprus, from where she could keep a closer watch on Russian ambitions.

Greece gained nothing from all these agreements and changes, nor were her requests given much attention concerning the Greek-inhabited areas of Epiros, Thessaly, Macedonia, and Crete. Turkish reluctance to consider Greek demands even though the Powers were in favor, led the frustrated Greeks to mobilize again in 1880. The Powers intervened once again and forced the Greeks and the Turks to negotiate an agreement in May 1881, finally gave Thessaly to Greece as well as the Arta region of Epiros. Another 300,000 people were added and a quarter more territory.

National Bankruptcy

Events during the next two decades or so were dominated by the rivalry of two Greek prime ministers who alternated with each other in office several times. Charilaos Trikoupis was a British-style liberal whose conservative economic and political reforms were constantly undone by the demagogic Theodoros Deliyannis. The faltering Greek economy was supported by a number of heavily discounted foreign loans, the debt-servicing of which required nearly half of the total budget by 1893. Trikoupis was finally compelled to declare national bankruptcy.

Yet another revolt on Crete in 1896 led to political as well as additional financial disaster. By early 1897, the Greeks sent troops to Crete, and by April war was declared on Turkey. Troops led by Crown Prince Constantine were now sent to the northern borders. His younger brother, Prince George, commanded the troops sent to Crete. The Turks crushed the weaker forces under Constantine, bringing great antipathy by the people for the royal family. But on Crete the Great Powers intervened to prevent bloodshed and were able to convince Turkey to grant autonomy to Crete while remaining under Turkish suzerainty, with Prince George appointed high commissioner. Adjustments were also made to the northern borders for defense purposes, and Greece was forced to return to Turkey again some small areas of the territory in Thessaly she had gained in 1881. Moreover, she was forced to pay Turkey reparations of four million Turkish pounds, which she could not afford at all.

The next few years saw much guerilla action from the Greeks, Serbs, and Bulgars, each of whom tried to increase their influence on Ottoman-controlled Macedonia, and the Turks fighting all of these. Crete, too, witnessed continued discontent, not having gained her much-coveted union with Greece during the eight years Prince George served as high commissioner. He resigned in 1906 in a dispute with a strong Cretan politician from whom much more would be heard, Eleftherios Venizelos (b.1864-d.1936).

In Macedonia, another revolution was born, specifically in Thessaloniki, this time against the Turkish Sultan Abdul Hamid II, by young Ottoman officers of the military stationed there who became known as the "Young Turks." This event in July, 1908, was taken advantage of by the Cretans a month later, resulting in another declaration for union with Greece by the Cretan assembly. A military revolt in Greece headed by a group called the "Military League," in part inspired by the actions and success of the Young Turks, toppled a weak Greek government in mid-1909. After imposing a number of reforms, the Military League finally dissolved itself in favor of Venizelos, who was summoned to Athens inviting him to become Prime Minister of Greece in October, 1910.

The problems of a disastrous Greek economy with widespread unemployment beginning around 1890 and until the first World War, led to extensive emigration, almost entirely to the United States. Some 350,000 left their country, amounting to a fifth of the total population. About an equal number of Greeks also emigrated from adjacent Greek populated areas still under Ottoman occupation, proceeding to America as well.

THE BALKAN WARS
(1912 and 1913)

The making of Greece, its territorial growth, its role in World War I, and in some considerable measure the disaster that was to come in Asia Minor in 1922, are all inextricably associated with the person of Prime Minister Eleftherios Venizelos. As a political leader he contributed greatly in achieving autonomy for his native Crete by November, 1898. First

MAP 7.3 FIRST BALKAN WAR (1912-1913)

Greece persisted in its efforts to regain areas occupied by Turkey containing Greek nationals. She allied herself with the Balkan Christia
states of Montenegro, Serbia, and Bulgaria, also seeking their freedom from the Ottoman Turks. In a first Balkan War, they drov
Turkey nearly entirely out of Europe.

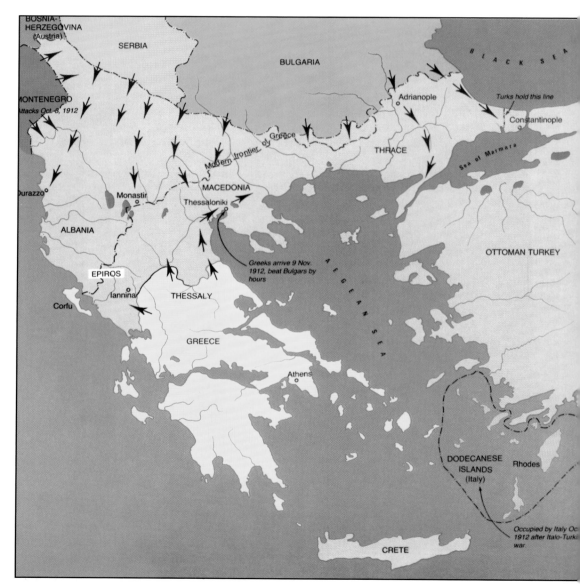

MAP 7.4 **SECOND BALKAN WAR** (1913)

change of government in Turkey renewed the war. Greece and Serbia did not trust Bulgarian ambitions. This second war won
them settled their control of territories, and Turkey retook a part of eastern Thrace from Bulgaria. Albania was created by the
reat Powers to keep Serbia out of the Adriatic.

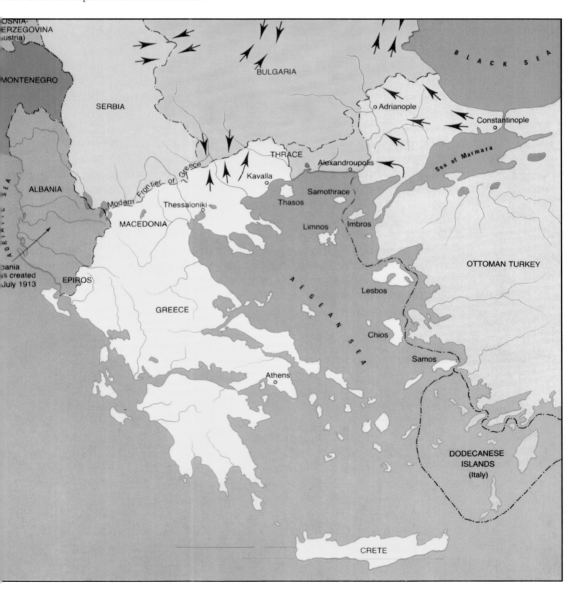

called to form a government in Athens in 1910, he continued to dominate Greek politics for more than two decades. He was prime minister several times during this period. His policies regarding the Balkans and against Ottoman Turkey ultimately resulted in freeing northern Greece and the large islands of the eastern Aegean, as well as Crete. When his influence finally waned, after a lifetime in Greek politics, he went into a self-imposed exile to Paris in 1932, where he died in 1936, aged 72.

The Young Turks revolt of 1908 sought a number of reforms in their country and reinstatement of the 1876 Turkish constitution. But this further disruption contributed to the already substantial weakening of the Ottoman government and set a number of events into motion. Taking advantage of the circumstances, Bulgaria declared her independence; Austria annexed Bosnia and Herzegovina; the Serbs and the Montenegrins plotted their independence, as well; the Albanians revolted; and the Cretans once again declared their union with Greece.

The ambitions of another government were also set into motion at this time, that would eventually contribute greatly to the problems of Greece. Italy was seeking colonies abroad to settle her substantial population. Taking advantage of Turkey's internal problems and the revolts in that country's Balkan territories, Italy declared war on Turkey in 1911 and sent troops to occupy Turkey's possessions in Libya. The Italians also attacked Turkish forts in the Dardanelles and occupied the unprotected Greek-populated Dodecanese islands off the southwest Asia Minor coast, strategically located for Italy's next steps to come. Peace was declared in 1912, but Italy continued to occupy the islands under the terms of the settlement with Turkey. Italy also had ambitions regarding Albanian territory as far south as the province of Epiros, the southern portion of which had a substantial Greek population and which area Greece also coveted. How these interests would affect Greece are developed in the paragraphs that follow.

The Balkan League

In the meantime, Greece and the Balkan nations were combining their forces into a Balkan League to force Turkey to release the areas containing their own nationals, and to insure superior strength against Turkish armies. Many thousands of Greek volunteers of the Diaspora returned to their homeland to fight for Greece, most of them from the United States. On October 8, 1912, Montenegro attacked, Serbia and Bulgaria declared war on the seventeenth, and the Greeks on the eighteenth. The Turkish forces were overwhelmed. Within two weeks they were being driven out of Europe. The Bulgarians occupied northern Macedonia and Thrace and were pushing toward Constantinople; the Serbians were forcing the Turks out of Serbia; and the Greeks were taking possession of the remaining areas occupied by Greeks in Thessaly and western Macedonia. The Greeks and the Bulgars conflicted over the occupation of Macedonia and its principal city of

Thessaloniki. The Greeks entered the city abandoned by the Turks only hours before the Bulgars would have been there. The Greeks also sent an army into Epiros to liberate this area, including Ioannina, its largest city; and the Greek navy took control of the Aegean.

Two months later, the Turks sued for peace, and although the Balkan allies signed an armistice with Turkey on December 3, 1912, Greece refused to join in, not having liberated all the areas she desired. The Young Turks objected to the peace terms and took over by force from the Turkish government that had signed the armistice, renewing the war in January. The Balkan allies continued to overwhelm the Turkish forces, and hostilities were brought to a halt again in May.

But this was not the end of the war. The Serbs and the Greeks suspected Bulgarian ambitions, and in June 1913, they signed a mutual defense pact. As they had anticipated, Bulgaria attacked the Serbs to gain more territory, and the Greeks and the Serbs drove them out of Macedonia and western Thrace. The Turks now took advantage of the circumstances and recovered areas of eastern Thrace they had lost to the Bulgarians, including Adrianople (present-day Turkish Edirne). Bulgaria sued for peace a month later. In the end, the Bulgarians had gained very little for their troubles, but they managed to keep a most strategic strip along the northern Aegean from Alexandroupolis to the Maritza River, an area that Greece also coveted.

Greece gained a substantial territory: Ioannina and southern Epiros (although she lost a part of northern Epiros with much Greek population to the creation in July 1913 of an independent Albania by some of the Great Powers to keep Austria-Hungary out of the Adriatic Sea); the coastal strip of Macedonia to Kavalla; the large islands of Lesbos, Chios, and Samos in the east Aegean; and Crete. The population and surface area of Greece had doubled.

In this atmosphere thoughts were rekindled for "the Great Idea". (See p.187). Greek euphoria even took as an omen the ascendency to the Greek throne of Crown Prince Constantine, after King George was assassinated in Thessaloniki by a madman on March 18, 1913. The last Byzantine Emperor had been Constantine XI Dragases. Some people also called the first modern Greek king Constantine I, Constantine XII, anticipating that he might lead them back to the glories of the Byzantine Empire. It did not happen. Would the new Constantine (II) become the XIII?

WORLD WAR I
(1914-1918)

Greece was euphoric over the success of its armies in the Balkan Wars of 1912 and 1913. The results enabled her to substantially increase her northern and island territories with their Greek populations. The policies of her dynamic Prime Minister Eleftherios Venizelos had triumphed. His statesmanship had highly impressed the British leaders, winning their cooperation in Greece's in dealings with Turkey. When World War I broke out

Escaping Serbian troops Dec. 1915   Final assault by Allies aided by Greeks May-Sept. 19:

MAP 7.5 FIRST WORLD WAR (1914-1918)

Greece remained out of the war because of political conflicts between the pro-German King Constantine and the pro-Entente Prim Minister Venizelos. She finally entered in the last year of the war when Constantine was forced to abdicate. Greece regained h Thracian territory from pro-Axis Bulgaria, and was to obtain the rest of this area to its present borders in 1919. But it was unable hold on to territory in Epiros with much Greek population.

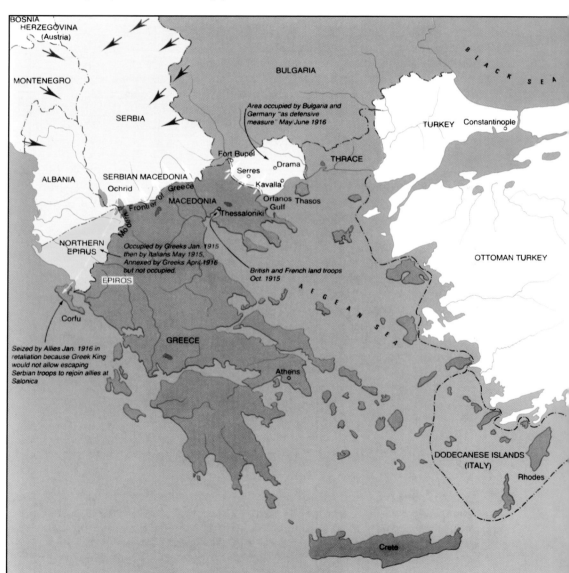

in August 1914, with Austria attacking Serbia, Venizelos eagerly offered the services of Greece to fight on the side of the *Entente Cordiale* (Britain, France, and Russia) against the Central Powers (Germany and Austria-Hungary). King Constantine did not agree with the offer of his Prime Minister, but in any event, the *Entente* turned down possible Greek participation in order to avoid provoking Bulgaria and Turkey into joining the Central Powers. However, by November 1914, Turkey had aligned herself with Germany.

In January 1915, the British conducted exploratory talks with the Greek government about the possibility of giving up a portion of its newly acquired area in Macedonia (which included the cities of Kavalla, Drama, and Serres), in exchange for unspecified territory in Asia Minor surrounding Smyrna, heavily populated for centuries by Greek-speaking Orthodox Christians, that is to say, Greeks. This strategy was being considered by the British in an urgent effort to win over Bulgaria at this politically critical time, enticing her with additional frontage on the Aegean Sea, which she much desired. The prospect of adding Smyrna and its hinterland to Greek territory greatly tempted Venizelos. But King Constantine objected to the vague terms and the idea of giving up another valuable area recently gained with Greek blood. The matter ceased to be an issue as in any case Bulgaria declared for the Central Powers on October 4, 1915.

The eagerness of Venizelos to support the British especially and the *Entente* in general was opposed by King Constantine, who felt that the best course for Greece was one of strict neutrality. But Venizelos never wavered from the view that the *Entente* would help Greece to continue to expand her territory to include the remaining areas containing predominantly Greek population in northern Epiros and the Asia Minor coast. He could see that this expansion would ultimately make Greece the major power in the Mediterranean. But the king, who as a young man had studied at the Berlin Military Academy, and in 1889 had married Sophia, the sister of Kaiser Wilhelm II of Germany, was of a different view. His high regard for the Germans caused him to conclude that Greece would be a loser on either side. The whole country was divided on what stance to take, and the argument wavered from one side to the other of the difficult question. Britain, France, and Russia were the Protecting Powers of Greece's territorial integrity; they were also allies against Germany. Yet, many in Greece believed that Germany and her partners were militarily stronger. Could Greece afford to remain neutral? Would she be served better by entering the war? Where did Greece's best interests lie? Nevertheless, pro-Venizelists considered the king to be pro-German, and relations between the king and his prime minister were beginning to be seriously strained. Controversy raged throughout Greece over the issues.

Another incident early in 1915 accelerated the break between Venizelos and the king, each of whom were unwilling to accept the other's views. The *Entente* planned an attack on the Dardanelles and again Venizelos offered Greek troops in support in his zeal to gain the good will of the allies to support his vision for Greek territory in Asia Minor. The king was at first persuaded by the idea, but on the arguments of other key advisors he changed his mind, and Venizelos resigned in protest on March 6. These and other disagreements between the two in this tense critical period for Greece over several years, and the king now ignoring the constitutional powers and prerogatives of his government headed by Venizelos, led to a damaging permanent break in relations between them that came to be known as the "National Schism" (in Greek: *Ethnikos Dichasmos*).

The Royalist Government

Other events were also beginning to take place that would strongly affect Greece as well. The British and French were courting Italy to join the *Entente*. This resulted in the Treaty of London of April 1915, the terms of which were unknown to Greece at the time. According to the treaty, Italy would definitively receive the Greek Dodecanese Islands, which she had occupied since 1911. They promised Italy "a just share in the Mediterranean adjacent to the Province of Adalia," in case Turkey should be partitioned, and planned for a partition of Albania more favorable to Italy than to Greece. In fact, Britain and France offered Italy an area in Turkey conflicting substantially with that area they had also proposed to Greece; they also offered Italy the area of northern Epiros, in Albania, with its Greek population. In May, when Italy finally entered the war on the side of the *Entente*, she immediately took possession of Albania, northern Epiros included, replacing Greek troops then occupying the area since the Balkan Wars. Meanwhile, the *Entente* was also continuing to woo the Bulgarians with offers of Greek territory in Macedonia, without any agreement on the part of the pro-Constantinist Greek Government that had taken over from Venizelos.

In June, 1915, new elections were held in Greece. They were easily won by Venizelos. For the next two months, the royal palace announced that King Constantine was ill, so that Venizelos could not take office until August. By the end of September, Bulgaria mobilized and entered the war, siding with the Central Powers, and she immediaterly attacked Serbia. Greece also mobilized. Under the terms of the Greco-Serbian Mutual Defense Pact of 1913, Greece was to come to the aid of Serbia against Bulgaria, provided Serbia would furnish 150,000 troops for the front. Occupied on the Austrian frontier, Serbia could not do so, and Venizelos obtained the agreement of the British and French that the Greeks would make up the deficit. The king again objected to the involvement of Greece, thus personally repudiating his country's defense pact with Serbia. The allies meanwhile proceeded to land 100,000 troops in Thessaloniki, quickly digging in on a line from Ochrid to the Gulf of Orfano (see Map 7.6). The irate king requested the resignation of Venizelos. The collapse of relations between the two was now final.

The *Entente* continued to pressure Greece to enter the war, at one time the British offering her Cyprus as an inducement, the island having a population that was more than 80 percent Greek. Cyprus, we should remember, was being administered by Britain as they had agreed with Turkey since 1878. But when Turkey joined the Central Powers, at the end of 1914 the British formally annexed the island. However, King Constantine's government was not tempted by the offer. The Serbian armies were defeated by the Austro-Bulgarian pincer and had to flee toward the sea across the rough mountainous terrain of Albania. France flagrantly disregarded Greek neutrality by occupying Corfu to create a regrouping area for the Serbs. Constantine continued to oppose the *Entente*, refusing to allow the Serbs to travel across Greek national territory to join the allied troops in the Thessaloniki area. More serious, at the request directly to Constantine by the German general staff, his government surrendered Fort Rupel on the Struma River to German and Bulgarian forces, exposing the *Entente* 's Macedonian flank. Greek esteem of the *Entente* dropped still lower with the British and French losses and withdrawal from the Dardanelles campaign, and by their failure to prevent the defeat and occupation of Rumania, which had joined the *Entente*. By June 1916, the *Entente* demanded the mobilization of the Greek army, being suspicious that Greece might even join the Central Powers, and the dismissal of the unsympathic Greek government and dissolution of its parliament. Showing his unity with Britain and France and anticipating where events might lead, Venizelos also announced that it would not be possible for his own political party to cooperate with the Greek government in power.

The Country Divided

In this tense atmosphere, on August 30, 1916, pro-Venizelist officers in Thessaloniki initiated a revolutionary movement against the Greek government. A month later Venizelos left Athens for his native Crete, where he was received enthusiastically. After a triumphant tour of the Aegean islands, he arrived in Thessaloniki, where he announced the formation of a provisional government. Greece was now effectively divided in two, one part under Constantine in Athens and the other in Thessaloniki under Venizelos, who had the support of most of the armed Greek forces there as well as the allied armies.

In this awkward position, King Constantine's "neutrality" began now to lean increasingly toward the Central Powers. To further emphasize their demands to truly neutralize the Greek forces if they could not be committed to their side, the British and French landed 1800 troops at Piraeus with orders to march to Athens. They were met by Greek forces on the way, and the ensuing battle resulted in many casualties on both sides. The allied troops were withdrawn, but severe reprisals against pro-Venizelists followed in Athens. The British and French now blockaded areas of Greece loyal to the king, namely the Peloponnese and southern Rumeli (a name given to northeastern Greece), the other areas of the country that were acquired after the Balkan wars being pro-Venizelist.

Italy saw a rival in Venizelos, however, and began to demand greater concessions from Britain and France. In April 1917, an agreement was concluded between the three allies at St. Jean de Maurienne (between Grenoble and the Italian border), whereby Britain and France would agree to give Italy the Turkish city of Smyrna and the area surrounding it, in addition to that of Adalia, if Turkey were to be partitioned. Clearly this conflicted directly with promises to the loyal Venizelos. But though the terms of the Treaty of London of 1915 had finally become known to the Greeks, the new agreement had not.

The Russian revolution, March 1917, toppled the Tsar and hastened the need for drastic action by Britain and France. In a final act of pressure on Greece, in June they demanded the abdication of King Constantine, in their role as Protecting Powers and in view of the king's obvious failure to act as a constitutional monarch. But Constantine did not abdicate; he left Greece for Switzerland, accompanied by his son Crown Prince George. His second son Alexander, became the provisional King of Greece.

Venizelos Returns

W ithin days of Constantine's departure, Venizelos returned to Athens as Prime Minister once again. He lost no time. On July 2, 1917, Greece declared war on the Central Powers. At the same time, a severe purge of anti-Venizelists took place. It was not until May 1918, that Greece was able to mobilize an army of 250,000. In the summer of 1918, the Greek forces joined British, French, and Italian armies in the final assault of the war in the Balkan area. In September, Serbian Macedonia was recovered, and the armies advanced farther into Serbia and into Bulgaria. By September 30th, Bulgaria signed an armistice, and Turkey capitulated a month later. On November 11, Germany also accepted an armistice. World War I was over. The Greek armies greatly helped in this final phase at the cost of 6,000 soldiers dead and 25,000 wounded. But World War I also resulted in a loss reported to amount to 130,000 civilians.*

Venizelos had at last been able to help the *Entente*. This put Greece in a position to seek the support of the Powers against a defeated Turkey. But the policy of Venizelos' government in this matter was to result in the country's greatest post-war catastrophe.

---

* This staggering number of Greek civilian losses is surprising considering hardly any of the war was fought on Greek soil. A review reveals that for the most part it came from the displacement on account of the war of about 270,000 civilians from Macedonia and western Thrace, and from the area around the Greek-Albanian border. Only an estimated 140,000 are said to have returned within the borders of Greece. The rest were considered lost, but not necessarily killed.

THE GREAT IDEA
Catastrophe in Asia Minor
(1919-1922)

The star of Greek fortunes was ascending. The country's greatest enemies, Turkey and Bulgaria, were on the losing side in the World War of 1914 to 1918. Despite frustrating opposition by King Constantine, Prime Minister Venizelos had at last been able to free Greece to join the *Entente* and contribute to the allies' final victory, thus assuring his country of their good will, which future plans would require. Following closely after the rapid and substantial growth of Greek territories as a result of the 1912 and 1913 Balkan Wars, all these events whetted irredentist or even imperialist appetites for what was formally called "The Great Idea": a Greece "of the five seas and the two continents."

Greece never having been a free nation until its independence from the Ottomans in 1833, and considering the dynamic history of the Greek people over the previous hundreds of years, to say nothing of its rich ancient heritage, what should be the borders of a Greece in modern times? The large Greek populations living in Epiros, Macedonia, Thrace, and western Asia Minor led many Greek leaders to think about boundaries roughly including these areas. The domination over the Romans of the Greek language, culture, and religion during Byzantine times, reinforced it. The collapse of the Ottoman government made it a possibility. It was time for the Greeks to occupy their rightful place in the world. Venizelos and his supporters were especially zealous to pursue and achieve this goal, but every patriotic Greek was caught up in this national fantasy. How to accomplish it and personality clashes were the bases of political differences; nearly everyone was unanimous on the desired result.

Venizelos lobbied hard at the 1918 Paris Peace Conference, urgently presenting his views for an expanded Greece, especially to include the large Greek communities in western Turkey. No more propitious an opportunity could be imagined. At the same time, his desires were made even more compelling by a real need to protect the Greeks in that part of Asia Minor. These people had been subjected to harsh treatment by the Turks during World War I. While they had not suffered the wholesale genocide meted out by the Turks to the Armenians earlier, during the four years of the war an estimated 450,000 Greeks were expelled or fled for their lives from their homes in the cities on the Asia Minor coasts, proceeding mostly to Greece. Incidents continued in which many were killed.

Venizelos had especially impressed David Lloyd George, the British Prime Minister, who strongly supported him. Of course, the greatest problem for Greek aspirations on Turkey were the colonial designs of Italy to take possession of a large part of southwestern Anatolia (Map 7.7), which had been confirmed by the allies in two separate formal treaties in 1915 and 1917. Italy was well aware of Venizelos' efforts and the greater sympathy shown by the allies toward the Greeks. To insure their mandate over the southwest region of Turkey, in March 1919 Italy

MAP 7.6 THE GREAT IDEA

Following World War I, the ambitions of Greece were to take possession of all territories containing Greek population, including
Aegean coast of Asia Minor, all of Thrace, the Dodecanese islands, and part of Epiros. It refrained from including Constantinople
its claims knowing that the European Powers would want that city and the Bosphorus to be international.

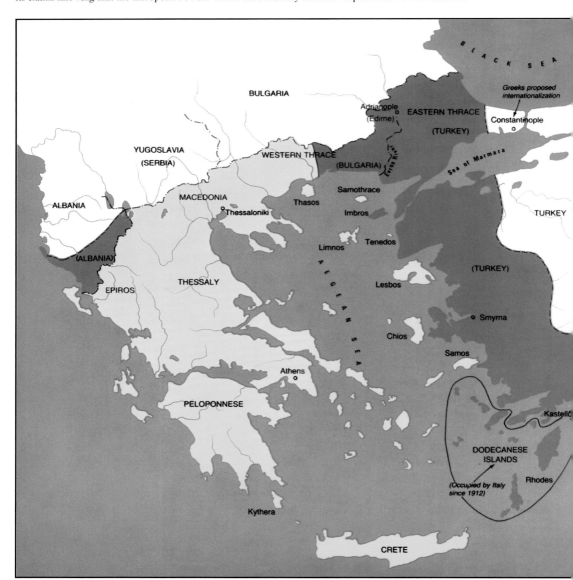

preempted possible contrary decisions of the British, French, and Americans, by landing troops at Antalya, on the Turkish southern coast, and marching them toward Smyrna. An alarmed Venizelos immediately appealed to Lloyd George. The British Prime Minister had already made up his mind to help Venizelos in his desire to add Smyrna and its hinterland to Greece. Initially, he favored occupation of the area by Greek forces to protect the large Greek population there. Greek annexation of the zone was a different consideration still being discussed among the allies. Lloyd George's counterparts were less sanguine. Prime Minister Georges Clemenceau of France was generally sympathetic toward Greece, but foresaw problems. The American President Woodrow Wilson remained aloof to these maneuverings. Indeed, Lloyd George's advisers were very pessimistic about the wisdom and possible success of a Greek presence in Asia Minor, and they so reported to their prime minister.

Nevertheless, the arbitrary move on the part of the Italians strengthened Lloyd George's resolve. His conviction also persuaded Clemenceau and Wilson, and on May 6, 1919, they agreed that Greek forces should immediately occupy Smyrna. Escorted by British and French naval units, Greek transports ferried her troops toward Smyrna, and on May 15, they landed a Greek army on the Asia Minor coast for the first time since Alexander the Great nearly 2300 years earlier. The panygeric reception by the Greek populace in Smyrna justified the Greek government's actions. They had come to liberate their fellow Greeks.

Almost immediately during the same day, the landing was marred by incidents between the Greek forces and Turkish soldiers, irregulars and rabble. Nearly 100 persons were killed on both sides and several hundred wounded, of which the greater part were Turks. Many more Turks were beaten and taken prisoner. These-out-of-control incidents brought forth bitter protests from Turkish authorities as well as worried demands for order from Greek officials and community leaders. Over the next two weeks, as the Greek occupation spread north to Ayvali and south to Aydin, a continued lack of restraint on both sides caused these outbreaks to multiply.

The allies had expected that the Greek landing was to be a "peacekeeping" mission, though how they could fail to anticipate the possible consequences of the pent-up emotions in the Greeks, and the Turks' reaction to an invasion force, is unclear. But soon it became apparent that the Greeks lacked the required military and administrative organizations to handle the mission with success, and this and the mishaps quickly gave the allies considerable misgivings about the outcome of the effort. The events also awakened a new sense of patriotism in a Turkish population depressed by decades of national weakening culminating in defeat in World War I. In the circumstances, what leadership was not forthcoming from the Sultan now came from a new Turkish personality to emerge, General Mustapha Kemal.

Mustapha Kemal

Originally a member of the Young Turks and participating in the revolution of 1908, which sought to create a constitutional government in Turkey, Kemal went on to become an experienced and high-ranking military officer with strong political interests. Seeking to keep him out of the capital to reduce his opposition to his government's stand on events that were taking place, he was appointed Inspector General for the Eastern Provinces. This occurred about the same time the Greeks landed at Smyrna. Meeting with nationalist-minded groups, Kemal soon organized them into a national revival movement in defiance of a weak Sultan, Mehmed VI. Kemal formalized his movement into a National Congress, culminating by February 1920 in a declaration of independence from the government in Constantinople. He established a new capital in the center of the country at Ankara and vowed not to allow Turkey to be partitioned or controlled by the various European interests.

It was disastrous for Greece that the allies' finalization of peace terms with Turkey following the end of World War I were so long delayed. The months passing caused the allies to weaken in their support of Greece against Turkey and the Kemalist national movement to be strengthened. Events possibly leading to a prolonged and costly new war in Asia Minor could be foreseen, which in no way could serve allied interests in the area. Venizelos kept up the pressure to conclude a peace agreement in Greece's favor, especially on his friend Lloyd George. Yet Venizelos was warned by Lloyd George that the British people would not tolerate imposing the treaty on Turkey if it meant a continuation of hostilities — Venizelos could not count on British aid in those circumstances. The Italians did not want the treaty at all. Nevertheless, Venizelos was adamant that Greece alone could impose the treaty.

By mid-June 1920, a Turkish nationalist attack on the British position on the Ismid peninsula at the eastern end of the Sea of Marmara gave Greece the chance to demonstrate her military effectiveness. At the request of the allies, Greece sent her troops to their aid. The troops advanced east from their agreed-upon holding line and occupied an area from the old capital at Bursa south to Alashehir and east to Ushak. For good measure in late July they also mopped up nationalist forces in Thrace and entered Adrianople (Edirne). In this optimistic atmosphere the Treaty of Sèvres was finally signed on August 10, 1920. Signing for the Turkish government were the Sultan's representatives, but Kemal's nationalists would not agree to go along.

Venizelos' efforts had succeeded. Almost beyond belief, the Treaty provided that Greece was to receive most of Thrace; sovereignty over the Aegean islands acquired during the Balkan Wars including Imbros and Tenedos flanking the Hellespont; the Gallipoli peninsula; in a separate agreement with the Italians, the Dodecanese Islands except for Rhodes (and most likely eventually that island as well); and Smyrna plus a substantial hinterland, subject to a decision for Greek or Turkish sovereignty after a five-year-period under Greek administration. The Straits were to be under an international commission dominated by the Great Powers, and Constantinople was to continue as Turkey's capital, but with a garrison of troops from the allies.

Two days following the signature of the Treaty, Venizelos was leaving Paris for Athens in triumph. At the Gare de Lyon train station, two pro-royalist Greek officers shot and wounded him in an assassination attempt. At the news fanatical pro-Venizelists in Athens reacted in a number of ugly incidents, among which was the murder of a staunch royalist member of the Greek parliament, Ion Dragoumis. The matter was never investigated, and the known perpetrators were never brought to trial. The significance of these events was that the allies were further disaffected by the lack of maturity of Greek politics. Having been obliged at the time by circumstances to sign the Treaty of Sèvres, subsequently none of the allies ratified it; nor did Turkey. The Treaty remained a piece of paper the contents of which only Greece celebrated, rather overoptimistically and prematurely.

Accelerating the downhill slide of Greek fortunes, on September 30, King Alexander was bitten by a pet monkey in the palace garden. Less than a month later he died of blood poisoning, at age 27. Although Alexander had been ineffectual, his presence had at least kept a lid on the royalist-Venizelist feud. However, his death affected the political atmosphere in Greece dramatically. Leaving no heirs as he had married a commoner, the throne was offered by Venizelos to Alexander's younger brother, Prince Paul. But he would not accept, reminding everyone that his exiled father King Constantine had not abdicated, nor had his older brother, Prince George, renounced his rights to succession.

General elections scheduled to be held on November 14, suddenly became the focus of new conflict between the supporters of Venizelos and those of King Constantine. Venizelos announced that if he lost the elections, he would retire from public life. The war-weary Greek people opted for change. To the surprise of many, Venizelos won only 118 out of the total of 369 seats. The crushing defeat obliged Venizelos and a number of his closest supporters to leave the country. Having been out of office for several years, it was the turn of the royalists to sack the Venizelist appointees in government, the judiciary, education, and the armed forces. Of course, the 1500 or so pro-royalist officers were returned to the military and the several hundred pro-Venizelist senior officers removed or placed in minor posts. The impact on affairs in Asia Minor, with an army at war, was to have a devastating effect.

The new government prepared for a plebiscite on the return of King Constantine. Remembering his pro-German posture during the war, the allies warned the Greek government that if he should be returned to the throne, they would cut off all aid to Greece. Nevertheless, the vote on December 5, 1920, was overwhelmingly in favor of Constantine's return, and he arrived from his three-year exile in Switzerland two weeks later.

Anticipating the likelihood that events in Asia Minor could go from bad to worse, a conference was called by the allies in London in late February 1921, inviting delegations from Greece and Turkey. The object was to try to stop the hostilities and to ease the harshness on Turkey of the terms of the Treaty of Sèvres. Both the Sultan's government and the Kemalists attended, but in separate delegations. However, neither the Greeks nor the Turks would budge from their respective positions, and the conference ended in failure. Meanwhile, the French and Italians took the opportunity to conclude private agreements with the Kemalists, in recognition of their mounting strength.

MAP 7.7 DISASTER AT SMYRNA (1919-1922)

A collapsing Turkey, on the losing side of World War I, fired the ambitions of Greece to claim Greek-populated territories of tha[...]
country. Italy, which had also been on the Allied side, likewise claimed portions of Turkey. When Italy preempted its demands b[...]
landing troops in Antalya, in March, 1919, Greece persuaded the Great Powers to allow her to occupy Smyrna and hinterlan[...]
This led to a war with Turkish forces organized under General Mustapha Kemal, which Greece lost.

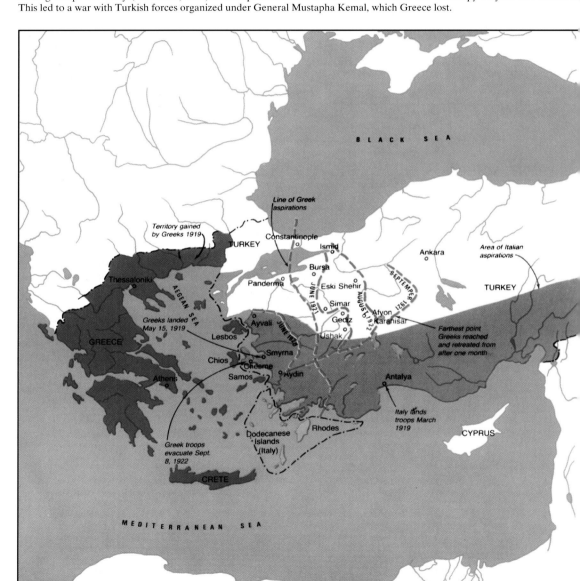

The Final Effort

What could not be won at the conference table the Greeks now decided to win on the battlefield. Earlier, in December 1920, the Greeks had advanced to Eski Shehir on a probing drive, and finding hard resistance, they retired to their former positions. In March 1921, the advance was more in earnest, but so was the defense by the entrenched Turkish nationalists, this time better prepared and equipped like a regular army. The surprised Greeks were beaten back, suffering their first major defeat in their modern history. Recriminations followed, and the Greeks began to realize that they were caught in a major trap. They were unlikely to win and keep any large area of Asia Minor as an invading army, but unless they crushed the nationalists, they could not even hope to hold a piece of Turkey even as defined in the Treaty of Sèvres, namely Smyrna and its hinterland. Everything they had done before would have been wasted. Furthermore, the futility of their position was underlined by the centuries-old Greco-Turkish enmity, which now resulted in repeated acts of brutality by each side, unrestrained in the atmosphere of war.

Not willing to go backwards, the Greek government decided to go forward against Kemal and Ankara. The army was increased, reinforced, and reorganized. King Constantine himself arrived in Smyrna in early June 1921, to lead the new effort (largely as a figurehead). In July, the Greek army again advanced on Eski Shehir and Afyon Karahisar, and this time they were successful. The Turkish army retreated, but in the certainty that as the Greek lines became extended, their own advantage would increase significantly.

The principal objective was Ankara, and the Greeks convinced themselves that if they could capture this nationalist capital, they would have destroyed the Turkish resistance and victory would be theirs. On August 14, 1921, the Greek assault began. In an all-out effort they managed to reach the Sakaraya River and the area near Polatli, about 40 miles (65 kilometers) from Ankara, before the exhausted Greek armies halted in the first days of September. The casualties on both sides were enormous, but the Turks remained undestroyed. The enemy now strongly counterattacked, and the Greeks fell back to where they started from, at Eski Shehir, stalemated and low on military hardware, and their country in difficult financial straits.

A year later, having gathered strength and aided by a supply of arms from Russia, Kemal Pasha began his final offensive at the end of August 1922. Overwhelmed, the Greeks retreated nearly 120 miles (200 kilometers) and tried to hold their lines. When that failed, the retreat became a rout. The armed forces were finally evacuated from Chesme, near Smyrna, September 8 to 14, and the massive Greek population tried to flee in panic before the avenging Turks. It is estimated that as many as 30,000 civilians lost their lives, and more than a million refugees fled to Greece as the Greek, Armenian, and European quarters were burned to the ground in a huge fire. These new refugees joined half a million or so Greeks who had fled earlier. The large Greek presence in the area had lasted nearly three millenia but it was now substantially at an end. The Great Idea was another one of the victims.

The sequel was predictable. A military coup in Greece on September 26 resulted in the abdication of King Constantine, who departed for Sicily, where he died four months later. Crown Prince George became King George II. Kemal Pasha became president of a republican Turkey in 1923 and he continued to be reelected, remaining in office until his death in 1938. (He eventually became known as *Atatürk*, or "father of the Turks.") He succeeded in removing all foreign interests from Turkey, including the attempt to internationalize the Straits. Under the terms of the new Treaty of Lausanne, signed in July 1923, Turkey also kept the strategic Greek-populated islands of Imbros and Tenedos that had been given to Greece under the Treaty of Sèvres three years earlier; and she was also allowed to keep European Turkey to the Maritza River. The Greeks held on to the rest of Thrace (an area gained from Bulgaria after World War I), under the Treaty of Neuilly of November 1919.

An exchange of minorities followed, adding to the population of Greece that had increased to 2,600,000 in 1907, and was to increase to 6,200,000 by 1928. In Athens itself the population doubled between 1920 and 1928, and particularly after the headlong evacuation from the Asia Minor coast of September 1922. For decades many thousands of displaced people were forced to live in shantytowns at the edges of Athens.

BETWEEN CATASTROPHE AND WAR
(1922-1940)

The Greek army was humiliated by its defeat in Asia Minor. Even as they left the Turkish coast in late September 1922, a small group of officers on a battleship steaming towards Athens, declared a revolution against King Constantine and the parliamentary government of Greece. Leaflets were dropped by plane over the capital even before the officers landed in Greece. The Revolutionary Committee demanded the abdication of the king; the resignation of the government, the dissolution of the chamber of deputies, and their replacement by a Revolutionary Government of officers of the armed forces. Purging themselves of their guilt for the catastrophe in Asia Minor was one part of their goal; these officers were also strongly motivated by their anti-royalist-pro-Venizelist passions. The guilt they felt was mixed with anger; it must be remembered that most of the senior officers engaged in the war in Turkey had been replaced with pro-royalists after Venizelos lost the November 1920, elections.

As mentioned in the preceding section, Constantine reluctantly abdicated and departed for Palermo, Sicily, on September 30, 1922 (where he was to die only four months later). His eldest son, Crown Prince George, was sworn in by the Revolutionary Government as King George II, even though many prominent pro-Venizelists, civilians and military, protested the continuation of the monarchy. Venizelos had been absent from Greece and had been living in Paris, to where he had self-exiled himself after losing the November 1920, elections. Now the Revolutionary Government invited him to formally represent Greece in the peace negotiations with Turkey to be held in Lausanne, Switzerland, and he accepted. He served the country ably in conducting this delicate mission. Greece's borders with Turkey were confirmed. Venizelos also dissuaded the stronger-minded Greek officers from proceeding with a plan to attack Turkey once again to drive them out of eastern Thrace as far as Constantinople and the Bosporus. Most importantly, the treaty provided for the massive population exchange that became necessary.

The Revolutionary Government was determined to put the blame for the Asia Minor disaster squarely on the administration that had been in office. they lost no time in arresting eight of the key ministers. Despite the strong objections of the Powers, especially Britain, these were quickly tried by military courtmartial, and as soon as they were found guilty, six were executed, the other two receiving life sentences. In continuation of the anti-royalist sentiment, Prince Andrew, brother of the deposed Constantine, was also tried by courtmartial for failure in his command in Turkey of the Greek Second Army Corps. He was found guilty and was permanently exiled from Greece. An abortive royalist military coup took place in Macedonia in October 1923, led by the ultra-royalist General Ioannis Metaxas. This led the Revolutionary Government in December to request King George II to leave Greece until a plebescite could be held to decide on the future of the monarchy. (He was not to return until 1935, twelve years later.)

Elections were held that restored constitutional rule, and the Revolutionary Government stepped down in January 1924, with Venizelos returning as prime minister. But his stay in office lasted barely a month, and he resigned again over the monarchy issue and the pressure by others to create a republic, leaving his country once more, in disgust. The political turmoil continued and worsened during the next several years, the republican government deposed by a military coup, followed by yet another, and then another republican government.

Finally, in March 1928, conditions changed once again to when Venizelos could return to Greece and form a new government. This lasted until the spring of 1932, during which time Venizelos very ably negotiated better relations between Greece and its neighboring countries. But the disastrous economic depression that spread throughout the world at that time included Greece as well, and more political unrest resulted. Governments changed several times during the next three years. Venizelos was now 71 years of age and exhausted; his power was coming to an end. He again left for Paris (where he was to die in March, 1936). This gave the royalists their chance again. A plebiscite in November 1935, restored the monarchy, King George II returning to the Greek throne once more. He asked the loyal and able General Ioannis Metaxas to form a new government. But continued political problems and a Communist threat led Metaxas to taking dictatorial powers, which authority the king supported. This was the government that was installed in Greece when World War II broke out in Europe in 1939. This new conflict would soon envelop the nation.

WORLD WAR II
(October 28, 1940 - October 31, 1941)

Greece tried to remain neutral in World War II. The sympathies of King George II were with Britain, but his country's economy had become increasingly dependent upon Germany. In any event, Greece was in no condition to take part in a war. She was still suffering from the world economic depression, and the continued political unrest in Greece kept the military dictatorship of General Ioannis Metaxas in power, endorsed by the king who felt this manner of rule was necessary for Greece at this time.

Italy had already occupied Albania in April 1939, even though its Fascist dictator Benito Mussolini had not yet declared his country's intent to enter the war. Perceiving his ambitions and those of Germany, Britain and France offered Greece a guarantee for her territorial integrity if she would remain neutral, an offer they had also made to Poland and Rumania. Greece accepted this protection and continued her neutral role. In June 1940, Mussolini joined Hitler in the war. As the junior Axis partner, he wanted to show Hitler that he was an able confederate, and he tried to provoke Greece out of her neutrality by a number of incidents. In August 1940, Mussolini accused Greece of supporting Britain and demanded she renounce the agreement with the allies. In that same month, the Greek naval cruiser *Elli* called at the island of Tinos during its highest religious holiday, paying a visit to the famous holy shrine there. In a sneak attack, the Italians torpedoed and sank the cruiser in the harbor. Mussolini also massed more than 150,000 troops on the Albanian border, and the Greek government was only able to place about half that number of its own ready to oppose them. In that tense condition on October 28, 1940, at the undignified hour of 3 AM, the Italian ambassador delivered an ultimatum from his government to Metaxas, to expire at 6 AM of the same say. Before its expiration and without waiting for an official reply, Italian troops invaded Greece across the Albanian border.

Mussolini had expected an easy victory. His troops had penetrated less than 20 miles (30 kilometers) into Greek territory against light resistance when the Greeks counterattacked. In spite of the cold and snow in that mountainous region, by the end of 1940 and early 1941 the Greeks had fought their way into Albania, and by March about one third of Albania was in Greek hands. Hitler did not wait for the outcome, In mid-December 1940, he issued a directive launching "Operation Marita" to mass German divisions in pro-Axis Rumania and then move across the territory of another partner, Bulgaria, and into Greece if necessary. Bulgaria had joined in the Axis Tripartite Pact (Germany, Italy, and Japan), and Yugoslavia also felt compelled to join on March 24, 1941. But the Yugoslav government was overthrown two days later by a military coup by officers who opposed this decision. Now Germany had to invade both Yugoslavia and Greece.

The combined invasion of Yugoslavia by Germany and Italy started on April 6,1941, and capitulation came eight days later. Simultaneously, the Germans attacked Greece. Meanwhile, the British landed nearly 60,000 troops in Greece from North Africa. But this proved to be of little help; the powerful German war machine was relentless. By the end of April, Greece fell, and the

— Italian Invasion   — German Invasion (1941)

— Greek counter-attack   — British evacuation (28 April 1941)

– – – – — Farthest Greek penetration   — German airborne landings (20 May 1941)

MAP 7.8 SECOND WORLD WAR (1940-1944)

Greece's neutrality was shattered by the Italian invasion across the Albanian frontier. The Greeks fiercely driving the Italians back forced Germany itself to invade and occupy Greece in April 1941. Greece remained under German, Italian, and Bulgarian occupation until October 1944; some of her areas remained under foreign occupation until the end of the war.

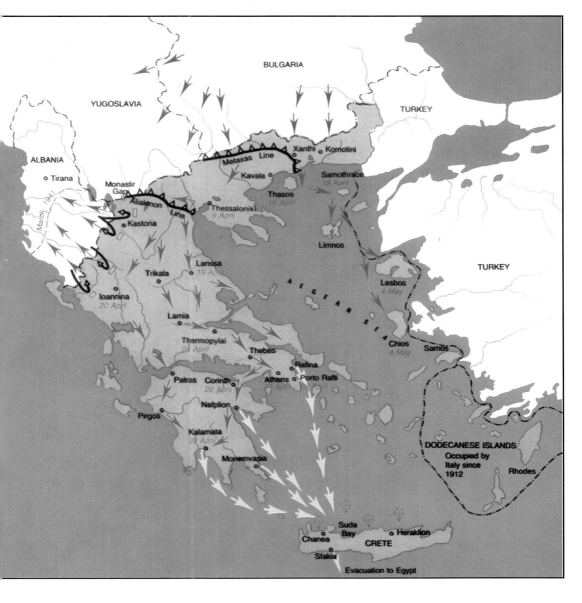

king and the government fled to Crete, along with about 42,000 British troops who had to leave the rest of their companions behind.

Crete became the next target for the Germans. While the large island was difficult to assault, its strategic position in the Mediterranean made this action necessary. The two poorly equipped Greek divisions there were reinforced by 30,000 British soldiers left there. Germany attacked with over 20,000 crack parachutists and glider-borne troops starting May 20, supported by 600 aircraft. By the end of May, the Germans were victorious but had lost 7,000 of their men in the fierce fighting against a loss of about 3,000 British and Greek soldiers. Several thousand Cretan civilians were killed in the fighting and in heavy reprisals by the Germans on a determined and courageous population defending their homeland. Fifteen thousand of the remaining British troops managed to be evacuated to Egypt along with King George II and his government. Eighteen thousand British and Greek soldiers had to be left behind.

But the real loss to Germany was time. The Greek invasion had used up nearly two precious months during which time Hitler's "Operation Barbarossa," the attack on Russia, was delayed. The German troops ran into the dreadful Russian winter at the end of the year before they could win their hard-fought campaign, resulting in appalling losses and contributing to the ultimate defeat of Germany.

Greece suffered a great famine in 1941 and 1942, under harsh conditions brought about by the combined German, Italian, and Bulgarian occupation. It is estimated that more than 300,000 Greeks died of famine. Resistance by Greek partisans also cost thousands of civilian lives in hostile actions and reprisals.

THE CIVIL WAR
(September 1943 - October 1949)

T he brutal civil war that was to take place in Greece 1943-1949, was rooted on the communist movement that began to make its appearance after the first World War. The few Greek communist leaders sent to establish the communist party in their country were educated and trained in Russia, itself the product of the Bolshevik revolution of 1917. The party grew very slowly and it made little impact to establish itself as a legitimate Greek political entity of any consequence. But the poor political and economic conditions in Greece resulting from the overwhelming forced emigration of Greeks from Otoman Turkey, followed by the world economic depression, and finally the World War II itself and occupation by the Axis powers (Italy, Bulgaria and Germany), provided a fertile atmosphere for the aggressive communists.

Greece's northern neighbors of Albania, Yugoslavia and Bulgaria had been ruled by monarchs before the war. Influenced by communist Russia, each of these countries were taken overe before the end of the war by their own communist regimes. At first, the geographical and political focus of attention in Greece was for a communist take-over of Macedonia in the north. While the intervention in Greece was almost entirely by Greek communists, they were greatly supported by their neighbors to prepare for the armed conflict that would be neeeded to achieve their aims. The war itself enlarged their opportunities.

A number of Greek resistance groups had been created during the war. The largest of these was the communist-led National Liberation Front (EAM in Greek initials), which had a large military arm, the National Popular Liberation Army (ELAS). The communists and their sympathizers had prepared well to take advantage of the war and the resulting political weakness in Greece. A complex number of events and the liberation of Greece from its Fascist occupiers and the devastating civil war that followed are briefly summarized:

- In the summer of 1943, as the tide of the war began to change, EAM-ELAS moved against the other Greek resistance groups, virtually eliminating them, except for EDES (National Republican Greek League), a much smaller but strong non-communist group. This was the first step by the communists in their strategic plan to eventually take over the entire country.

- Italy collapsed in September 1943, and the Germans disarmed and ordered their forces out of Greece, but not before the disenchanted Italian army left behind large quantities of arms. These fell into the hands of resistance groups, largely ELAS.

- The war was now going badly for the Germans, losing their Italian allies, and the Rumanians changing sides. Turkey also severed its ties with the Axis. The German army began to evacuate from Greece in August 1944, their troops being needed elswhere, and EAM-ELAS took over as they left. They thus occupied 90 percent of the countryside.

- Political differences decimated and made the Greek army ineffective. The British knew the communist danger, and sent 5,000 troops to Greece under General Ronald Scobie. By October 1, 1944, they moved into Patras, and by October 12, they arrived in Athens as the Germans evacuated. George Papandreou, the Greek prime minister-in-exile, arrived October 18 to take charge. The British troops were the only tangible obstacle to a complete takeover of the country by EAM-ELAS.

- The last Germans evacuated northern Greece October 31, 1944, along with the Bulgarians. However, the Germans still retained Crete and a number of strategic Greek islands until their country surrendered to the allies on May 9, 1945.

- On December 3, 1944, at a mass rally in Constitution Square in the center of the city, shooting broke out and the fight began for control of Athens between ELAS and the British together with a brigade of Greek army and many police. Thousands of civilians participated on both sides. The battle lasted a month and most of the capital came into ELAS hands. They slaughtered and executed thousands of their countrymen.

• Despite this dangerous and tense atmosphere, Winston Churchill, the British prime minister, and Anthony Eden, his foreign minister, arrived in Athens Christmas Eve1944, meeting briefly with American and Russian representatives, to bolster the shaky Greek government. Over the next two weeks, the British forces prevailed in heavy fughting and ELAS finally accepted a cease-fire on January 11, 1945. But the communists were by no means defeated; they only changed tactics. An agreement was reached whereby they would give up the fight in order to be allowed to be recognized as an official political party.

• A massive counter-communist movement took place during 1945 and 1946. Thousands were killed, some legally and others by secret death squads, and 70,000 were prosecuted for their activities in EAM-ELAS. Some called the period "The White Terror."

• In the Fall of 1946, a full-fledged civil war broke out with the Greek communists, now supported by Albania, Yugoslavia, and Bulgaria, invading Greece from refuge in these countries. As the British were in no condition to continue to help Greece, the tattered Greek army was assisted by American military aid, requested by President Harry Truman of the United States Congress on March 12, 1947, and granted in May. This was in the initial amount of US$400 million; the program became known as the "Truman Doctrine." (Turkey was also a recipient.)

• U.S. military aid was accompanied by American advisors starting November 1947, and in February 1948 General James Van Fleet became head of the joint United States-Greek military advisory and planning group. The British also sent similar noncombatant missions.

• Over the period 1947 to 1948, the Greek communist combatants were slowly being driven out of Greek territory, to the mountainous areas close to the Albanian and Yugoslavian borders from where they had been receiving their military supplies. They dug in there desperately. The Greek Marshal Alexandros Papagos, head of the Albanian campaign that had driven back the Italians at the start of the war, took over as commander-in-chief in January1949. It took many vicious battles until late in the summer of 1949 for the government forces to win at last. In no small way the tide was also turned by Tito's breaking with Stalin, which left the Greek communists on the fence. They respected Moscow but needed Yugoslavia, as a result of which they were neglected by both. Yugoslavia closed its borders to them in July. They finally withdrew their remaining forces of several thousand across the border into Albania, and the civil war ended in October.

• The civil war produced nearly 100,000 casualties, and perhaps another 100,000 people fled or were forced across the northern frontiers. More than

28,000 children between the ages of three and fourteen were also taken forcibly across the same borders into the Eastern Bloc countries,* ostensibly to "protect" them from deprivations or harm from the Greek government "fascists". Ten percent of the total Greek population of about 7,000,000 sought safety in the already overcrowded cities of Athens, Thessaloniki, and others.

The brutal civil war, coming on the heels of the World War II occupation, greatly affected Greece for many years into the postwar period. Poverty, politics, and a greatly depressed economy, did not allow the bitter experiences of the war to be easily forgotten.

Yet, a byproduct of the war and its loss by the Axis was the formal return to Greece on March 7, 1947 of the Dodecanese islands, which had been under Italian rule since the Italo-Turkish war of 1910 to 1912. This completed the area of modern Greece as we know it today.

---

* This became know to the horrified Greeks as the *pethomazoma*, or the child-gathering or abduction.

Eight

Summary of the Formation of the Modern Greek State (1832-1947)

THE EARLY GREEK PEOPLE ON THE PENINSULA AND islands lived in separate city-states that coexisted or at times warred with each other. There was little need for formal boundaries, so there were none, or for the creation of a nation of cities. Populations being small, for the most part there was room for everyone. Some of these people also left their mother cities at times and migrated in search of more space, safety, adventure, or to create an independent community that better suited to the colonists' needs. In this respect, Greece was not different from other places and peoples in ancient times. Over the centuries, some of the Greek states covered larger areas for varying periods, and during the reign of Philip II of Macedonia, his conquests and alliances unified for a time the larger part of the Greek peninsula (see Chapter Four). It did not stay together long after Philip's death in 336 BC, his son Alexander soon leaving his native land to conquer Persia, from which expedition he never returned. In a manner of speaking, the cities in the area that includes what we now call the nation of Greece were unified for the first time in 146 BC, under Roman occupation. This territory remained under one conqueror or another for nearly 2000 years.

The formation of the modern Greek state was a process that started only in 1821 and ended in 1947. Described in greater detail in separate headings in this volume, the six major liberations of Greek territory are summarized below (see also Chapter Seven).

THE LIBERATION OF MODERN GREECE

1832. The revolution of 1821 ended in 1832 with the independence of a part of Greece consisting of the Peloponnese, an area of mainland Greece stretching between and below the cities of Arta and Volos, as well as the Sporadic and Kykladic islands in the Aegean Sea. Britain, France, and Russia among the Great Powers of Europe, determined how much of Greece was to

MAP 8.0 LIBERATION OF GREECE (1830-1947)

Greece achieved its present borders in six steps, as shown on the map and as summarized in the text.

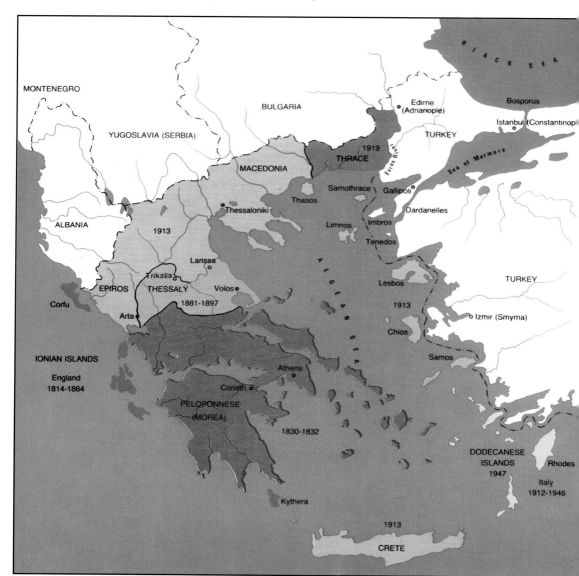

be liberated as they also undertook to guarantee the independence of this area from Turkey. With the concurrence of Greek leaders, they also selected a 17-year-old Bavarian, Prince Otto (Othon in Greek), to place on a previously nonexistent Greek throne, in an attempt to give the Greeks the unity they could not create for themselves under a democratic system of government. The Greek leaders also had little or no experience conducting a democratic administration, and even less inclination to cooperate with each other for a common purpose.

1864. Theoretically independent but under the protection and administration of Britain, which had captured them from the French in 1814, the seven Ionian islands off Greece's western coast in the Adriatic Sea were voluntarily ceded to Greece by the British in 1864 in an act of good will. The occasion was the Protecting Powers' offer and the Greek acceptance of 17-year-old Prince George as their second monarch, son of King Christian IX of Denmark, the Greeks having become disillusioned with King Othon, who was finally forced to abdicate after nearly thirty years rule, leaving no heirs.

1881. The continued deterioration of the Ottoman State and its inability to calm its European Balkan territories which were in constant revolt, helped to bring into focus the strong nationalistic and territorial ambitions of the Greeks. The weak Ottoman condition was also of interest to the Russians, whose Tsar Nicholas I (1825-1855) had called Turkey "a sick man, a very sick man." In 1853, Russia invaded the Turkish-held Danubian provinces to gain access to eastern Europe and the Black Sea. Turkey declared war on Russia and was joined by Britain and France as they were fearful of Russia's expansionist aims. This resulted in the Crimean War of 1853-1856. In 1876, the Balkan provinces of Bosnia and Herzegovina rebelled against Turkey, and the Serbs and Montenegrins came to their aid. When they were defeated by the Turks, the Russians saw this as a new opportunity and another Russo-Turkish war was begun in 1877. Greece could also see that unless she pressed her claims for the areas toward the north, others would occupy these predominantly Greek-populated territories. Finally, in 1881, Greece sent irregulars to stir things up in Thessaly; she mobilized her troops in 1877 and again in 1880 to press her claims, but she could not succeed on her own. Britain and France again intervened and forced Turkey to negotiate with Greece. As a result, Turkey yielded to Greece the territory from Arta east and including most of Thessaly, in 1881.

1912 and **1913.** It took two wars against Turkey for Greece to gain additional territory. In 1912, Greece joined Montenegro, Serbia, and Bulgaria, forming the Balkan League. Their purpose was to drive the Turkish armies out of European territories containing their own nationals. They were substantially successful. Greece liberated much of the area she desired in Epiros and Macedonia, but competed with Bulgaria for the area along the Aegean coast from Thessaloniki to the east. In June 1913, Greece and Serbia joined in a mutual defense pact against suspected Bulgarian ambitions. Their suspicions proved correct, and a short war with Bulgaria after she attacked Serbia enabled Greece to acquire parts of western Thrace and additional northern territories. Though Turkey also regained the eastern Thracian area lost to Bulgaria in these wars to the Maritza River (Turkish=Meriç R.; Greek=Evros R.), Bulgaria was able to keep the area on the Aegean Sea from the Maritza to the Nestos Rivers, which Greece also desired. Nevertheless, the peace agreement with Turkey also liberated the remaining large islands in the eastern Aegean Sea, as well as Crete.

1919. Bulgaria and Turkey had joined the Central Powers in World War I and were on the losing side when the war ended in 1918. Greece had been kept out of the war because of the pro-German sentiments of King Constantine I, neutralizing the strongly pro-*Entente* maneuverings of Prime Minister Eleftherios Venizelos. But Greece finally entered the war in May 1918, and participated in the final assault in the Balkans. The prize for her efforts was the Aegean-fronting area between Kavalla and the Evros River, gained from Bulgaria by the Treaty of Neuilly signed November 1919.

1947. Recognizing the weakness of the Ottoman government, Italy had attacked Turkish possessions in Libya in 1911, then occupied the Greek-populated Dodecanese islands then part of the Ottoman-held territories, strategically located for her expected grab of southwestern Anatolia, should Turkey be partitioned. The Italo-Turkish war resulted. Though a peace agreement was signed, Italy was able to retain these islands. This came about becaise Italy had joined the *Entente Cordiale* in World War I, and Turkey had joined the Central Powers, so there was no chance of the *Entente* forcing Italy to give the Dodecanese islands to Greece. But in World War II, Italy had joined the Axis and Greece the Allies. The British occupied the islands in 1944 after the Germans, Italians, and Bulgarians retreated from Greece, and they remained there until 1946. In a formal agreement with Italy in 1947, the islands were turned over to Greece, these becoming the last territory added to make up the Greek state as we know it today.

Nine

Greek Religion

THE DEVELOPMENT OF GREEK RELIGION FOLLOWS A complex path over a period of 2000 years, from polytheism to the Olympic deities, through the "mystery religions," and the less dramatic but spiritually very important philosophical monotheism, arriving finally at Christianity. To trace this complex path in detail is beyond the scope of this volume, but we will briefly review the principal elements.

CULTISM AND THE OLYMPIC DEITIES

Ancient Greek religion was polytheistic, a Greek word meaning the worship of many gods. In addition to developing concepts of their own gods from throughout the Greek world, at that time the Greeks were also influenced by earlier cultures in Asia Minor and Egypt with which there was contact. Mycenaean clay tablets discovered at Knossos in Crete and at Pylos in the western Peloponnese, dating from about 1300 BC, contain the names of many of these Greek gods, so it is obvious that some of these had existed from even before that early date.

Greek religion involved more than the simple worship of statues. Through their religion the Greeks attempted to understand the natural mysteries of the world in which they lived, or to appeal to the supernatural for help in events beyond their own control. They honored their deities by placing statues depicting them in temples and shrines. But very often these statues were erected as a matter of civic adornment and pride rather than for the purpose of religious worship. Well known impressive examples were the Parthenon on the Akropolis hill in Athens displaying inside an enormous standing statue of Athena, the city's patron goddess; another was the figure of the huge seated Zeus in the main temple at Olympia. Many others were more modest but also well fashioned. Over the centuries, certain gods became more important than others, and a hierarchy of gods began to emerge.

Two persons in archaic Greek history are responsible for creating a more clear and common understanding and acceptance of the cultist religions, and especially what came to be popularly known as the "Olympian family," as will be described. These were the poets Homer, who lived in the first half of the eighth century BC, and Hesiod, who lived in the second half of the same century; the writings of both of these came down to us substantially intact.

In those early days, the ancient world evolved a more or less personal and word-of-mouth view of the cultist concept. Most likely there were some more formalized oral traditions passed on through the bards and poets of ancient times, at a time when writing hardly existed at all and there was no way for people to be literate. It took millenia for writing to be widely adopted as a means of communication. But by the eighth century BC, Homer's dramatic description of the Trojan war had appeared in writing. In poetic form, he described not only the battles and the heroes but the participation of the gods in many events and incidents; he made clear the gods' characters and their relationships to each other. Homer's *Iliad* and *Odyssey* became the first texts widely disseminated by being copied by hand over and over again, that helped to guide the masses into a more uniform concept of their cultist religion based on anthropomorphic gods, that is, those that had the form of man.

The gods were said to live on Mount Olympos, the highest peak in Greece, and their rulers were king Zeus and queen Hera. The pantheon consisted of twelve principal gods and some lesser ones; each was associated with a particular responsibilty. For example, Athena was the goddess of wisdom; Poseidon, god of the sea; and so on. (See the following page). The gods were given human personalities. They had nobility and pettiness, they had passions, and they played tricks on each other. They helped certain mortals or brought them to grief; they took sides and they competed with each other. In general, they were lively examples of human beings, but they were also immortal and had extraordinary powers. They took other forms at will, changing into mortals or animals as might suit them, and could appear anywhere or to anyone as they chose. In the mythical cosmos there were nymphs and nereids, demigods of whom one parent was a god and one a mortal, such as the hero Achilles in Homer's *Iliad*. There were the half-god-half-animal figures such as satyrs and centaurs, combining human and animal characteristics; and some mortals who had divine powers. Ancient poets, writers, and playwrights, wrote the gods and half-gods into their epics and plays, and freely interpreted their actions and personalities, and how they affected their heroes and the course of events. The creation of these stories, their lively embellishment and interpretation over the ages, gave rise to a group of stories known as "myths."

Hesiod's *Theogony* is a different kind of book. In it the author sets out his concepts of the mythological origins of the world, the geneology of some 300 gods, and he describes the events that led to the rule of the Olympian kingdom by Zeus.

The human need to understand events, and, especially, to seek guidance for future actions, very early led to the development of oracles housed in beautiful shrines, the most famous of which was that at Delphi dedicated to Apollo, the god of light. This shrine was attended by priestesses skilled in creating

The Olympian Gods (mythology)

Notes: The principal gods are shown in bold type. Some women were mortals. The Titans were earlier gods. As may be seen, Zeus was not only king of the gods, but sired many of them, plus quite a few demi-gods and mortals.

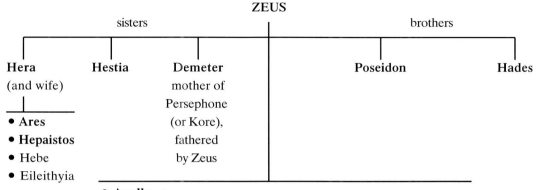

ZEUS

| sisters | | | brothers | |

Hera
(and wife)

Hestia

Demeter
mother of
Persephone
(or Kore),
fathered
by Zeus

Poseidon

Hades

- **Ares**
- **Hepaistos**
- Hebe
- Eileithyia

- **Apollo** ⟩ twins, mother was Leto, a Titaness.
- **Artemis** /
- **Hermes**, mother was Maia, a Titan daughter.
- **Athena**, mother was Metis, a Titan daughter, first wife of Zeus.
- **Dionysos**, mother was Semele, a mortal eastern princess.
- **Aphrodite**, mother was Dione, second wife of Zeus.
  (According to some legends, Aphrodite, meaning
  "foam-born," rose from the sea of no parents.

Some other consorts and children of Zeus

- EURYNOME: daughter of Okeanos; mother of the three Graces, godesses of charm and beauty in life.
- EUROPA: eastern princess, brought to Crete on bull's back (Zeus in disguise); four children.
- ANTIOPE: Theban princess; two sons.
- DANAË: Argive princess; bore Perseus.
- IO: daughter of river god Inachos; one son.
- LEDA: Spartan queen, coupled with Zeus who took the form of a swan; two sons, and one daughter, who was Helen of Troy.
- THEMIS: Titaness; three girls, the goddesses of order in nature, the Horai (Hours)
- ALKMENE: Mycenaean princess; bore Herakles (Hercules).
- MNEMOSYNE (Memory): Titaness; bore the nine Muses, goddesses of the intellectual arts.

The Principal Gods (and Roman equivalents)

- ZEUS (**Jupiter**): king of the gods.
- HERA (**Juno**): queen of the gods.
- HESTIA (**Vesta**): goddess of the hearth.
- POSEIDON (**Neptune**): god of the sea
- HADES (**Pluto**): god of the underworld.
- ARES (**Mars**): god of war.
- DEMETER (**Ceres**): goddess of agriculture

- APHRODITE (**Venus**): goddess of love and beauty
- HEPHAISTOS (**Vulcan**): god of fire.
- APOLLO (**Apollo**): god of light (the sun).
- ARTEMIS (**Diana**): Goddess of the hunt, youth, the moon.
- HERMES (**Mercury**): the god's herald.
- ATHENA (**Minerva**): goddess of wisdom and battle.
- DIONYSOS (**Bacchus**): god of fertility and wine.

an awe-inspiring atmosphere. The oracles uttered their answers in riddlelike statements to questions posed by supplicants, or they prophesized the future for them. So impressed and awed were the ancients by these rituals, that if the prophesies turned out to be wrong, they blamed their own misinterpretations rather than blame the oracle. Soothsayers and seers were also developed to explain to their patrons the true meaning of certain omens, or to gove advice on what actions to take. Sacrifices of animals, or even humans, or some other ritual would be performed to appease or appeal to one of the gods.

Down the centuries, the Romans adopted and developed a polytheistic religion similar to that of the Greeks they would eventually dominate politically beginning in the second century BC. Though early Roman religious concepts did not see their gods as having human characteristics, Jupiter and Juno were more or less equivalent to Zeus and Hera; Minerva equated to Athena; Ceres was Demeter; and so on. In some cases the Romans adopted the Greek god without change, as for example Apollo.

MYSTERY RELIGIONS

The character and actions of the gods as described by Homer were intended to interest and amuse and not to cause fear. Though what they stood for helped explain the mysteries of nature, people in the ancient world began to need something more from which they could derive spiritual satisfaction. The deities did not entirely satisfy emotionally, especially as philosophical thought developed and man began to think more intelligently about his own afterworld. The Greeks were not the first to feel this need, and a number of religious ceremonial practices became familiar to them from the east, especially during the great colonization period of the eighth to the sixth centuries BC. The results were the creation of a number of "mystery religions." These grew into prominence during classical times and were popular during the long Roman period, until Christianity was formally accepted by the Roman Emperor in AD 392.

Among the principal mystery deities, most of which were related to fertility, were: Demeter, goddess of grains and especially corn, of the harvest, mother-earth; her daughter Persephone (known also to the Greeks as Kore), who was also goddess of vegetation; and Dionysos (also called *Bakchos* in Greek, and *Bacchus* in Latin), god of the trees and the grapevine and wine-making, and therefore also of fertility. Apollo was another highly regarded figure of the mysteries, being god of light and therefore the sun, of inspiration, of music and song.

The mysteries themselves consisted of secret rites, held annually such as in the spring or at harvest time, or when the wine was ready for drinking. The ceremonies might begin with purification of the devotees, such as by a ritualistic bath in the sea, then in procession bearing figures and relics they would proceed to the temple of the god where the secret rites would be held. All this was accompanied by dancing and singing and some sort of religious drama acted out for the benefit and pleasure of the worshippers. The whole was intended to be uplifting and inspiring. Bulls, goats and pigs were sometimes sacrificed during the rites as objects of fertility.

The main mystery sites were at Eleusis near Athens, dedicated to Demeter and her daughter Persephone (Kore); at the island of Delos, dedicated to Apollo; at Delphi, dedicated to Apollo and later also to Dionysos; and at the island of Samothrace, dedicated to the "Great Gods," the *Kabeiroi* (in Latin the *Cabiri*), later to Demeter also as mother-goddess — all associated with fertility. Many of these mystery religions were practiced in elaborate temples, but another such religion known as Orphism (after the mythical god Orpheus), scorned the trappings of ritual and its followers met in the open or wherever to discuss aspects of their faith and to teach it to others.

Also popular, and dating from archaic times, were religious celebrations that involved formal athletic and cultural contests. The Olympic Games are well known, having been resumed in modern times as purely athletic contests (see p.220). But they also were religious rites in ancient times. Other such games and festivals were held the best known of which included the Pythian festival at Delphi; the Isthmian at the eastern side of that narrow neck not far from Corinth; the Nemean games, at a site near Mycenae on the Peloponnese; the Delian festival on Delos island. Not so formal, but no less important as religious rites and rituals, were other unscheduled athletic contests held in thanksgiving or to honor an important event, such as victory in battle. Homer wrote about such contests held by the Greek warriors at Troy in the thirteenth century BC, for example, and historians accompanying Alexander the Great during his conquests in Persia nearly a thousand years later also recorded athletic contests associated with religious ritual.

Pre-Christian polytheistic beliefs had lasted 2000 years and had taken a very strong hold on the minds of the people, in various forms. But as early as the sixth century BC, a form of monotheism was already being developed in the ancient Greek world by a number of philosophers such as Herakleitos, Anaxagoras, Protagoras, and Sokrates, identifying God with Logos (mind or reason), Beauty, First Mover, Unknown God, and so on. The freedom of expression of the Greeks and their natural urgency to examine, question, talk about, and form philosophies about such basic elements as the natural phenomena, and living, thinking, and dying, made the Greeks especially receptive to the spiritual movement when it appeared called Christianity.

CHRISTIANITY
Saint Paul
(c. 10 AD-c. 67 AD)

The Christian religion emerged in Hellenized Judea (Palestine) under Roman rule and its adherents suffered much before it eventually won over polytheism. The Roman-occupied Greek world, especially the Greek peninsula, continued its pagan beliefs and rites and was not

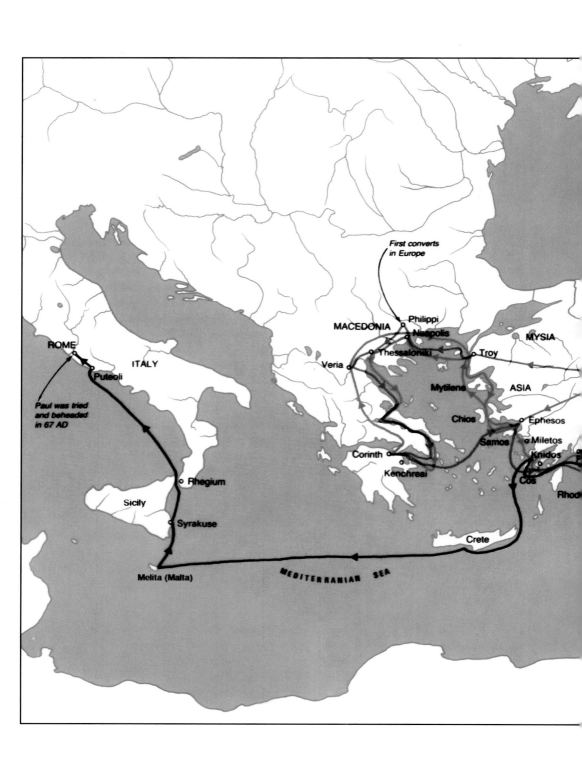

First converts
in Europe

MACEDONIA
Philippi
Neapolis
Thessaloniki
Veria
Troy
MYSIA

ROME
Puteoli
ITALY
Mytilene
ASIA

Paul was tried
and beheaded
in 67 AD

Chios
Ephesos

Samos
Miletos

Corinth
Knidos

Kenchreai
Cos

Rhegium
Rhod

Sicily

Syrakuse

Crete

Melita (Malta)

MEDITERRANEAN SEA

First Journey 46-48 A D, with Barnabas

Second Journey 49-52, with Silas and Timothy

Third Journey 53-57, with Timothy and Erastus

Journey to Rome 59-61, arrives Spring 62

MAP 9.0
SAINT PAUL'S MISSIONARY
JOURNEYS

Saint Paul made three missionary journeys to make
converts to Christianity. His second journey was to
Greece, where he made the first European converts.

immediately affected by the events concerning Jesus Christ and his teachings. His trial and crucifixion in Jerusalem in AD 33, were civil problems of the Roman administration there, as were the trials and executions of other Christian leaders.

The twelve first-rank disciples of Christ were known also as his "Apostles," a Greek word meaning "envoys," in the sense that they were sent forth to spread his teachings. There were other apostles as well; one of these, Saint Paul, is a most important figure in this early missionary work, first bringing Christianity to polytheistic Greece in AD 49. (See Map 9.0).

Although Saint Paul was not one of the original twelve disciples and in all probability never knew or even saw or heard Jesus at all, he is considered by many to be the leading figure in the Christian faith after Christ himself. He was not always so. Born in Tarsus in southern Asia Minor around AD 9, and named Saul, he became a zealous defender of his Jewish faith against the teachings of Christ, who was considered to be a revisionist Jew who had proclaimed himself as the Messiah. But the message and teachings of Christ did not die with his crucifixion and death in AD 33. Four years later, Saul was sent to Damascus by the Jewish high priests in Jerusalem to help counter the persisting new belief. On the way, suddenly Saul had a blinding vision and as he fell down he heard the voice of Christ address him directly, "Why do you persecute me?" Temporarily blinded and emotionally drained, he was led to Damascus where he gradually recovered his vision. The experience affected him deeply and caused him to convert to Christianity abruptly and completely. He was baptized and his name changed to Paul. He soon became the most energetic, gifted, and persuasive missionary of the new faith. Originally directed to those of the Jewish faith, Saint Paul's missionary work found greater success among the gentiles (i.e., those not Jewish), so much so that he became known as "the apostle to the gentiles."

In the spring of AD 49, Saint Paul arrived in Greece on the first missionary journey to preach the Christian faith by anyone on European soil. He was accompanied by Saints Silas, Timothy, and Luke. Saint Paul made his first converts to Christianity in Philippi, which was then the principal town of the Romans in Macedonia. He continued his trip visiting Thessaloniki, Veria, Athens, and Corinth, making many converts among the Jews and the gentiles. This first journey to Greece lasted two-and-a-half years, until the fall of 51. Saint Paul was successful in starting Christian communities in each place he visited except in Athens, where people were less receptive. Athens appalled Saint Paul because of its numerous pagan temples, shrines, and idols. Although he was invited to formally address the Greek philosophers and their followers and to explain the Christian beliefs, they were not convinced and preferred their Epicurian and Stoic philosophies. Even so, some prominent Athenians were impressed and accepted Christianity.

Saint Paul also made other missionary journeys, to Cyprus and to the Greek cities of Asia Minor, including Ephesos and Troy, as well as to Rhodes and Crete. He returned to Macedonia and Corinth twice more. In some of these places he suffered much opposition from the zealots of the established and traditional Jewish religious communities, and was at times beaten, arrested, jailed, and brought before Roman magistrates on formal complaints. Sometimes he had to flee to escape these indignities. But the converts he made increased in numbers and grew into Christian communities. He kept in touch with them by letters on the faith and with his own visits or those of others he sent to them from time to time.

The Jewish high priests continued their campaigns against Paul, and in 58 he was again brought before the Roman magistrates in Jerusalem on various charges, he was jailed for two years in Caesarea, in Asia Minor. When he eventually realized that he would never receive a fair trial in the atmosphere of this area, he exercised his right as a Roman citizen and requested trial in Rome. There he was first kept under house arrest for an extended period, during which time he continued his teachings by letter. Finally, he had the misfortune of still being in Rome when Emperor Nero (54-68) made the Christians the scapegoats for the great fire that destroyed much of Rome in 64. Paul became one of the victims a short time later, and he was sentenced and executed by beheading in 67.* But the churches he founded remained and grew.

THE SPREAD OF THE CHURCH

C hristian communities throughout the Empire grew steadily between AD 70 and the beginning of the fourth century. They did not grow unopposed, for waves of persecution took place at the hands of pagan Roman emperors, starting with Nero. The early Christians were looked upon with suspicion and even hatred by others. Their persecution by the Roman state had its basis, at least in part, by the refusal of the Christians to worship the state pagan gods, and in other ways related to their religion, disobeying Roman law. A popular Roman spectacle in those times was placing unrepentant Christians into an arena together with hungry and ferocious wild animals. In spite of all this, churches continued to be established, and Christians worshipped openly, for the most part, and the power of the church continued to spread.

Christians increased in number substantially to where, by the year 300, it is estimated they comprised 5 to 10 percent of the total population in the Western Roman Empire and an even greater proportion in the Eastern Empire. This caused some of the emperors to feel that the church threatened the imperial authority of the state. Christian persecution came to a climax under Emperor Diocletian, in the period 301 to 305. Christian churches were destroyed, their books burned, priests jailed, and all were required to sacrifice to the official state gods on pain of death. But Diocletian went too far. Most likely in recognition of political trends, his successor, Galerius, in 311 issued an edict shortly before his death officially tolerating the Christian religion throughout the empire and allowing the reconstruction of the churches.

The final breakthrough for the Christians came in 312, when Emperor Constantine (later to be known "the Great") on his way to Rome with his army

---

* Also during Nero's persecutions, Peter, the first among the Apostles and one of Christ's disciples, was brought to Rome, where he was crucified head down in AD 64 , when he was about 70 years old.

to do battle for control of the empire, is said to have seen the sign of the cross over the sun and the message "in this sign conquer." Constantine soundly defeated his rival, resulting in his becoming the senior Augustus. He considered the victory to be a confirmation of his vision. By 313, Constantine and his fellow Augustus Licinius issued the "Edict of Milan," by which they granted complete freedom to the Christians and restored all church properties previously confiscated.

Finally, after first putting down Licinius and becoming sole emperor, in 324, Constantine decided to build a new imperial capital in the east at the site of ancient Byzantium, calling it New Rome, though people came to call it after him, *Constantinoupolis*, or Constantinople. No polytheistic shrines would be allowed there nor any but Christian rites. The city was completed in 330 and became Constantine's capital of the eastern empire. With the decline of the western empire due to the invasions of Germanic tribes, the creation of this city became a significant factor in the growth of the church. In addition, in 325 Constantine called for the first Ecumenical Council of the Church, to be held in Nikaia, and this began the intimate association of the Byzantine throne with the church, as explained in Chapter Six.

Over the next fifty years, in spite of more repressions of Christians during the reign of Julian, the church grew to when Theodosius I (379-395), declared Christianity the official state religion, in 392. It was the turn of paganism to be persecuted.

THE OLYMPIC GAMES
(776-BC-AD 393)

The Olympic Games are conducted today as a purely international athletic competition. The event as originally created was also an athletic competition, but with very important religious and political emphasis. Because it has come down to us from nearly 3000 years ago, a brief description of the ancient history of the event, will be of interest.

Olympia is the name of a religious site that was installed in the western Peloponnese, Greece, beginning in the first millenium BC, although legend colors its true origins. By the ninth century BC, it became a shrine dedicated to Zeus, in whose glory the athletic games were held. Beginning in 776 BC, the games were held every four years for the next twelve centuries. The games embodied the ancient Greek philosophy of "a sound mind in a sound body."

Our knowledge of Olympia and the games comes to us from many ancient sources. The site was discovered in modern times only in 1766, but serious investigations did not begin until 1829, by a French team of archeologists. It was no easy matter. The site was found buried under 13 feet (4 meters) of material washed down through the centuries from Mount Kronos just north of the location and by heavy and frequent flooding of the Kladeos River to the west and the Alpheios to the south. A number of heavy earthquakes during the centuries had also taken their toll on the temples there.

The Olympia site was brought to its present state by more than fifteen years of work by German archeologists, beginning in 1874, which was continued by them until recently despite a number of interruptions. All sculptures and artifacts that were excavated are in the small Olympia Museum on the grounds, or in the National Archeological Museum in Athens. The ruined temples and other structures were reassembled as well as possible, providing the modern visitor a good impression of how the site looked orginally.

The frequent political rivalries and wars between the Greek city-states were put aside for thirty days on the occasion of the Olympic Games each four years. in a spirit of truce that was respected and taken very seriously by all in spite of their differences. The competitions were open only to qualified men and boys whose native tongue was Greek. The winners of the formal athletic events having their names inscribed in permanent records. They were honored by everyone. In addition to the athletic contests, other cultural events also took place during the festivities. The finest Greek authors and artists participated and presented their works for the entertainment and appreciation of all.

The Olympia site reached its zenith in the fifth century BC, a number of beautiful temples having been installed there by that time. In addition to the many large and small temples, numerous fine sculptures from donors adorned buildings and were mounted on pedestals located along the walks and elsewhere on the grounds. Of course, the large Temple of Zeus was the main attraction, inside of which was the gigantic seated ivory-and-gold statue of Zeus (over 40 feet high, or13 meters). It was made by Pheidias, the famous Athenian sculptor also responsible for the Parthenon on the Akropolis in Athens. The huge statue of Zeus was considered one of the Seven Wonders of the ancient world (see p.104). The modern museum at Olympia contains a small but carefully made scale model of the site as it may have looked at the time, as well as a sampling of the sculptures and other artifacts found in the excavations.

Olympia remained relatively untouched throughout antiquity. The Slavs invaded the area in AD 267 and caused some damage, but the games continued to be held as before. Theodosius I, the first Roman Christian Emperor (AD 375-395), banned all pagan rites in AD 393, and the games came to an end. His successor, Theodosius II, went further and ordered the pagan temples to be pulled down. By the eighth century of our era, this, plus invasions of Germanic and Slavic tribes as well as natural disasters, had destroyed Olympia completely. The site continued to be hidden until the remains were again uncovered and restored more than a thousand years later.

Baron Pierre de Coubertin of France initiated efforts and took the lead to revive the olympic spirit in modern times. This resulted in the first modern games being held in 1896 at the ancient stadium in central Athens, beautifully reconstructed in gleaming white marble for the purpose through the efforts and donations of various individuals, Greek and foreign.

So important and consistent were the Olympic Games that by the fourth century or so BC, dates were reckoned by the games. Thus, one would refer to an event as having taken place, say, in 90.2, or two years after the 90th Olympiad. This was based, as we have seen, on the first Olympiad in 776 BC of our calendar, the games being held each four years thereafter.

THE HOLY MOUNTAIN: MOUNT ATHOS

A description of religion in Greece would not be complete without including a brief mention of Mount Athos, that easternmost finger of the Chalkidiki peninsula in northern Greece. Mount Athos has been operating for at least twelve centuries as a restricted, wholly self-administered and self-sustaining community of Eastern (Greek) Orthodox priests and monks.

Strabo and Herodotos wrote that Persian King Xerxes, bringing his invasion fleet to Greece (see Map 2.2, p.42) in 481 BC, ordered the cutting of a canal across the narrowest and lowest point of the isthmus, at about the location of the present town of Roda. This was ordered allegedly because in 492 BC the Persian general Mardonius, bringing a Persian army and fleet to invade Greece, had lost 300 ships and 20,000 men in rough seas off Cape Akrothoos. Historians have been unable to find documentary proof that this canal was ever dug by the Persians, or if started it was ever completed. No physical trace of it has been found, either. Some say that ships may have been hauled across the isthmus by rolling them on logs the 1.5 mile (2.4 kilometer) distance.

In the Eastern Roman Empire, Christian monasticism, or the retreat from life to live a solitary existence and seek communion with God to achieve the salvation of one's soul, formally began in the fourth century AD. This came into being as a result of persecutions of Christians by the Roman state over the preceding three centuries. Even earlier, monastic communities existed in Egypt, Syria, and Asia Minor as well as in Palestine and Constantinople. Many of these communities were destroyed or abandoned as a result of religious persecutions, by the Arab invasions, as well as by hostilities during Byzantine times, especially during the "iconoclastic period (726-842 AD).* During this period many monks fled to Mount Athos.

Monasteries Established

The Islamic conquests that began in AD 632 included many important Christian centers and their surrounding areas (Damascus 635, Jerusalem 638, Alexandria 646, Cyprus 648, Rhodes 654, among others). This caused many monks from these places to flee to the area of what was to beginning to be called the Holy Mountain, a ragged, mountainous, sparsely inhabited area in northern Greece. This religious exodus continued through the periods of more Arab conquests of the area, and because of their attacks on Constantinople itself 673 to 678 and 717 to 718. Its isolation

---

* The period reflected strong opposition by the state and some religious leaders to the veneration of images, or icons, in order that the humanity of Christ and other religious figures could be emphasized. After raging for over a century, the controversy eventually died down. One lasting effect, it led to the stylized depiction of the figures on the icons by Byzantines artists in order that they should not look too lifelike. As art, the style has been much admired, to the present day.

MAP 9.1 HOLY MOUNTAIN: MOUNT ATHOS (LOCATION)

This rugged and mountainous terrain, sparsely populated, was occupied by Christian monks escaping oppression in Byzantine Asia Minor and other areas during the iconoclastic period in the seventh century AD. The area was formally designated an excusively religious site by Byzantine Emperor Basil I in AD 885 and remains so to this day.

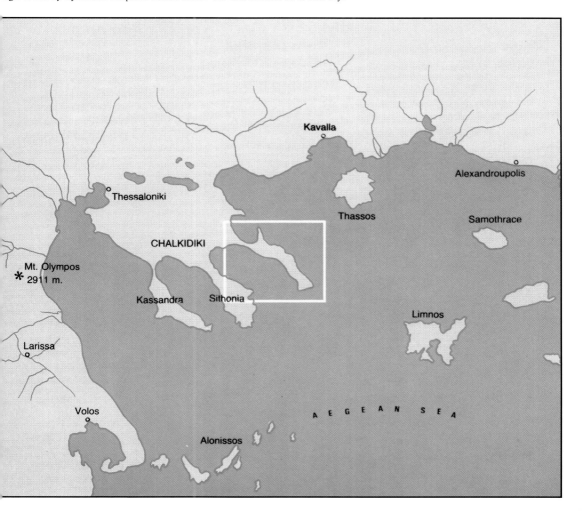

MAP 9.2 HOLY MOUNTAIN: MOUNT ATHOS (DETAIL)

Twenty large monasties are located throughout the peninsula, connected by dirt roads. The capital in the center is Kariai, reache
from the port of Daphne.

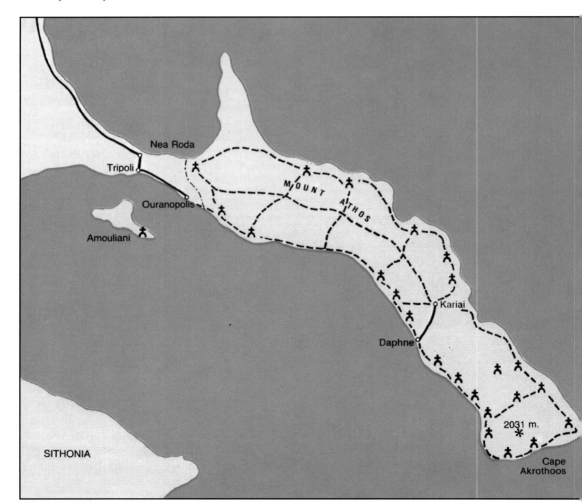

appealed to those in search of a meditative religious life. (The word "monk" comes from the Greek word *monachos* meaning one who is alone.) However, little factual information is known of the earliest years of Mount Athos.

Recorded history first shows that monks from Mount Athos took part in a council convened in Constantinople by the Byzantine Empress Theodora in 843. In 885, by *chrysobull** of Emperor Basil I the area was set aside as areligious retreat. All others were forbidden to remain in the zone. Although the whole peninsula was known as *Ayion Oros*, that is, the Holy Mountain, from an early date in its formal religious development, the name was officially adopted in a chrysobull of Byzantine Emperor Constantine IX Monomachos in 1046. The name Mount Athos is in fact the name of the highest peak at the southernmost end of the peninsula, but the name is also popularly used to designate the entire area.

Succeeding Byzantine emperors financed the construction of a number of large, well-built monasteries. Beautiful religious artifacts, ornaments, and illuminated documents were created by those living there, or were donated by others. The first elaborate monastery was the Great Lavra, founded about AD 963, through the efforts of Athanasios the Athonite, who was a friend and confessor to Emperor Nikephoros Phokas (963-969). The construction of many other monasteries and lesser buildings soon followed, and a total of about 40 were built altogether, with a monk population reaching a peak of about 40,000. No females reside on the peninsula, nor are any permitted to visit there. No female animals are allowed either, any bigger than chickens or cats.

Pirates and other marauders raided Mount Athos over the centuries, but, ironically, it then prospered under the recognition and respect of the Turkish sultans from 1453 to 1821. However, the church's support of the Greek insurgents in the 1821 revolution brought Mount Athos much suffering at the hands of the Turkish Muslims. The area became independent from the Ottomans along with that part of Greece after the Balkan War of 1913.

Today, the peninsula is an autonomous Greek Orthodox monastic dependency of Greece. A special visa is required to visit there. The Holy Mountain now has twenty monasteries: seventeen Greek, one Russian, one Bulgarian, and one Serb. There are also some lesser hermitages. The total number of monks is now fewer than 1500. The Holy Council that administers its own government at Kariai in the center of the peninsula, consists of one deputy from each of the twenty monasteries.

Meteora

There are numerous other Greek Orthodox monastic retreats in Greece, many of which are no longer in use. Some of these may be visited. The most spectacular is at an impressive site called Meteora. This is a monastic Greek Orthodox community near Kalambaka in central Thessaly, established originally about AD 1336. The community eventually grew to thirteen

---

* Chrysobull: an imperial edict affixed with a golden seal (Greek "chryso," Latin "bulla").

monasteries, with its supplementary buildings, all constructed on the tops of gigantic and spectacular perpendicular sheer, dark grey rock pinnacles, like tusks, some hundreds of feet high and most accessible only by a winch lift. Meteora was originally supported by the Serbian conquerors of Thessaly. In the eighteenth century, the area began to decline as a monastic retreat and is now largely a tourist curiosity. It is still administered by the Greek Orthodox Church, with only four monasteries open, operated by a handfull of monks to accommodate casual visitors.

Epilogos

THE GREAT IDEA

I f since their country's independence the Greek people had a dream that affected the history, mood, and economy of their nation, it was the concept of expanding their borders to become a facsimile of the Byzantine Empire, if not becoming the empire itself. Who could blame them? This was the last grand view of Greek presence and dominance in their recent history. Nor could they forget the great accomplishments of the Classical and Hellenistic Periods. As we have seen, this dream became "The Great Idea" — "a Greece of the seven seas and two continents."

The people of Greek heritage were always proud of their ancestors' ability to have achieved a highly developed ancient culture that made a major impact on a civilized world to modern times. They were convinced that someday they would recover not only the land of their forefathers but all that area where Greek people settled and resided for more than 2500 years. It was a dream that began to seem possible to convert into reality when, following the initial independence of 1832, large territories and Greek population were acquired in systematic steps from a declining Ottoman Empire, and added periodically to a growing Greece (see Chapter Eight).

Even earlier, one of the first to widely proclaim this dream was the patriot Constantine Rhigas, born about 1757 at a town near ancient Pherai in Greece (north of Athens). He was well educated, a true intellectual, and served in a number of important posts with prominent Greek officials in the Balkans. Inspired mostly by the French Revolution, in 1797 he published a revolutionary manifesto describing his ideas on the formation of a Hellenic Republic which would include the diverse peoples of Turkish-occupied Europe (Thrace and the Balkans), the Danubian provinces of Moldavia and Wallachia, Greece itself and the Aegean islands, and Asia Minor. He suggested that the capital would be at Constantinople. His treatise included a description and a map, a constitution, and a national anthem. Three thousand copies of his manifesto were distributed to the enthusiastic Greeks over a wide area, his anthem was popular among them, and he originally founded the *Philiki Etairia* (Society of Friends), where these and other patriotic themes were discussed by the members. (The *Etairia* did not become the secret revolutionary society until later, in 1814.) But Rhigas' patriotic fervor led to his being arrested in Vienna in 1798, turned over to the Turkish authorities in Belgrade, and he was killed by them there. His martyrdom fanned the flames of other patriots, and kept the idea alive of an enlarged Hellenic Republic molded on the Byzantine Empire.

Also before the 1821 revolution, the Phanariotes were able to position themselves into ruling the Vlach Danubian provinces under the nose of the Ottoman sultan, whose semiautonomous territory it was. Having been able also to insinuate themselves in key roles in the sultan's court over many decades, the now weakening Ottoman government inflated the dreams of many Greek nationalists. Referring to that period, the prominent English Byzantine historian Steven Runciman has written: "Soon, the older Phanariotes hoped, there would be such disorder in the central administration that *even the Turks would be content to let the Greeks take over the government.*"* (Italics mine.) The war of independence of the Greeks in 1821 was to be a general uprising of all the Eastern Orthodox faithful in the Danubian provinces and in all Greece. Would a Greek takeover in western Turkey be far behind?

This first Greek attempt to realize The Great Idea was shattered when the Greek uprising in the Balkans in 1821 led by Phanariote Prince Alexander Ypsilantis was quickly crushed by Turkish armies. The Orthodox Christians in the Balkans did not rise, and the failure of this military effort discouraged the Greek populations from doing the same. Instead of their taking over the Ottoman government, the Phanariotes in Constantinople were brutally wiped out by the Turks in revenge. But Greek perseverance was finally rewarded by an expanded Greece.

By the end of the second Balkan War of 1913, which again substantially expanded Greek national territories, about 60 percent as many Greeks still lived outside the newly-formed Greek boundaries as lived within Greece itself. Nearly two million of these lived in western Asia Minor and in Turkish Thrace. The energetic and ambitious Prime Minister of Greece, Eleftherios Venizelos, went to the Paris Peace Conference in December 1918 following the end of World War I a month earlier. He presented a claim on behalf of his people and nation for a part of Turkey in western Anatolia and Thrace that very nearly equalled in area that comprised Greece itself at that time (see Map 7.7, p.192). If the area he claimed did not also include the city of Constantinople, it was not from modesty on the part of the Prime Minister, but because he understood that the Great Powers would insist that this strategic city and the Bosporus it

---

*Steven Runciman, *The Great Church in Captivity* ; (Cambridge University Press, 1968) p.396.

guarded connecting the Black Sea with the Sea of Marmora and the Mediterranean, would remain either neutral or under international control.

Another aspiration for The Great Idea was also shattered when the Greek armies invading Asia Minor in 1919, to ensure their possession of Greek-populated Smyrna and its hinterland, were finally routed by the forces of General Mustapha Kemal Pasha. There are many thousands of persons of Greek heritage living today whose parents were among the one-and-a-half million Greeks fleeing in panic for their lives in 1922 from the avenging Turkish troops. The many-generations-old residency in Asia minor for many came to an abrupt end, and they made their way to Greece. The Greek economy, never strong, reeled from the impact of having to provide for these people. A military government took over in Greece from the king that was deposed and his cabinet ministers who were blamed for the failure in Asia Minor. To make up for the humiliation they suffered at losing the war, they actually planned to attack the Turks once again in eastern Thrace and push them entirely out of Europe, including Constantinople. But these Greek officers were dissuaded by Venizelos himself, who saw that Greece had more to lose than to gain by this action, and thus ended the last dream of The Great Idea.

Other National Problems

In other ways, too, Greek nationalistic pride inadvertently made an impact on their country. Many thousands of Greeks lived in Egypt for many generations saw no need to be anything but Greek citizens. They were stunned when the nationalistic Egyptian premier Gamal Abdul Nasser declared in 1952 that they would have to take Egyptian citizenship. Thousands chose to leave for Greece.

The specter of the avenging Turks loomed up again in 1974 when Greece and independent Cyprus attempted a political union. In response, the Turks promptly invaded Cyprus and took military possession of the northern 40 percent of the island on behalf of a less than 20 percent Turkish minority, who had lived in their own or mixed communities dotted throughout Cyprus. There was no Greek Cypriot army, and the Greek forces were too far away to be able to come to their aid. Anyway, the Greeks did not have the military might of Turkey, whose population is five times that of Greece.

Other major problems of Greece in recent history include the royalist-antiroyalist rivalry that has led in the past to sometimes untimely changes in leadership. As the government changed so did a large number of people in key positions. This practice is normal in many countries when political parties change. But in comparison with other nations, the replacement of government and semigovernment officials goes to a much deeper level in Greece, affecting most key positions and some not so key as a matter of patronage, including political figures, military officers, many civil servants, and key figures in government-controlled banking and industry. The negative impact is compounded on the political and economic well-being of the country. What happens is that good order and systematic growth is replaced by an atmosphere in which everyone waits for his turn and opportunity to benefit — having been deprived when others were in power.

The rivalry of the political left and right has also been another debilitating element in modern Greece. Who can forget the brutal civil war of 1943-1949? The view of the Greek military that communism was again threatening the nation in1967 resulted in their overthrow of the democratic government and the departure of the young king, Constantine II. The fiercely independent and outspoken Greek people were shocked by the stern military atmosphere imposed on the country by the Junta, where a critical statement overheard in public, or some other offense, could lead to imprisonment on a barren Greek island, and, in some instances, beatings and torture. But the economy prospered for a while. Many Greeks in later and more liberal times following the joyous overthrow of the Junta reflected that, after all, maybe things were better when a strong government imposed firm measures for the common good on a sometimes unruly and self-seeking populace. Once again, a plebiscite by the newly installed democratic government in1974 terminated the monarchy.

Greek Emigration

When Greece was being newly created, bit by bit, large Greek population inflows from outlying areas had to be accommodated. Some were peaceful movements, and others more violent such as the already mentioned forced migrations from Asia Minor in 1922. Equally significant were the large population outflows that emanated from Greece itself during its modern history. The rapidly expanding economies of certain countries needed workers not available in sufficient numbers from their own indigenous populations. Among other peoples, Greeks left their own country and went to these nations in large numbers. Many returned, but the large majority subsequently stayed in those foreign lands. Today, nearly half as many persons of Greek origin live abroad permanently, as live in Greece itself. The following table is indicative, but represents only the numbers that actually left Greece, not their growth within their newly adopted lands.

Greek Emigration (Based on Greek government statistics.)

To United States 1890-1985	700,000
Greeks from Turkish-occupied Greece and from Turkey proper.	400,000
To Canada 1890-1985	200,000
To Australia 1890-1985	500,000 (some sources say over 700.000)
To Germany 1821-1940	50,000
To West Germany 1949-1985	400,000 (even more worked there and then returned to Greece)
To Russia before WW I	800,000
WW I-1985	400,000
To Argentina to 1985	40,000
Brazil to 1985	50,000
England to 1985	5,000 (Plus 100,000 Cypriots)
France to 1985	30,000
Belgium to 1985	30,000
South Africa to 1985	50,000
Elsewhere to 1985	200,000
TOTAL	**3,905,000**

Greek society today is trying to cope with its never-ending economic and political problems, for the country is more vulnerable than other western countries to these changing conditions. It still depends largely on tourism and remittances from abroad for its hard currency. Recent entry into the European Economic Community has been helpful, and is beginning to help raise Greece's economy approching those of other European nations.

Meanwhile people of Greek origin abroad continue to have their affectionate ties with Greece and a deep sense of pride for their heritage. People of Greek heritage permanently living abroad maintain their Greekness by many means, such as clubs, cultural societies, and, especially, through the Greek Orthodox Church. Churches and their other facilities in America, Canada, Australia, and elsewhere provide spiritual as well as ethnic centers. These are growing in numbers.

A BIOGRAPHICAL NOTE

Just before the turn of the century, my paternal grandfather was mayor of his town of Aghios Konstantinos on the island of Samos and a member of the Senate, the island having virtual autonomy from the Ottoman government since 1559. He owned some fertile land, a provisions shop and two sailing boats that traded between the islands and Asia Minor nearby, carrying his own goods and freight for others. One of his boats carrying barrels of wine was run aground and smashed by the neglect of a drunken captain who had tapped the cargo enroute. The other suffered a similar fate shortly later in a heavy storm. In those days there were no insurance companies in Samos to help guard against possible dangers. Having to be personally responsible for the secure delivery of the freight as well carrying the risk for the safety of his own boats, these tragic mishaps suddenly turned my prominent grandfather into a debtor. Other families with better fortune from these same beginnings evolved into wealthy shipowners. My grandfather left Samos to escape imprisonment for debt and went to Rumania, a Greek Orthodox country with many Greeks at that time. He returned home two years later, my strongminded grandmother having somehow fixed things. But he soon died of pneumonia. He left nine children, the eldest of which was a son 15 years old. My father was the second son, aged 13.

To find work in that village and in those times, without resources of your own, was nearly impossible. A few years later the eldest brother left to find work in America where labor was greatly in demand. A family usually had to borrow to obtain the fare necessary for one of their sons to make the costly voyage. In those days to repay a debt was considered a primary obligation to keep up the honor of the family — a particularly sensitive point for my father's family. So a lengthy period was spent working abroad just to break even, and then the others at home still depended on the support of those working in America, and for the fare to bring them there as well.

When my own father went to America in 1907 (Samos was then still part of the Ottoman Empire; it was not freed until 1913), he joined his brother and other countrymen of his working in Peabody, Massachusetts, one of the many factory towns in the northeast welcoming immigrant labor. He arrived at Peabody in the morning and went to the house where his brother and friends were living. When they came home at the end of the working day, my father saw that they were all dressed in black. He was startled. "Who died?" he asked fearfully. "Nobody died," they replied, "these are our work clothes". They worked in a leather tannery and wore black because of the dyes. My father was stunned. "Is this America?" he asked in bitter disappointment. The natural beauty and warm friendliness of his native but impoverished island was replaced with the harsh reality of factory life in America.

Eventually my father married a young woman, also from Samos, and had a family. By this time, my father became relatively successful and owned a business. In 1930, he took us all back to visit his native land. The joy he felt to return after an absence of 23 years was infectious. I was only a little boy at the time, but I remember the trip vividly —everybody's hospitality and warmth, relatives and friends alike. The sense of identity my parents felt in their native land did not exist for them in the melting pot of America. When we returned to America several months later, there was a feeling of sadness in my parents that even I could sense without then understanding the reason. Vacationing was one thing, to return to Samos again to live permanently was out of the question. The economics had not changed very much, and my parents were out of tune now with the realities of that society. It must have been irrationally tempting to my father, as why else would we have stayed the long months that we did?

My father never went back to Greece again. He was never completely reconciled with living in America either, whatever its bounty, although he was always grateful for its freedom and opportunity.

What would all of these people who came to America by the millions from many lands have done without it? And how could America have grown and prospered without them?

Appendix

FOR FURTHER READING

T he general reader has available many interesting books to expand his knowledge of Greek history. The more advanced reader might seek primary sources or more detailed and scholarly texts intended for study not amusement. The suggestions I make here for the most part favor the more easily readable material, from the vast number of fine books available. The list covers specific periods and subjects. Some of these listed were used to prepare the material contained in this volume, as were many others too numerous to mention here. It is not felt that my omission to mention the many fine books on this broad subject requires any apology.

As the original language of **Hellenika** is English, the references are those available mostly in the English language.

The Bronze Age

T wo very good books on this period written by eminent historians, and with maps and illustrations, are published in Greece by Ekdotike Athenon S.A., Athens, as part of its sixteen volume set called **The History of the Hellenic World**. Unfortunately only the first two volumes are currently available in English. Volume 1, **Prehistory and Protohistory** (to 1100 BC), and Volume 2, **The Archaic Period** (1100-479 BC). Ekdotike Athenon also publish other excellent and well- illustrated volumes on the ancient period and a full list may be obtained from the publisher at Omirou Street 11, Athens 135, Greece.

For general reading, see **The Minoan World**, by Arthur Cotterell; Michael Joseph, Ltd., London, 1979; and the biography of Sir Arthur Evans, **The Find of a Lifetime** by Sylvia L. Horwitz; Weidenfeld & Nicholson, London 1981.

A fictionalized account about the Schliemanns, **The Greek Passion** by Irving Stone, is a somewhat dry but adequate book about the Mycenaean and Troy excavations, widely available in paperback editions. Mine is a Signet book; The New American Library, New York, 1976. A more scholarly reference on this period is **Mycenaean Greece** by James T. Hooker; Routledge and Kegan Paul, London,1976. See also **Schleimann of Troy - Treasure and Deceit**, by David A. Traill, St. Martin's Press, New York, 1995.

Homer and Mythology

B ooks covering the Homeric period are numerous and fascinating, starting of course with the **Iliad** and the **Odyssey** which are available in many editions. See those published in paperback by Penguin Books. Almost all of the ancient history and classical period book publishers have brought out volumes about Homer's writings, and the interested reader will have no difficulty selecting among them. Remember that Homer wrote in poetic form, and translations of this material are available. The most recent editions are those prepared by Robert Fagles, with excellent long scholarly introductions by Bernard Knox, 1991 and 1996. Most casual readers prefer the prose versions prepared by a number of prominent writers.

The adventures of Odysseus, in particular, have occupied many modern writers who have tried to determine where the events could have taken place geographically. One of these books, **The Voyages of Ulysses** by photographer Erich Lessing; McMillan, London, 1966, compares the Odysseus travels and adventures as analyzed by Victor Bérard, a French scholar, and Ernle Bradford, an English scholar, sailor and writer of many lively historical books on the Mediterranean world. Lessing also includes commentaries on the Homeric period by several other well-known historians. With excellent color photographs, the whole is a fine treatment of the subject. Bradford wrote another account of the subject **Ulysses Found**, but this is out of print.

There are numerous accounts describing the myths and legends of the ancient Greek world. Well known editions are those of Edith Hamilton, **Mythology**, and by Thomas Bullfinch, of the same title. Another excellent volume is **Gods and Heroes - Myths and Epics of Ancient Greece**, by Gustav Schwab; Pantheon Books, Inc., New York, 1974. All these are printed and reprinted. One of my favorites is **Myths of the Greeks and Romans** by Michael Grant; Mentor books, The New American Library, New York 1962. Professor Grant is a prolific and extensive writer on the classical Mediterranean world, and all of his writings are heartily recommended.

Thera

The cataclysms in antiquity at the island of Thera (modern-day Santorini) was the subject of an international conference held in 1978 in London, attended by leading vulcanologists, seismologists, archeologists, geologists, historians, and others. The Proceedings of this conferences were published in a two volume set under the title **Thera and the Aegean World**, London 1978 and 1980. For the serious student of this event nothing else is better documented, if these could be found. For the more general reader some other texts are available, **The End of Atlantis**, by J.V. Luce; Paladin books, Granada Publishing Co., St. Albans, Herts., England, 1970; and **Atlantis** by A.G. Galanopoulos and E. Bacon; T. Nelson, London, 1969.

Greek Expansion Overseas

The subject of Greek expansion overseas is well described in John Boardman's **The Greeks Overseas**; Penguin, 1964. **The Phoenicians** by Donald Harden; Pelican Books, Penguin, 1971, is recommended for the subject of their own colonization, that includes a description of their contact with the Greeks.

The Persian Wars

For this subject, including many other descriptions of the period, **The Histories of Herodotos** is must reading; Penguin Books, England. The Persian Wars are described in readable form in **Persia and the Greeks - The Defence of the West 546-478 BC,** by A.R. Burn; Edward Arnold Publishers Ltd., London 1962. Also see **The Greeks and the Persians** by Hermann Bengtson; Weidenfeld and Nicolson, London, 1968. Recommended as well is the Cambridge Ancient History series, Volume IV, **The Persian Empire and the West**. All the volumes of this series covering other periods of Greek and Roman history are excellent references.

The Golden Age of Greece

So many books are available on the Golden Age of Greece, the Classical Period, and the emergence of democracy there, that it is difficult to select those which will satisfy the needs of the general reader. An excellent small book ontroducing the ancient Greek civilization and why and how it achieved what it did, is **The Greeks** by Prof. H.D.F. Kitto; Penguin, 1951. This book has been reprinted 32 times as of this writing and has sold more than 1,500,000 copies --an unheard of success for this type of subject matter. See **Pericles of Athens and the Birth of Democracy,** by Professor Donald Kagan, Free Press, New York, 1991. This classical historian has also written the definitive modern history of the Peloponnesian War, in four volumes. Also available on the period is a more academic small work **The Emergence of Greek Democracy - The Character of Greek Politics 800-400 BC,** by Prof. W.G. Forrest; Weidenfeld and Nicolson, London, 1966. Also interesting is **Democracy and Classical Greece** covering the period 500-300 BC, by J.K. Davies, Fontana books, England, 1978. An attractive and well-illustrated book on the ancient Greek world is the **Atlas of the Greek World** by Peter Levi; Facts on File, Inc., New York, and Phaidon Press Ltd., Oxford, England, both 1981.

The list of other volumes on this subject is endless, as it is the period that has most fascinated scholars and historians. Not to be neglected are a number of volumes published by that great quality and classical publisher in England, Thames and Hudson.

Alexander the Great

The travelling exhibit from Greece on recent and older Macedonian grave-findings of the Philip-Alexander period, brought forth some new volumes on a well-written-about subject. Alexander's father Philip is less well known, as are his achievements, which gave Alexander the impetus to produce his own extraordinary accomplishments. **Philip of Macedon** by a number of Greek scholars is handsomely produced and well researched;

Ekdotike Athenon, Athens, 1980. Also recommended is **The Search for Alexander** by Robin Lane Fox; Little, Brown and Co., Boston, 1980. A very good account on the period is **Alexander the Great** by Ulrich Wilcken in an edition introduced and annotated by Eugene N. Borz; W.W. Norton, New York and London, 1967. Among the many books on Alexander are those of N.G.L. Hammond who has spent a lifetime on this subject, culminating with **The Genius of Alexander the Great**, University of North Carolina Press, 1997. For serious readers on Alexander the Great, see the volume by Nancy J. Burich containing an annotated bibliography, Kent State University Press, 1970. A must for Alexander buffs is Mary Renault's **The Nature of Alexander;** Pantheon, New York, 1975. Her fictionalized and imaginative accounts about Alexander will interest the general reader and are good casual reading: *Fire From Heaven,* about the young Alexander; *The Persian Boy,* on Alexander's later life; and *Funeral Games,* about his death and his successors.

The Hellenistic Age

Among the books on this important period, highly recommended are **The Harvest of Hellenism** by F. E. Peters; Simon & Schuster, New York, 1970; and **From Alexander to Cleopatra**, By Michael Grant; Charles Scribner's Sons, New York, 1982. Also of interest are **Hellenistic Civilization** by Professor W.W. Tarn; Meridian books, The New American Library, New York. See also **The Hellenistic World** by F.W. Walbank; Harvard University Press, Cambridge, Massachusetts, 1981; and **Hellenistic Culture**, Fusion and Diffusion, by Moses Hadas; W.W. Norton & Company, New York and London, 1972.

The Roman and Byzantine Empires

This period has also been the subject of a vast quantity of writings. Some of the easier-to-read references are mentioned here. An **Atlas of the Roman World** is recommended, part of the series mentioned above in the references to the Golden Age; Facts on File in New York and Phaidon Press in Oxford, 1982. A fine illustrated volume for the general reader is **The Birth of Western Civilization, Greece and Rome;** Thames and Hudson, London 1964. One of the basic references for the Byzantine period is George Ostrogorsky's **History of the Byzantine State;** Basil Blackwell, Oxford, 1956. Most stimulating are the several books by the well-known Sir Steven Runciman, **Byzantine Style and Civilization; The Eastern Schism; The Fall of Constantinople 1453;** and **The Great Church in Captivity.** See also **Byzantium, Its Triumphs and Tragedy** by René Guerdan; G.P. Putnam & Sons, New York, 1957. A very important aspect of Byzantine civilization is covered by Rev. Dr. Demetrios J. Constantelos, **Byzantine Philanthropy and Social Welfare;** Rutgers University Press,

1968. Very readable are the three volume series on Byzantium by Lord John Julius Norwich 1989,1991, and 1996.

Medieval Greek History

Another era of great interest in Greek history is the medieval period. Professor Deno J. Geanakoplos has written a fine college text, **Medieval Western Civilization and the Byzantine and Islamic Worlds** -Interaction of Three Cultures; D.C.Heath and Company, Lexington, Massachusetts, 1974. There are many good accounts of the crusader period, especially Steven Runciman's **A History of the Crusades;** Penguin books, England. (It was principally the Fourth Crusade that affected Greece, and the events that followed.) A definitive reference work on the period which covers also the events between the crusades and the crusader kingdoms is a six-volume series by the University of Wisconsin Press, **A History of the Crusades.** The Frankish and Venetian occupation is minutely covered in **The Latins in the Levant** - A History of Frankish Greece (1204-1566) by William Miller; E.P. Dutton, 1908; reprinted by AMS Press, New York, 1979. Also recommended is **Mediaeval Greece** by Nicolas Cheetham; Yale University Press, 1981. See also The **Decline of Medieval Hellenism in Asia Minor and the Process of Islamization through the Fifteenth Century,** by Dr. Speros Vryonis Jr.; University of California Press, Berkely, Los Angeles, and London, 1971.

Some insights into the role of Venice in the Mediterranean which affected the Greek world is contained in **A History of Venice** by John Julius Norwich, Allen Lane, London, 1982.

The Ottoman Empire

A very good reference on this period including events concerning Greece and the Greeks is the **History of the Ottoman Turks** by E.S. Creasey, London, 1878. It is mostly out of print; I have a reprint by Khayats, Beirut, Lebanon, 1968. Highly recommendable are the books of Lord Kinross, especially **The Ottoman Centuries: The Rise and Fall of the Turkish Empire;** William Morrow and Co., New York, 1977 (paperback edition, 1979).

The Revolution of 1821

The Greek revolution of 1821 is very well covered in the **Greek Struggle for Independence 1821-1833,** by Douglas Dakin; B.T. Batsford Ltd., London, 1973. Another good account is **The Greek Phoenix** by Joseph Braddock; Constable, London 1972. For an eye-witness account read **Makriyannis** - The Memoirs of General Makriyannis 1797-1864, edited and translated by H.A. Lidderdale; Oxford University Press, 1966. A well-illustrated volume is **The Greeks - Their Struggle for Independence** by Peter H. Paroulakis; Hellenic International Press, Darwin, Australia, 1984.

Two books recommended for their description of the participation of the Philhellenes in the revolution, are **That Greece Might Still Be Free** by William St. Clair; Oxford University Press, 1972; and **The Greek Adventure** by David Howarth; Collins, London, 1976.

Smyrna – Catastrophe in Asia Minor

Ionian Vision - Greece in Asia Minor 1919-1922, by Michael Llewellyn; Allen Lane, London 1973, is highly recommended, containing a good account of the Greek vision of "The Great Idea", as well. Also worth reading are **The Blight of Asia** by George Horton, New York 1953; and **The Smyrna Affair** by Marjorie Housepian; Harcourt Brace Jovanovich, New York 1966. Other references I used were written in the Greek language.

Greek Religion

References on mythology have already been covered in the paragraph on Homer above. Another excellent and more scholarly work is by the French Professor Jean-Pierre Vernant, **Myth and Thought Among the Greeks;** Routledge & Kegan Paul Ltd., London, 1983. For the story of St. Paul, see **St. Paul**, by Michael Grant; Charles Scribner's Sons, New York, 1976. Another good small book is **St. Paul in Greece,** by Otto F.A. Meinardus; Lycabettus Press, Athens, 1973. We have already mentioned above, but it is worth repeating for it covers the history of the Greek Orthodox church during the four centuries of Ottoman rule, **The Great Church in Captivity,** by Sir Steven Runciman; Cambridge University Press, 1968. Another good book by Professor D.J. Constantelos is **Understanding the Greek Orthodox Church - Its Faith, History, and Practice;** Seabury Press, New York, 1982. Also recommendable is **The Greek Orthodox Church,** by Timothy Ware; Penguin Books, England, latest version 1983.

The history of the ancient Olympic games is beautifully presented in **The Olympic Games** published in English in a well-illustrated volume by Ekdotike Athenon, Athens. Another good small book on the subject was published in 1980 by the British Museum in London at the time of an exhibition shown there, **The Ancient Olympic Games,** by Judith Swaddling.

Other

Many other references are available, from easy narrative accounts to definitive references. The above list is intended for the general reader who may not want to read the weightier tomes for his pleasure and to add to his knowledge of the long history of the Greeks. Two short modern continuous histories are also worth mentioning, **A Short History of Modern Greece** by Richard Clogg; Cambridge University Press, 1979, covering the period 1204 to about 1978; and **Modern Greece, A Short History,** by C.M. Woodhouse; Faber and Faber, London 1977, covering the period from Constantine the Great (324), to 1976. Special recommendation is made to those readers interested in what is likely the best description of a most brutal and devastating period in modern Greek history, the civil war of 1944-1949. This is **By Fire and Axe** - The Communist Party and the Civil War in Greece, 1944-49, by an eminent Greek parliamentarian and many times minister, Evangelos Averoff - Tossiza. It was originally published in French (**Le Feu et la Hache**), Editions de Breteuil, Paris, 1973. Published in many languages, the English Language edition by Caratzas Brothers, Publishers, New Rochelle, New York, 1978.

Historical Atlases

For those that like maps, historical atlases were published, without text, prepared by Martin Gilbert; Weidenfeld and Nicolson, London, and McMillan, New York. These are not exclusively on Greece, but references also include the history of the Greek world. The **Ancient History Atlas** by Michael Grant, by the same publishers, covers Greece and Rome in the period 1700 BC to 565 AD.

Military history atlases are also available and the many wars of the Greeks and Romans are covered. These were prepared by Arthur Banks, Seeley Service, London. A beautiful book for war buffs of the Graeco-Roman periods is **Warfare in the Classical World** by John Warry; Salamander Books, England, and St. Martin's Press, Inc. New York, 1980. It contains drawings, maps, photographs, and good battle descriptions.

Ancient Sources

For those that want to read from ancient sources, in addition to the other references mentioned in this volume, your library will probably have a copy of the two-volume set of **The Greek Historians,** The Complete and Unabridged Historical Works of Herodotus, Thucydides, Xenophon, Arrian, edited by Francis R.B. Godophin; Random House, New York, 1942. The commentaries preceding each of the translations are very interesting, and the works contained are highly readable. The two-volume edition of the Loeb Classical Library includes the works of many of the classical Greek authors; Harvard University Press, 1979. For those that want to go further into original sources for particular periods, the bibliographies in many of the books mentioned above, will provide that information.

For an excellent book on samplings of the works of many of the Greek authors of the classical age, see **The Classical Greek Reader**, edited by Kenneth J. Atchity, Henry Holt, New York, 1996.

THE GREEK KINGS
(1833-1974)

1833-1862 **Othon,** (Greek for Otto), b.1815, d.1867, second son of Ludwig I, King of Bavaria. He was made king of Greece by the Great Powers when he was 17 years old. He married Amalie of Oldenburg, Germany, in 1836. A bloodless revolution on September 3, 1843 obliged the king to convene a national assembly and draw up a constitution, which became official March 16,1844. But the authoritarian-minded king never fully accepted the role of his being a constitutional monarch, and another revolution led to his being deposed October 23, 1862. He died in his native Bavaria five years later.

1863-1913 **George I,** b.1845, d.1913, second son of King Christian IX of
1920-1922 Denmark. He was installed as "King of the Hellenes" on October 23, 1863 when he was 17 years old, again by the intervention of the Great Powers. England returned the Ionian islands to the Greeks in 1864, as an act of good will at their accepting the new king. He married Grand Duchess Olga in1867, daughter of Grand Duke Constantine, the younger brother of Tsar Alexander II of Russia. He ruled a "crown democracy" under a new constitution in 1864 (revised in 1911). He was assassinated in Thessaloniki in March 1913 by a madman.

1913-1916 **Constantine I,** b. 1868, d. 1922, eldest son of George I and Olga,
1920-1922 he succeeded to the throne March 18, 1913 following his father's assassination. He married Sophia in 1889, sister of Kaiser Wilhelm II of Germany. World War I led to a bitter dispute between the pro-German king and his Prime Minister Eleftherios Venizelos, who was for the *Entente Cordiale*. The Protecting Powers forced the king to resign in June 1917 and he left the country for Switzerland accompanied by his son, Crown Prince George. They left the younger son, Alexander, as interim king. Constantine returned to the throne December 1920 following the death of Alexander and a plebiscite that overwhelmingly favored his return. After the disastrous Graeco-Turkish War in Asia Minor, a military revolt in September 1922 deposed him, and he left the country. He died four months later in Palermo, Sicily.

1917-1920 **Alexander,** b. 1893, d. 1920, second son of King George I of Greece and Olga. He married a commoner, Aspasia Manos, in November 1919, against his government's wishes. He became interim king when his father and older brother left for exile June 1917. He was bitten in the palace garden by a pet monkey and died of blood poisoning on October 20, 1920.

1922-1923 **George II,** b. 1890, d. 1947, eldest son of King Constantine I and
1935-1941 Sophia. He married Elizabeth of Rumania in 1921, sister of Prince Carol,
1946-1947 later King Carol of Rumania. They were divorced in 1935. He
became king September 27, 1922, when his father was deposed. In
December 1923, general elections greatly favored Venizelos reviving
the old controversies (see Chapter Seven) and the military
government asked George II to leave for a short time until the
constitutional question was resolved, and he did so without
abdicating. A plebiscite in 1924 established a republic by a 70 percent
vote, and the king remained abroad. Another plebiscite in November
1935 restored the constitutional monarchy, and George II returned
to the throne from his exile in Rumania and London. When
Germany invaded Greece in World War II, the king fled to Crete in
April 1941, and a month later to Cairo and then London. The civil
war in Greece in 1943 prevented the king from returning until after
a plebiscite in September 1946 which overwhelmingly returned him
to the throne again. But he died on April 1, 1947.

1947-1964 **Paul,** b. 1901, d. 1964, the third and youngest son of King
Constantine I and Sophia. He married Princess Frederika of
Brunswick, Germany in 1938. He became king on the death of his
brother George II in April, 1947. The king and queen were very
popular after the civil war in 1949 for their role in aiding the victims.
However, by 1963 they were the center of great controversy caused
by internal political currents which were strongly anti-monarchy.
Queen Frederika, especially, was the target of much leftist-generated
abuse because of her outspoken Germanic authoritarianism in
contrast to the king's gentle nature. She was chased in the street by
a leftist organized mob during a visit to London, and had to flee on
foot before she was rescued. Paul died of cancer in March 1964.

1964-1967 **Constantine II,** b. 1940, son of King Paul and Frederika. He
married Princess Anne-Marie of Denmark after he assumed the throne
upon the death of his father. When a military junta overthrew the
government in 1967, the king's feeble attempt to oust the junta led to
his fleeing the country in December 1967. The junta was dissolved in
1974, and Greece returned to a constitutional government. A
referendum on December 8, 1974 on the subject of a republic or a
monarchy for Greece, found 70 percent of the votes for a republic,
ending royal rule of Greece.

A LIST OF OTTOMAN RULERS

Osman I 1288-1326
Orkhan......................................1326-1359
Murad I......................................1359-1389
Bayezid I 1389-1402
(Interregnum)............................1402-1413
Mehmed I 1413-1421
Murad II 1421-1451
Mehmed II (the Conqueror)........1451-1481
Bayezid II..................................1481-1512
Selim I 1512-1520
Suleiman I (the Magnificent)........1520-1566
Selim II.....................................1566-1574
Murad II 1574-1595
Mehmed III...............................1595-1603
Ahmad I 1603-1617
Osman II...................................1618-1622
Mustapha I................................1622-1623
Murad IV 1623-1640
Ibrahim.....................................1640-1648
Mehmed IV...............................1648-1687
Suleiman II 1687-1691
Ahmad II...................................1691-1695
Mustapha II...............................1695-1703
Ahmad III..................................1703-1730
Mahmud I 1730-1754
Osman III 1754-1757
Mustapha III 1757-1773
Abdul Hamid.............................1773-1789
Selim III....................................1789-1807
Mustapha IV 1807-1808
Mahmud II.................................1808-1839
Abdul Mejid 1839-1861
Abdul Azziz 1861-1876
Abdul Hamid II 1876-1908
Mehmed V 1909-1918
Mehmed VI................................1918-1922
Mustapha Kemal: elected first president
   of Turkish Republic ......October 29, 1923

MEDIEVAL FEUDAL LORDS OF THE
GREEK PENINSULA AND ISLANDS

Beginning in 1204, after the Franks and Venetians conquered Constantinople, the Greek peninsula and islands came under a feudal rule that lasted three to four centuries. Some events of this period are described in the text (see Chapter Six). This appendix listing the principal areas and the successions of rulers, gives an indication of how the area was divided and under whom. It should be understood that while some areas remained under the fairly stable control of their lords for long periods, borders changed at frequent intervals, and holdings were sometimes passed from one family to another, or sold, leased, taken by force, or abandoned.

When the Byzantine rule in Constantinople came to an end after the attack of 1204, there were neither imperial nor local armed forces to protect these areas, and no resources with which to build fortifications. The Greek people that lived on the Greek peninsula and islands found themselves under various Latin feudal lords instead of the Byzantine governors they had before. Though the Byzantine Empire itself was retaken from Frankish rule by Michael VIII 57 years later, in 1261, the Byzantines were in no condition to win back most of the areas they had lost. The Greek peninsula and islands remained under the control of their foreign feudal lords until the stronger, more numerous, and aggressive Ottoman Turks took possession of the entire area about three centuries later.

During this period, most of the Greek mainland was under the rule of Byzantine Michael I Dukas Angelos Komnenos and his heirs (see p.144-5); Athens and the Attika peninsula, as well as most of the Peloponnese, were under Frankish lords; a wedge of the Peloponnese from Mystra (south of Sparta) southeast to Monemvasia and the Mani on the Aegean coast was taken back by the Byzantines from the Franks in 1262; and the Venetians controlled the large islands of Euboia and Crete, most of the islands of the Aegean Archipelago, along with the western Greek islands from Corfu south, and a number of fortified cities ringing the Peloponnesian coast.

Of course, other adventurers and conquerors (Florentines, Genoese, Pisans, and other Latins) occupied some islands at various times between 1204 and the Ottoman takeover by the fourteenth and fifteenth centuries. Turkish and Arab corsairs, and miscellaneous pirates, plundered the Aegean islands and coastal Greek cities, at will. So serious and frequent were these raids that some islands were entirely depopulated for long periods.

These lists have been adapted from **The Latins in the Levant** (A History of Frankish Greece, 1204-1566) by William Miller.* The lists and references have been somewhat refined and expanded from other sources, but the complexity of this period is such that the information is offered as indicative rather than precisely complete.

---

* E.P. Dutton and Company; New York, 1908.

Princes of Achaia (the Peloponnese, or Morea)

Guillaume I of Champlitte 1205-1209
Geoffroy I of Villhardouin..1209-c.1229
Geoffroy II of Villhardouin c.1229-1246
Guillaume II of Villhardouin 1246-1278
Charles I of Anjou...1278-1285
Charles II of Anjou...1285-1289
Isabelle of Villhardouin...1289-1306
    with husband Florent of Hainault...................................1289-1297
    with husband Philip of Savoy 1301-1306
Philip I of Taranto..1306-1313
Mahaut of Hainault..1313-1321
    with husband Louis of Burgundy.....................................1313-1316
John of Gravina (Anjou) 1322-1333
Robert of Taranto 1333-1364
    with wife Catherine of Valois 1333-1346
Marie of Bourbon 1364-1370
Philip II of Taranto 1370-1373
Joanna I of Naples 1373-1381

    Achaia leased to the Knights of St. John.................................1376-1381

Jacques of Les Baux..1381-1383
Charles III of Durazzo 1383-1386
Ladislas of Naples 1386-1396
Pierre "Bordo" of St. Superan 1396-1402
Maria Zaccaria (regent)...1402-1404
Centurione II Zaccaria...1404-1430

Dukes of Athens

Othon of la Roche (Burgundy)..1208-1225
Guy I of la Roche 1225-1263
John of la Roche...1263-1280
William I of la Roche..1280-1287
Guy II of la Roche..1287-1308
Walter of Brienne 1309-1311

    Under the Catalan Grand Company 1311-1388

Roger Deslaur 1311-1312
Manfred..1312-1317
William II of Randazo...1317-1338
John II of Randazo 1338-1348
Frederick I of Randazo 1348-1355
Frederick II (III of Sicily)..1355-1377

Pedro (IV of Aragon)..1377-1387
John III (I of Aragon)...1387-1388
Nerio Acciajuoli (of Florence)..1388-1394

    Under the Venetians 1394-1402

    Under the Florentines 1402-1456

Antonio I..1403-1435
Nerio II 1435-c.1439
Antonio II...c.1439-1441
Nerio II (restored)..1441-1451
Francesco I..1451-1456
Francesco II 1455-1456

Despots of Epiros (Byzantines)

Dynasty of the Angelos Komneni 1204-1318
Michael I Dukas Angelos Komnenos...1204-1214
Theodore...1214-1230
Manuel 1230-1236
Michael II..1236-1271
Nikephoros I..1271-1296
Thomas..1296-1318

    Under the Roman Orsini Family,
        Counts of Cephalonia...1318-1339, 1356-1359

Nicholas..1318-1323
John II...1323-1335
Nikephoros II...1335-1339
                                                                 1356-1359

Epiros came again under Byzantine rule during the period 1339 to 1349; then Serbian rule (1349-1356), after which Nikephoros II Orsini came back to power briefly. The Serbian ruler Simeon Urash then reoccupied the area, calling himself "Emperor of the Greeks and Serbs." He turned the northern part over to his son-in-law, Thomas Peliubovish, who ruled briefly, then was under Albanian rule until 1418, when it was united under the Anjou counts of Cephalonia, who had ruled the island since 1194.

Dukes of the Archipelago

Marco Sanudo, a nephew of Doge Enrico Dandolo, Venetian leader who had helped the crusaders take Byzantine Constantinople in 1204, won for himself by force of arms the large and fertile Greek island of Naxos in the center of the Aegean Sea, and with his supporters, proceeded to take the surrounding islands, creating what was called the "Duchy of the Archipelago." Over a short period of time, and creating a number of fiefs, the Duchy included the islands of Naxos, Antiparos, Paros, Kimolos, Ios, Kythnos, Sikinos, Siphnos, Syra, Anaphe, Santorini (Thera), Astypalaia, Tinos, Mykonos, Skyros, Skopelos, Seriphos, Keos, Cerigo (Kythera), and Cerigotto (Andikythera); and, later, Andros.

Dynasty of Sanudo

Marco I (Venetian)	1207-1227
Angelo	1227-1262
Marco II	1262-1303
Guglielmo I	1303-1323
Niccolo I	1333-1341
Giovanni I	1341-1361
Fiorenza (Duchess)	1361-1371
with husband Niccolo II Sanudo "Spezzabanda"	1364-1371
Niccolo III dalle Carceri	1371-1383

Dynasty of dalle Carceri

Francesco I Crispo	1383-1397
Giacomo I	1397-1418
Giovanni II	1418-1433
Giacomo II	1433-1447
Gian Giacomo	1447-1453
Guglielmo II	1453-1463
Francesco II	1463
Giacomo III	1463-1480
Giovanni III	1480-1494

    Under Venice directly 1494-1500

Francesco III	1500-1511

    Under Venice directly 1511-1517

Giovanni IV	1517-1564
Giacomo IV	1564-1566

    Taken over by the Ottomans, they gave rule of the Duchy to
       Joseph Nasi (a Portuguese of Jewish faith) 1566-1579

Lords of Corfu

Under Venice 1199-1214

Under Despots of Epiros...1214-1259

Manfred of Sicily 1259-1266
Chinardo.. 1266
Charles I of Anjou...1267-1285
Charles II of Anjou 1285-1294
Philip I of Taranto 1294-1331
Catherine of Valois
   with husband Robert of Taranto 1331-1346
Robert of Taranto 1346-1364
Marie of Bourbon... 1364
Philip II of Taranto 1364-1373
Joanna I of Naples...1373-1380
Jacques of Les Baux...1380-1382
Charles II of Naples...1382-1386

Under Venice 1386-1797

Palatine Counts of Cephalonia
(Including Zante —modern Zakinthos)

Dynasty of the Orsini family 1194-1324

Maio 1194-1238
Richard 1238-1303
John I..1303-1317
Nicholas 1317-1323
John II 1323-1324

    United with Ahaia under the Angevins (Anjou) 1324-1357

Leonardo I Tocco (related to the Orsini family) 1357-1377
Carlo I..1377-1429
Carlo II 1429-1448
Leonardo III..1448-1479
Antonio...1481-1483

Venetian Colonies

Modon and Coron	1206-1500
Argos	1388-1463
Navplia	1388-1540
Monemvasia	1464-1540
Lepanto (Naupaktos)	1407-1499
Negroponte (Euboia)	1209-1470
Pteleon	1323-1470
Aegina	1451-1537
Tinos	1390-1715
Mykonos	1390-1537
Northern Sporades	1453-1538
Corfu	1194-1214; 1386-1797
Cephalonia	1483-1485; 1500-1797
Zante (Zakinthos)	1482-1797
Cerigo (Kythera)	1363-1797
Sta. Maura (Levkas)	1502-1503
Athens	1394-1402
Patras	1408-1413; 1417-1419
Naxos	1494-1500; 1511-1517
Andros	1437-1440; 1507-1514
Paros	1518-1420; 1531-1536
Amorgos (part of)	1370-1446
Maina (the Mani peninsula)	1467-1479
Vostitsa (Aeghion)	1470
Candia (Crete)	1210-1645
and some parts until	1669

THE EAST ROMAN (BYZANTINE) EMPERORS AT CONSTANTINOPLE

<u>Ruled</u>

Constantinian Dynasty (AD 324-363)
Constantine I (Constantius), the Great (b.285-d.337) 324-337
Constantius II (317-361), son of Constantine I 337-361
Julian the Apostate (331/2-361), nephew of Constantine I...............361-363

Inter Dynasty (AD 363-378)
Jovian (c.331-364) 363-364
Valens (c.328-378), brother of Roman Emperor Valentinian I 364-378

Theodosian Dynasty (AD 379-457)
Theodosius I (347-395), with son Arcadius 383-395 379-395
Arcadius (377-408), son of Theodosius I...395-408
Theodosius II (401-450), son of Arcadius 408-450
Marcian (396-457), married sister of Theodosius II 450-457

Leonine Dynasty (AD 457-518)
Leo I (400?-474) 457-474
Leo II (468-474), grandson of Leo I, emperor at age 6...........................474
Zeno (? -491), son-in-law of Leo I, father of Leo II........................474-475
Basiliskos (? -477), usurped throne of brother-in-law, Zeno 475-476
Zeno, restored 476-491
Anastasios I (430?-518)...491-518

Justinian Dynasty (AD 518-602)
Justin I (c.450-527) 518-527
Justinian I (483-565), husband of dynamic Empress Theodora 527-565
Justin II (? -578), nephew of Justinian I...565-578
Tiberius I (? -582) 578-582
Maurice (c.539-602), married daughter of Tiberius II 582-602

Inter Dynasty (AD 602-610)
Phokas (? -610)..602-610

Heraklian Dynasty (AD 610-711)
Heraklios (c.575-641)..610-641
Constantine III (612-641), son of Heraklios, ruled three months.............641
Heraklonas (636-641?), younger son of Heraklios, co-ruler with
  his elder brother Constantine III 641
Constans II Pogonatos (630-668), son of Constantine III..................641-668

Constantine IV (652-685), son of Constans II....................................668-685
Justinian II (669-711), son of Constantine IV 685-695
Leontios (? -705), (later executed by Justinian II) 695-698
Tiberius II (? -705), (deposed and executed by Justinian II).............698-705
Justinian II, regained throne 705-711

Inter Dynasty (AD 711-717)
Philippicus Bardenes (Varden)(? -after 713)...................................711-713
Anastasios II (? -721) 713-715
Theodosios III (? -after 717) 715-717

Syrian (or Isaurian) Dynasty (Iconoclasts) (AD 717-802)
Leo III (c.675-741) 717-741
Constantine V Kopronymos (718-775), son of Leo III......................741-775
Leo IV (749-780), son of Constantine V...775-780
Constantine VI (770-after 797), son of Leo IV................................780-797
Irene (752-803), wife of Leo IV, earlier ruled with son......................797-802

Inter Dynasty (AD 802-820)
Nikephoros I (? -811), died in battle, son mortally wounded............802-811
Staurakios (? -811), son of Nikephoros I, died of wounds...................811
Michael I Rhangabes (? -c.845), son-in-law of Nikephoros I.............811-813
Leo V (? -820)...813-820

Phrygian (or Amorian) Dynasty (AD 820-867)
Michael II (? -829) 820-829
Theophilos (? -842), son of Michael II...829-842
Michael III (838-867), son of Theophilos, crowned age four 842-867

Macedonian Dynasty (AD 867-1057)
Basil I (? -886)...867-886
Leo VI (686-912), son of Basil I, co-ruler with Basil I......................886-912
Alexander (830-913), son of Basil I, co-ruler with Leo VI 912-913
Constantine VII Porphyrogenitos (905-959), son of Leo VI..............913-959
Romanos I (c.872-948), co-reigned with Constantine VII.................920-944
Romanos II (939-963), son of Constantine VII................................959-963
Nikephoros II Phokas (912-969) 963-969
John I Tzimiskes (c.925-976) 969-976
Basil II Bulgaroktonos (958-1025), son of Romanos II.....................976-1025
Constantine VIII (c.960-1028), son of Romanos II, ruled jointly
    with brother Basil II until 1025..1025-1028
Romanos III Argyros (c.968-1034) 1028-1034
Michael IV (the Paphlagonian) (? -1041) 1034-1041
Michael V Kalaphates, reigned four months with Zoë 1041
Zoë (978-1050), daughter of Constantine VIII, married

Romanos III at age 50, then Michael IV at age 56, then at
age 64 with Constantine IX, co-ruled 1042-1050
Theodora (981-1056), younger sister of Zoë, ruled jointly..............1042-1055
Constantine IX Monomachos (c.980-1055), ruled with Zoë and
Theodora 1042-1055
Theodora, alone...1055-1056
Michael VI Stratiotikos (? - ?) 1056-1057

Inter Dynasty (AD 1057-1081)
Isaac I Comnenos (? -1059)..1057-1059
Constantine X Dukas (? -1067)...1059-1067
Romanos IV Diogenes (? -1072)...1068-1071
Michaael VII Dukas (? - ?), eldest son of Constantine X.............1071-1078
Nikephoros II Botaniates (? - ?) 1078-1081

Comnenian Dynasty (AD1081-1185)
Alexios I Comnenos (1048-1118)...1081-1118
John II (1088-1143), son of Alexios I...1118-1142
Manuel I (c.1122-1180), son of John II 1143-1180
Alexios II (1169-1183), son of Manuel I...1180-1183
Andronikos I (1118-1185), grandson of Alexios I............................1183-1185

Angeli Dynasty (AD 1185-1204)
Isaac II (c.1135-1204), son-in-law of Alexios I................................1185-1195
Alexios III Angelos (? -after 1210), brother of Isaac II...................1195-1203
Isaac II (restored) co-emperors with his son Alexios IV 1203-1204

Inter Dynasty (AD 1204)
Alexios V Dukas Murtzuphlos (? -1204)...1204

Constantinople under the Franks (1204-1261)
Baldwin I of Flanders (1171-1205) 1204-1205
Henry of Flanders (1174-1216), younger son of Baldwin 1206-1216
Peter of Courtenay (? -1219), brother-in-law of Baldwin 1217-1218
wife, Yolande (regent) 1218-1219
Conon of Béthune (regent)...1219-1221
Robert of Courtenay (? -1228), son of Peter..................................1221-1228
Baldwin II (1217-1273), son of Peter ....
with regent John of Brienne 1228-1237
Baldwin II, alone..1237-1261

Paleologi Dynasty (AD 1261-1453)
Michael VIII (1224?-1282), son of Andronikos Comnenos 1261-1282

Andronikos II (1260-1332), son of Michael VIII 1282-1328
Michael IX (c.1277-1320), co-emperor with his
    father Andronikos II 1294-1320
Andronikos III (1296-1341), grandson of Andronikos II 1328-1341
John V (1332-1391), son of Andronikos III 1341-1376
John VI Kantakuzenos (1291-1383), co-emperor with John V........1347-1354
Andronikos IV (? - ?), son of John V who deposed his
    father for three years...1376-1379
John V (restored) 1379-1391
John VII (1360-1410), son of Andronikos IV, usurped..........................1390
    throne six months, deposed, then served
    as co-emperor with Manuel II 1394-1403
Manuel II (1350-1425), son of John V 1391-1425
John VIII (1390-1448), son of Manuel II 1425-1448
Constantine XI Dragases (1404-1453), brother of John VIII 1449-1453

Nikaian Emperors (AD 1204-1261)
Theodore I Laskaris(c.1175-1222),son-in-law of Alexios III............1204-1222
John III Dukas Vatatzes (1193-1254), son-in-law of Theo. I 1222-1254
Theodore II Laskaris (1222-1258), son of John III 1254-1258
John IV Laskaris (c.1250-c.1261), son of Theodore II 1258-1261
Michael VIII Paleologos (1224-1282), co-emperor, ...1259-1261
    also Byzantine emperor, including Nikaia................................1261-1282

INDEX

Timetable of Greek History

	Bronze Age 2500-1100 BC			Iron Age	Geometric	Archaic	Classical		Hellenistic P
	2500	2000	1500	1000	800	600	400	300	200

History and Political

- Minoan Culture 2500-1400
- Mycenaen 1600-1100
- Thera cataclysms 1500-1450
- Dorian invasions 1100-900
- Indo-Europeans settle in Greece c. 1500
- Greek expansion onerseas 800-600
- First Olympic Games 776
- Tyrants rule 650-500
- Golden Age 5th century
- Solon's reforms c. 590
- Persian Wars 546-479
- Kleisthenes creates democracy 507
- Perikles 497-430
- Delian League created 478
- Peloponnesian War 431-404
- March of the ten thousand 401-400
- Ascendancy of Macedonia under Philip II 359-306
- Alexander's Conquests 356-323
- Successors' wars 323-306

Religion, Philosophy and Science

- Hsiod's *Hegemony* c. 750
- Plato 428-347
- Sokrates 469-391
- Hippokrates 460-c.375
- Aristotle 384-322
- Xenophon 430˙355
- Pythagoras c. 582-507
- Ptolemy I & II build Library and Museum at Alexandria

Art, Architecture and Archeology

- Palaces in Crete 1700-1500
- Parthenon 447-438
- Pheidias' statue of Zeus at Olympia mid 5th cent
- Tomb of Mausolos 353
- Temple of Artemis 323
- Kolossos of Rhodes 307
- Alexandria lighthouse 285-247

Literature and Theatre

- Honer's Iliad & Odyssey c. 800
- Aeschylos 525-456
- Pindar 518-436
- Sophokles 496-406
- Herodotos 484-420
- Euripedes 480-407
- Thukydides 455-400
- Aristophanes 450-385
- Sappho Beg. 6th cent.
- Menander 342-292
- Apollonios's Argonautica c. 250

Other Cultures

- Great Pyramids in Egypt c. 2700
- Old Kingdom in Egypt 2575-2134
- Hittites 1600-1200
- Middle Kingdom in Egypt 2040-1640
- New Kingdom in Egypt 1550-1070
- Carthage founded
- Etruscans evolve
- Rome founded 753
- Persian Empire founded 550
- Rome consolidates central Italy 290
- First Punic War 264-241
- Second Punic War 218-201
- Third P War 149-1
- Assyrian and Babylonian Empires 1800-600
- Phoenicians spread into Mediterranean 1100-700

Imperial Roman Period			Byzantine Period				Ottomans	Modern Period		
0 AD	200	400	600	1000	1200		1500	1800	1900	2000

Rome occupies Greece 146

Roman Empire's largest extent 2nd century

Constantinople built 324-330

Western empire collapses 6th century

Byzantine empire begins

Crete occupied by Arabs 823-961

Battle of Manzikert 1071

Constantinople conquered by Franks and Venetians 1204

Knights of St. John occupy Dodecanese 1310-1522

Catalan Grand Co. occupies Athens & Thebes 1302-1388

Ottoman conquest of Greece 1382-1699

Crusades 1095-1270

Revolt against the Turks 1821-33

Balkan Wars 1912-13

WWI 1914-1918

The Great Idea 1919-1922

WWI 1940-44

Civil War 1943-49

Saint Paul's Greek missions 46-57

Strabo c. 63 BC-AD 21 Plutarch 50-120

Christianity becomes state religion by order of Theodosius I 380

Mt. Athos designated religious area 585

Death of Muhammad 632

Schism of Great Church 1054

Haghia Sophia built in Constantinople 533-537

Cermans uncover Olympia 1876-1890

Mycenae 1876-1877

Schliemann discovers Troy 1871-1876

Corinth Canal 1881-1893

French at Delphi 1892-1903

Sir Arthur Evans discovers Knossos 1900-1940

Conquests of Islam 632-732